D1806966

Who Rules the Coast?
Policy Processes in Belgian MPAs
and Beach Spatial Planning

Who Rules the Coast?

Policy Processes in Belgian MPAs and Beach Spatial Planning

Dirk Bogaert and Frank Maes (eds.)

Maklu

Antwerpen-Apeldoorn

Dirk Bogaert and Frank Maes (eds.)
Who Rules the Coast?
Policy Processes in Belgian MPAs and Beach Spatial Planning
Antwerpen-Apeldoorn
Maklu
2008

187 pag. – 24 x 16 cm
ISBN 978-90-466-0174-7
D 2008/1997/
NUR

Maklu-Uitgevers nv
Somersstraat 13/15, 2018 Antwerpen, info@maklu.be, www.maklu.be
Koninginnelaan 96, 7315 EB Apeldoorn, info@maklu.nl, www.maklu.nl

CONTENTS

LIST OF FIGURES

LIST OF TABLES

INTRODUCTION

This book is the result of research that was funded by the European Interreg IIIB North-West Europe Program in the COREPOINT Project (Coastal Research and Policy Integration / 2004-2008) and co-sponsored by the Flemish Agency for Maritime and Coastal Services – Coastal Division and the Province of West-Flanders. Focus of COREPOINT is on integrated coastal zone management (ICZM). This publication provides an in depth analysis and assessment of the policy processes of two Belgian/Flemish case studies related to ICZM, stakeholder participation and spatial planning. The first case study analyses the process of designating Marine Protected Areas (MPAs) in the Belgian part of the North Sea (chapter 3). This was a difficult process since some initial mistakes were made. Due to the lessons learned the MPA's were finally designated in 2005. The second case study analyses the process of adoption of the Provincial Spatial Implementation Plans for Beaches and Dikes (PRUP) (chapter 5). The analysis in both cases is based on the 'Policy Arrangement Approach' with special attention to stakeholder participation. Quite some effort was spent in the organisation and processing of in-depth interviews with key stakeholders (state, market and civil society) involved. The authors are indebted to those stakeholders and governmental representatives, ranging from the former Minister for the North Sea, the Governor of the province of West Flanders, mayors of coastal municipalities, advisers of ministerial offices, civil servants (federal, Flemish, provincial and municipal), scientists, representatives of NGOs, representatives of the market (harbours, windmills…), who kindly and without hesitation were prepared to spent some of their valuable time for the interviews. Without their co-operation the publishing of this book would have not been possible.

The assessment of the policy processes leading to the designation of MPAs in Belgium and the adoption of the Provincial Spatial Implementation Plans for Beaches and Dikes (PRUP) are placed in their legal context. In chapter 2 the reader will find the international and national legal framework for designating and managing marine protected areas, with focus on the MPAs in the Belgian part of the North Sea. In chapter 4 a legal technical analysis is given regarding a relatively new instrument, the Spatial Implementation Plan (RUP), as applied to the Flemish beaches and dikes. Conclusions and recommendations can be found in chapter 6.

Finally, we would like to thank Ann Vanhulle for making the charts, Misjel Decleer for the pictures and Lieve De Meyer and Phil Gaskell for translating the Dutch text into English.

'Who Rules the Coast?' is a book providing insight in participation and governance processes on key activities, spatial planning and related policy objectives for the Belgian part of the North Sea and the Flemish beaches. The book is of interest for scientists, policy makers, civil servants on federal, regional, provincial and local level and all of those who make use of the sea and the beaches for their living or during their leisure time.

Frank Maes & Dirk Bogaert
Ghent, 21 March 2008.

CHAPTER 1

Research Questions, Framework for Analysis and Methodology

Dirk Bogaert and Dino Dewaen

1. Research Questions

This book analyses two policy processes on the Belgian coast: the designation of Marine Protected Areas (MPAs) in the Belgian part of the North Sea, and the Provincial Spatial Implementation Plans for Beaches and Dikes (PRUP). As these policy processes had been wound up by the time of the analysis, this is an ex-post policy evaluation. The question central to this research was: *'How did the policy process work and what was the role of participation?'*.

For policy evaluation a difference can be made between generic research questions and evaluation questions in the strict sense (Crabbé *et al.* 2006). Generic research questions include the full policy process and are relevant in all phases of the policy cycle. In this book the focus is on political and legal criteria. Examples of generic questions used during the research: *Did policy work in a participatory way? Did policy use an open and transparent or a closed and informal policy process? Is the policy legitimate? Is there support for the policy? Is the policy based on regulations of high quality?*

Despite the fact that policy processes are complex and difficult to reduce to simple series of successive phases (Sabatier *et al.* 1993), various sociologists and political scientists have made an attempt to formulate a policy cycle. Since Fuller and Myers (1941) many authors use phase divisions (*see among others* Parsons 1995). Reduced to its simplest form, the policy cycle can be defined in the following phases: setting objectives, instrumentation, implementation and effects. This makes it possible to formulate evaluation questions in the strict sense, linked to various phases in the analysed policy processes.

Examples of evaluation questions in the strict sense, used in this research:
- Setting objectives: *What is the problem that must be solved? Who formulated this as a problem?*
- Instrumentation: *Were there alternatives to the designation as MPA or to the establishment of a PRUP for reaching the same objective? Is an MPA/PRUP appropriate for achieving the objective set?*
- Implementation: *What implementation problems arose? How did the authorities and the target groups get on with each other? Which forms of participation were used? What opinions do the actors have of the policy? How did policy makers deal with possible implementation problems? Why did the policy finally reach its objective (or not)?*
- Effects: *Questions about intended and unintended (side-)effects of the policy (focus on participation). Which (un)intended changes can we see in the policy as a result of the designation of the MPAs? Were the objectives that were set reached?*

Finally, the aim of this book is also to formulate a number of recommendations on the basis of the lessons learnt from the analysis of both policy processes.

2. *Analysis Framework*

The framework of analysis is based on the 'Policy Arrangement Approach' (PAA) (*see among others*: Van Tatenhove *et al.* 2000; Bogaert 2004; Arts *et al.* 2006). "*A 'policy arrangement' refers to the temporary stabilisation of the organisation and the substance of a policy domain at a specific level of policy making.*" (Van Tatenhove *et al.*, 2000: 54). Both aspects, organisation *and* content, are inherently linked and deserve due attention in a policy analysis. In this research we follow the interpretation of Van der Zouwen (2006) in which '*policy domain'* is replaced by '*policy-making processes'*. As we shall demonstrate later in this book, the process of designation of MPAs is not, after all, limited to *one* policy domain (e.g. nature conservation policy). Developments in adjacent policy domains, such as energy and spatial planning, have an influence on the designation process that is the subject of our research. Furthermore, we do not limit the analysis to '*a specific level of policy making*', but we investigate the impact of policy developments at various levels of government. In concrete terms, for example, this relates to the impact of international legislation and regulations on the designation process of MPAs under study. In this regard specific attention will be paid to the analysis of the PRUP related to questions of hierarchy and subsidiarity.

Stability and change of arrangements, and the mechanism behind these, form the core of the analysis by means of the PAA. For the analysis of the content-related and organisational modelling, four dimensions are distinguished, of which the first three are related to policy organisation and the fourth to policy content (Van Tatenhove *et al.* 2000):
- The *actors* and their *coalitions* (and *opposition groups*) involved in the policy domain
- The division of *power* and *resources*
- The current *rules of the game*
- The current *policy discourses* and *policy programmes*

Under *actors* and *coalitions* we describe who is involved in the policy processes from different spheres of society: state (e.g. a politician, a civil servant...), civil society (e.g. an individual citizen, an association...) and the market (e.g. a port authority, the energy sector, the hotel and catering industry...) and to what extent there are interdependencies between these actors. Actors and coalitions participate in policy processes with an eye toward achieving policy objectives. In this the emphasis can be on supporting policy discourses used ('*supporting coalitions*'), or on making opposition in order to adjust these discourses ('*challenging coalitions*').

Patterns of interaction are also defined by *power* relationships between actors and vice versa. A second dimension that we include in the analysis is the division of power and influence between actors, in which power refers to mobilisation, distribution and use of resources, and influence to who defines the policy outcomes and how they are defined (Bogaert 2004). Through the distribution of resources, power refers to the input side of the policy process, while influence rather points to the output side (Arts 2001), namely who finally weighs in policy outcomes. By *resources* are meant, among other things, money, means, people, knowledge, expertise and competences.

"Rules prescribe appropriate behaviour in particular settings and thus are collective attributes. Procedures are those rules that determine how actors and organizations make all other rules" (Stone Sweet *et al.* 2001:7). At this level of abstraction a distinction can be made between three important aspects of *rules*: 'precision of prescription', 'formality' and 'authority' (Stone Sweet *et al.* 2001). Firstly, rules can be very strictly formulated, thus highly restricting the freedom of action of actors, or inversely, they can be very broadly formulated, leaving much freedom of action for the actors involved ('precision of prescription'). Secondly, rules can be particularly different in their formal character ('formality'). So they can vary from rather informal rules (customs), to much formalised rules that are reflected in legislation and define which actors are formally involved in the policy process. Thirdly, rules can vary in their compulsory nature ('authority'). In this view, non-observance of rules can only lead to absolutely nothing, to being blamed or to receiving a formal sanction. In the analysis we shall check which rules have been used in the respective policy processes.

Finally, attention will be given in the analysis to the *discourses* used. Hajer defines a discourse as: *"A specific ensemble of ideas, concepts, and categorizations that are produced, reproduced and transformed in a particular set of practices and through which meaning is given to physical and social realities"* (Hajer 1995: 44). Discourse refers to the opinions and reports of the actors involved, in terms of norms and values, problem definitions, and possible solutions. Attention will be given in the analysis to discourses used, the appearance of discourse coalitions and shifts in discourses.

The various dimensions are inextricably bound up with one another. Liefferink (2006) shows this in a tetrahedron, in which each corner represents a dimension.

Changes in one dimension can bring about changes in the other dimensions. So we see, for example, that a change in rules of the game on the entering into force of the Marine Environment Act (1999), not only led to the first designation proposals, but also to changing positions of actors and the appearance of coalitions of users of the North Sea *(see chapter 3).*

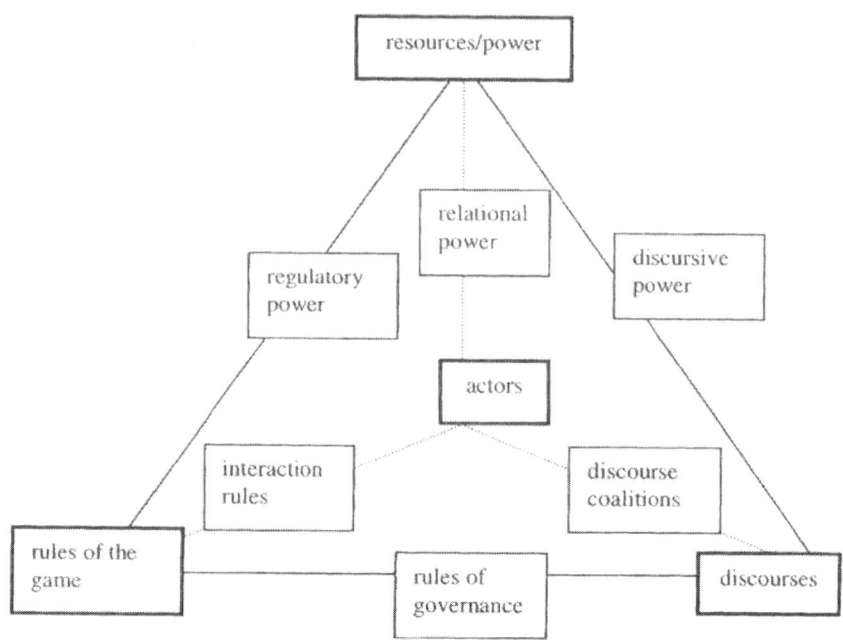

Figure 1: Four dimensions linked up with one another (Liefferink 2006)

In addition to attention to strategically operating actors, the PAA also focuses on the interaction with the structural level. Thus changes in coalitions, mobilisation of resources, discourses and rules of the game are not only the result of strategic actions and interactions of actors involved in the daily policy process, but these are also influenced by structural processes of change in society and politics (Bogaert 2004). With the generic research question formulated before we point to an important change, in scientific literature called the shift from 'government' to 'governance' (Marks 1992; Rosenau 2000). Alongside traditional arrangements with a dominant government and with rather classic forms of policy practise (top-down), there is the expectation that more and new interactive arrangements (negotiating state, bottom-up) may appear. We will examine if these shifts also occurred in the designation process of the MPAs, and the policy process for establishing the PRUP for Beaches and Dikes.

3. Research Methodology

For both the analysis of the designation process of MPAs in Belgium and the development of the PRUP for Beaches and Dikes we used case study research. An analysis by means of a case study using several research techniques and sources (triangulation), can lead to independent and trustworthy observations

(Swanborn 1987; Yin 1989). Moreover case study research allows for social phenomena to be studied in their context (Yin 1994).

Dependent on the objectives set, a distinction can be made between sorts of case studies.

All sorts of terms and distinctions are in circulation (among others Swanborn 1994). In this research a single case study is employed, because:
- A unique case is studied;
- The case is a representative case for the Flemish/Belgian situation;
- It is about a pilot project (without precedent) from which we can draw a number of lessons for the future.

Given the great importance of the diversity of sources, use was made of data triangulation through literature studies, documentary analysis (policy notes, reports of (in)formal consultations, legislation, press reports...) and in-depth interviews. The choice for a qualitative research design led to working with in-depth interviews with a relatively restricted number of respondents (18 for the MPAs and 18 for the PRUP) in the period October 2006 – April 2007. During the interviews we worked with a hybrid of open and half-structured interviews.

For the selection of respondents for the MPA analysis, the following criteria were used:

- Type of actor
  - State (federal, Flemish, local)
  - Civil society
  - Market
  - Science
  - Other
- Involvement in the designation process
  - Not involved
  - Involved
- Period of involvement
  - 1999-2003: first (unsuccessful) attempt at designation
  - 2003-2006: final designation
  - Whole period
- Sort of involvement
  - Initiator/initiative taker
  - Intermediary
  - Object
- Attitude to designation process
  - Positive (active or passive support)
  - Neutral
  - Negative (active or passive resistance/protest)

The selection led to a distribution of respondents across the following categories - representatives of the state (8), market (3), civil society (4), and scientists (3). For the federal government we interviewed a former Minister for the North Sea (2003-2005) and two officials from ministerial offices. We also interviewed the Governor of the Province of West Flanders and a mayor of a coastal municipality. Finally, 3 civil servants were interviewed (2 federal, 1 Flemish). For the market interviews took place with representatives of a port authority, the director of a planned off-shore wind energy project and a ship owner. For civil society there were interviews with representatives of a water sports federation, an anglers' association and a nature conservation organisation.

In selecting respondents for the PRUP analysis, the following criteria were used:

- Involvement in the designation process
  - Not involved
  - Involved
    - In informal preliminary consultation
    - In formal consultation PRUP1, PRUP2, PRUP3, PRUP4, ... PRUP10, all
    - In the whole procedure
- Sort of involvement
  - Initiator/initiative taker
  - Intermediary
  - Object
- Participation in public inquiry via comments and/or complaints (notice of objection)
  - None
  - Comments
  - Complaints
  - Comments and complaints
- Type of actor
  - State
  - Civil society
  - Market

The selection led to a distribution of respondents across the following categories: state (12), market (1) and civil society (5). For the Flemish authorities we interviewed a civil servant from the ministerial office of the Flemish Minister of Finances and Budget and Spatial Planning. In addition, we interviewed the member of the Provincial Executive of West Flanders in charge of spatial planning and two mayors of coastal municipalities. Finally, we also interviewed 8 civil servants (2 Flemish, 3 provincial and 3 municipal). For the market an interview took place with a manager of a surf club. For civil society interviews took place with representatives of a water sports federation, an association for the self-employed, and a nature conservation organisation. In addition, the chairpersons of two public advisory bodies were interviewed: the 'Provinciale Commissie Ruimtelijke Ordening' (PROCORO – Provincial Advisory Commission for Spatial Planning) and a 'Gemeentelijke Commissie Ruimtelijke Ordening' (GECORO) (Municipal Advisory Commission for Spatial Planning).

Digital audio recordings were made of the interviews. Before the interviews took place the respondents were expressly asked if they had any objection to this and were assured that anonymity was guaranteed. The interviews lasted between 1 and 2 hours on average. The audio recordings were subsequently written out in full. With the help of the software program NVivo7[1] the abundance of data was analysed. The interviews were coded via *'tree nodes'*, in which the tree diagram was based upon the dimensions distinguished within the PAA described above. Via *'coding summary reports'* the data were then compared with each other. Via *'queries'*, overview matrices were produced that make it possible to reproduce and compare the point of view of the interviewed respondents.

References

ARTS, B., P. LEROY & J. VAN TATENHOVE (2006). 'Political Modernisation and Policy Arrangements: A Framework for Understanding Environmental Policy Change'. *Public Organization Review* (6), pp. 93-106.

BOGAERT, D. (2004). *Natuurbeleid in Vlaanderen. Natuurontwikkeling en draagvlak als vernieuwingen?* Brussel: Instituut voor Natuurbehoud.

CRABBÉ, A., J. GYSEN & P. LEROY (2006). *Vademecum Milieubeleidsevaluatie.* Brugge: Vanden Broele.

FULLER, R.C. & R.R. MYERS (1941). 'The natural history of a social problem'. *American Sociological Review* (6), pp. 320-328.

HAJER, M.A. (1995). *The Politics of Environmental Discourse: Ecological Modernization and the Policy Process.* Oxford: Oxford University Press.

LIEFFERINK, D. (2006). 'The dynamics of policy arrangements: turning round the tetrahedron'. In B. Arts & P. Leroy (eds.), *Institutional Dynamics in Environmental Governance.* Berlijn: Springer.

MARKS, G. (1992). 'Structural policy in the European Community'. In A. Sbragia (ed.) *Euro-politics: Institutions and policymaking in the 'new' European Community.* Washington DC: The Brookings Institution.

PARSONS, W. (1995). *Public Policy: An Introduction to the Theory and Practice of Policy Analysis.* Aldershot: Edward Elgar.

ROSENAU, J.N. (2000). 'Change, complexity, and governance in globalizing space'. In J. Pierre (ed.) *Debating Governance; Authority, Steering and Democracy.* Oxford: Oxford University Press.

SABATIER, P.A. & H.C. JENKINS-SMITH (1993). *Policy Change and Learning: An Advocacy Coalition Approach.* Boulder: Westview Press.

STONE SWEET, A., W. SANDHOLTZ & N. FLIGSTEIN (2001). *The Institutionalization of Europe.* Oxford: Oxford University Press.

---

[1] *See*: http://www.qsrinternational.com/products_nvivo.aspx

SWANBORN, P.G. (1987). *Methoden van sociaal-wetenschappelijk onderzoek.* nieuwe editie. Boom: Meppel.

SWANBORN, P.G. (1994). 'Het ontwerpen van case-studies: enkele keuzes'. *Mens en Maatschappij* (3), pp. 322- 335.

VAN DER ZOUWEN, M. (2006). *Nature policy between trends and traditions: Dynamics in Nature Policy Arrangements in the Yorkshire Dales, Doñana and the Veluwe.* Delft: Eburon.

VAN TATENHOVE, J., B. Arts & P. Leroy (2000). *Political Modernisation and the Environment. The Renewal of Environmental Policy Arrangements.* Dordrecht: Kluwer Academic Publishers.

YIN, R.K. (1989). *Case study research: design and methods.* Newbury Park.

YIN, R.K. (1994). *Case study research: design and methods.* 2nd edition. Thousand Oaks: Sage.

The legal Framework for Marine Protected Areas in Belgium

An Cliquet, Dirk Bogaert and Frank Maes

1. Introduction

This chapter describes the legal framework for Marine Protected Areas (MPAs) in Belgium. First of all we will explain the concept of Marine Protected Areas. Then we will describe the international and European obligations that lie at the foundation of the Belgian legal framework. In the next part we will examine the Belgian legal framework and pay attention to possible pressure points. Finally we will give an overview of the implementation of the legislation related to the Belgian marine environment.

In this chapter we examine which process-related obligations or obligations relating to participation have possibly been included in international and national legislation with regard to protected areas. For some years now scientific literature and legislation have gradually been paying more attention to the changing needs of the management of protected areas and the role of participation in this. Kelleher (1999) for example refers in this respect to joint management ('management partnership') (Kelleher 1999). According to this author as well as to others it seems essential for the management of MPAs to involve local communities and other stakeholders (CBD 2004; Kelleher 1999).

In the next chapter we will then examine how this has been implemented in practice on the occasion of the designation of the MPAs in Belgium. Within the scope of this book no attention is paid to other international obligations relating to participation, such as for example the Aarhus Convention[1]. However this does not take anything away from the importance of those obligations.

2. The Concept of 'Marine Protected Areas'

The designation and the management of 'Marine Protected Areas' (MPAs) is not new (Gubbay 1995). The first MPAs were designated at the beginning of the 20th Century. The majority however have been designated during the past three decades (Agardy et al. 2003). There is no generally accepted interpretation of the concept of MPAs. On the international level different names are used, such as, for example, marine reserve, marine park and protected seascape (Wells & Day 2004; IUCN 2007), but moreover, the same names are also interpreted in a different way. The differences in the various types of MPAs have to do with the legal basis, the location, the objectives of the protection, the criteria for the designation of protected areas and the degree of protection (Cliquet 2001).

---

[1]   Convention on Access to Information, Public Participation in Decision-making and Access to Justice in Environmental Matters, Aarhus, 25 June 1998; in force since 30 October 2001; http://www.unece.org/env/pp/; ratified by Belgium by the Act of 17 December 2002, Belgian Law Gazette 24 April 2003.

During its 17th General Assembly in 1988 the IUCN adopted the following definition of an MPA: *"Any area of intertidal or subtidal terrain together with their overlying waters and associated flora, fauna, historical and cultural features, which has been reserved by law or other effective means to protect part or the entire enclosed environment"*[2].

In the context of the Convention on Biological Diversity the Ad Hoc Technical Expert Group (AHTEG) defined an MPA as follows: *"'Marine and coastal protected area' means any defined area within or adjacent to the marine environment, together with its overlying waters and associated flora, fauna and historical and cultural features, which has been reserved by legislation or other effective means, including custom, with the effect that its marine and/or coastal biodiversity enjoys a higher level of protection than its surroundings."* Areas within the marine environment include permanent shallow marine waters; sea bays; straits; lagoons; estuaries; subtidal aquatic areas (kelp forests, sea-grass meadow); coral reefs; intertidal muds; sand or marine salt flats and marshes; seamounths; deep-water corals; deep-water vents; and open ocean habitats. (CBD 2004: 7).

It is clear that just as for protected areas on the mainland there is no uniform typology of MPAs either. This makes comparison between different countries more difficult. The IUCN has made an effort to establish an overall classification of the various categories of areas. On the basis of various management objectives 6 area categories can be distinguished (IUCN 1994)[3]:

I. *Strict Nature Reserve/Wilderness Area*: managed for science or for wilderness protection;
II. *National Park*: managed for ecosystem protection and recreation;
III. *Natural Monument*: managed for conservation of specific natural features;
IV. *Habitat/Species Management Area*: managed in view of nature conservation through active management;
V. *Protected Landscape/Seascape*: managed for conservation of landscape/seascape and recreation;
VI. *Managed Resource Protected Area*: managed in view of the sustainable use of natural ecosystems.

This classification should make it possible to compare MPAs. But even this classification is not completely conclusive. According to Wood, cited in MPA News, there is little correlation between the IUCN area categories and the actual protection of the MPAs. This is caused by the fact that the names of the categories do not clearly correspond to the actual objectives of the category concerned (MPA News 2007). This is however rather due to the lack of understanding of the role of the categories than to problems with regard to their specific implementation in the marine environment (Wells & Day 2004: 36). Therefore, the guidelines for the area categories are currently under revision[4].

---

2   Resolution by the 17th General Assembly of IUCN: 17.38 Protection of the coastal and marine environment.
3   http://www.iucn.org/themes/wcpa/theme/categories/categories.htm.
4   http://www.parksnet.org/index.php?globalnav=detail&table=documents&id=1282.

Another problem is that it is not possible to classify one area under more than one category. This is for example the case with larger multiple use areas in which one or more 'no-take' zones are designated (MPA News 2007). These so-called no-take zones are zones from which it is prohibited to remove marine species, to modify, extract or collect marine resources (Wells & Day 2004), unless this is necessary for monitoring or research to assess the effectiveness of these areas (Jones 2006). These no-take zones have become an important instrument both for the conservation of marine biodiversity and for the management of fisheries. In many cases it will be possible to classify the no-take zones under the IUCN Categories I and II. However, it is also possible to designate no-take zones within a larger MPA, as for example the no-take zones in Lundy Island Marine Nature Reserve in Great-Britain. This area was also designated as a Special Area of Conservation according to the Habitats Directive and is classified under IUCN Category IV (Wells & Day 2004). The Special Protection Areas and Special Areas of Conservation designated according to the Birds and Habitats Directives will usually fall within IUCN Category IV, since these areas are designated in view of the conservation of specific habitats or species. In principle the Belgian MPAs (*see below*) also fall within this category.

3. International Obligations

The past few decades the growing attention to MPAs has also been translated into international treaties. In what follows we will describe the most important treaties and the resulting obligations and pay special attention to the repercussions for Belgium.

3.1 Ramsar Convention[5] (1971)

The Ramsar Convention, aiming at the protection of wetlands of international importance, contained for the contracting parties the first obligations with regard to MPAs. On the basis of the Ramsar Convention the contracting parties shall designate the suitable wetlands within their territory for inclusion in a *List of Wetlands of International Importance*. Article 1 of the Convention describes the notion of *wetland* as: "*areas of marsh, fen, peatland or water, whether natural or artificial, permanent or temporary, with water that is static or flowing, fresh, brackish or salt, including areas of marine water the depth of which at low tide does not exceed six metres*". Riparian or coastal areas adjacent to the wetlands and islands or bodies of marine water deeper than six meters at low tide lying within the wetlands, can also be included in the Ramsar list, especially where these have importance as waterfowl habitat (article 2, § 1, Ramsar Convention). This means that the Ramsar Convention also applies to coastal zones as

---

[5]   Convention on Wetlands of International Importance especially as Waterfowl Habitat, Ramsar, 2 February 1971 (hereafter: Ramsar Convention); in force since 21 December 1975; http://www.ramsar.org; ratified by Belgium by the Act of 22 February 1979, Belgian Law Gazette 12 April 1979.

well as in a part of the marine environment. As a consequence of the depth criterion in the definition, the implementation in marine areas is restricted to shallow, inshore marine waters.

The management measures that the Convention provides for are quite vague and leave the parties a great deal of room for interpretation. The Convention itself does not provide any measures with regard to participation in the designation, conservation and management of the Ramsar sites. Afterwards the topic of participation was also dealt with by the Conference of the Contracting Parties. Thus guidelines were developed for strengthening participation of local communities and indigenous people in the management of wetlands[6]. The series of Ramsar Secretariat Handbooks on the 'Wise Use of Wetlands', also pay attention to communication, education and public awareness (Ramsar 2007a) and to participation (Ramsar 2007b).

In Belgium various Ramsar sites were designated by the Royal Decree of 27 September 1984[7], and one of these was situated in the marine environment, the area of the 'Kustbanken' in the territorial sea (the Royal Decree speaks of the 'Vlaamse Banken' in the coastal waters). No specific measures for conservation or management were linked to the designation. The area falls entirely within the Special Area of Conservation 'Trapegeer-Stroombank', which was designated in 2005 (*see below*).

3.2 United Nations Convention on the Law of the Sea[8] (1982)

The Convention on the Law of the Sea does not mention MPAs as such, but it does mention measures that are necessary for the protection and the conservation of rare or fragile ecosystems, as well as the habitat of depleted, threatened or endangered species and other forms of marine life (article 194, § 5, Convention on the Law of the Sea). The Convention on the Law of the Sea does not create any new area categories, as is the case with other treaties such as the Ramsar Convention. The only exception to this is article 211, § 6 of the Convention on the Law of the Sea, providing for the possibility of establishing protected areas with respect to shipping. The Convention on the Law of the Sea does however determine the various marine jurisdictions and thus provides the basis on which the rights and duties of coastal states and other states are determined. These provisions are important to check which opportunities

---

6   Guidelines for establishing and strengthening local communities' and indigenous people's participation in the management of wetlands, Annex to Resolution VII.8, COP7, San José, Costa Rica, 1999.

7   Royal Decree of 27 September 1984 on the designation of wetlands of international importance, Belgian Law Gazette 31 October 1984.

8   United Nations Convention on the Law of the Sea, Montego Bay, 10 December 1982 (hereafter: Convention on the Law of the Sea); in force since 16 November 1994; http://www.un.org/Depts/los/convention_agreements/convention_overview_convention. htm; ratified by Belgium by the Act of 18 June 1998, Belgian Law Gazette 16 September 1999.

the coastal state has for the designation and management of MPAs (Cliquet 1996). In what follows we will briefly examine the possibilities for the territorial sea, the Exclusive Economic Zone (EEZ) and the continental shelf, since these are the most relevant areas for Belgium.

As a consequence of the sovereignty of the coastal state over its territorial sea the coastal state is competent to take measures with regard to the conservation and management of the natural resources and the natural values in its territorial sea. So the coastal state can designate and protect MPAs in the territorial sea. But when taking measures, the coastal state should take into account the right of 'innocent passage' for all ships.

In the Exclusive Economic Zone the coastal state has sovereign rights for the purpose of exploring and exploiting, conserving and managing the natural resources, of the waters superjacent to the seabed and of the seabed and its subsoil, as well as jurisdiction with regard to among other things the protection and preservation of the marine environment and marine scientific research. The designation of an MPA is a conservation measure and therefore a coastal state will be entitled to establish an MPA within the EEZ and to take measures, for example, with regard to fisheries or protection of species. The coastal state shall however have due regard to the rights of other states, such as the freedom of navigation. Navigation can only be restricted at international level.

On the continental shelf the coastal state exercises sovereign rights for the purpose of exploring and exploiting the natural resources. The exploitation is limited to the non-living natural resources and the living organisms belonging to sedentary species. Sovereign rights are not equal to the sovereignty that is exercised over the territorial sea. A coastal state can in principle designate an MPA on its continental shelf in order to preserve non-living and sedentary living resources. The measures can only concern the seabed and subsoil.

3.3 Convention on Biological Diversity[9] (1992)

The Convention on Biological Diversity (CBD) was signed at the 1992 UNCED Conference (United Nations Conference on Environment and Development) in Rio. During the preparation of this Convention there was mainly discussion about terrestrial biodiversity (resources of the tropical forests) and hardly about marine biodiversity. Still the CBD explicitly applies to marine areas. This appears from article 2 in which 'biological diversity' is described as the variability among living organisms from all sources including, inter alia, terrestrial, marine and other aquatic ecosystems and the ecological complexes of which they are part. The Convention applies to components of biodiversity in

---

[9]   Convention on Biological Diversity, Rio de Janeiro, 5 June 1992; in force since 29 December 1993; http://www.cbd.int; ratified by Belgium by the Act of 11 May 1995, Belgian Law Gazette 2 April 1997.

areas within the limits of its national jurisdiction (article 4, a, CBD), thus to the territorial sea and EEZ. Moreover the Convention also applies to processes and activities carried out under its jurisdiction or control, within the area of its national jurisdiction or beyond the limits of national jurisdiction, regardless of where their effects occur (article 4, b, CBD). As a consequence the Convention applies to activities on the high seas. In the marine environment the Convention must be applied in conformity with the rights and duties of states under the Law of the Sea.

According to article 8 of the Convention the contracting parties shall establish a system of protected areas or of areas where special measures need to conserve biodiversity. Although the Convention calls upon the contracting parties to establish protected areas, no new international list of protected areas is created, as for example the Ramsar list. An important target that was formulated in the context of the Convention is the 2010 target, in which the contracting parties agree to achieve by 2010 a significant reduction of the rate of biodiversity loss at the global, regional and national level[10]. A sub-target of the 2010 target requires that at least 10% of each of the world's ecological regions will be effectively conserved. From the Global MPA database (Wood 2007) it appears however that for the marine environment this target is as yet far from being reached: only 0,6% of the marine environment is currently protected (Wood 2006). Considering the rate at which MPAs are being designated it will still take until 2069 before the 10% target is achieved (MPA News 2005).

In 1995 specific attention was paid to the marine and coastal environment by the so-called Jakarta Mandate on Marine and Coastal Biological Diversity[11]. The recommendations of the Subsidiary Body on Scientific, Technical and Technological Advice (SBSTTA) urged parties to establish a representative system of marine and coastal protected areas[12]. These recommendations were supported by the Conference of the Parties in 1995[13]. The programme of work on marine and coastal biological diversity was adopted by the Conference of the Parties in 1998[14] and reviewed in 2004[15]. Particularly in the reviewed working programme of 2004 MPAs were examined in more detail[16]. It agreed to the

---

[10] COP 6 Decision VI/26, The Hague, 7 - 19 April 2002, Strategic Plan for the Convention on Biological Diversity; http://www.cbd.int/decisions/?m=COP-06&id=7200.

[11] COP 2 Decision II/10, Jakarta, 6 - 17 November 1995, Conservation and sustainable use of marine and coastal biological diversity; http://www.cbd.int/decisions/?dec=II/10.

[12] SBSTTA, Recommendation I/8; par. 11; http://www.cbd.int/recommendations/?rec=I/8.

[13] COP 2, Decision II/10, Annex I.

[14] COP 4, Decision IV/5, Bratislava, 4 - 15 May 1998, Conservation and sustainable use of marine and coastal biological diversity, including a programme of work; http://www.cbd.int/decisions/ ?dec=IV/5.

[15] COP 7, Decision VII/5, Kuala Lumpur, 9 - 20 February 2004, Marine and coastal biological diversity. Review of the programme of work on marine and coastal biodiversity; http://www.cbd.int/decisions/?dec=VII/5.

[16] Based upon the work of the Ad Hoc Technical Expert Group on MCPA's (UNEP/CBD/SBSTTA/8/INF/7) and the work of the SBSTTA (SBSTTA 8 Recommendation

concrete objective of establishing a system of MPAs by 2012[17]. Thus the target in the Plan of Implementation plan of the World Summit on Sustainable Development (2002) was accepted, i.e. the establishment of a network of MPAs by 2012 and the establishment of no-take areas[18].

The objective concerning marine and coastal protected areas in the programme of work on marine and coastal biological diversity is formulated as follows: *"The establishment and maintenance of marine and coastal protected areas that are effectively managed, ecologically based and contribute to a global network of marine and coastal protected areas, building upon national and regional systems, including a range of levels of protection, where human activities are managed, particularly through national legislation, regional programmes and policies, traditional and cultural practices and international agreements, to maintain the structure and functioning of the full range of marine and coastal ecosystems, in order to provide benefits to both present and future generations"*[19]. In the appendix to the programme of work this objective is further developed into operational objectives[20]. One of those objectives is to achieve an effective management of MPAs (operational objective 3.3.).

In the context of the CBD attention is also paid to participation. The programme of work concerning protected areas contains a specific chapter on governance, participation, equity and benefit sharing[21]. Thus by 2008 there should be full and effective participation of indigenous and local communities, as well as participation of relevant stakeholders in the management of existing and the establishment and management of new protected areas (goal 2.2.). The public awareness, understanding and appreciation of the importance and benefits of protected areas should be significantly increased (goal 3.5.). By 2012 all protected areas should be effectively managed, using participatory and science-based site planning processes, that incorporate clear biodiversity objectives, targets, management strategies and monitoring programmes, as well as a long-term management plan with active stakeholder involvement (goal 1.4.).

VIII/3, Montreal, 10 - 14 March 2003, Marine and coastal biodiversity: review, further elaboration and refinement of the programme of work;
http://www.cbd.int/recommendations/ ?m=SBSTTA-08&id=7056&lg=0).

[17] COP 7, Decision VII/5, Kuala Lumpur, 9 - 20 February 2004, Marine and coastal biological diversity. Review of the programme of work on marine and coastal biodiversity, par. 19; http://www.cbd.int/decisions/?dec=VII/5; COP 7 Decision VII/28, Kuala Lumpur, 9 - 20 February 2004, Protected areas (Articles 8 (a) to (e)), par. 18; http://www.cbd.int/decisions/ ?m=COP-07&id=7765&lg=0.

[18] Plan of implementation of the World Summit on Sustainable Development, par. 32, c. In: United Nations. Report of the World Summit on Sustainable Development. Johannesburg, South Africa, 26 August- 4 September 2002. A/Conf.199/20; http://www.unmillenniumproject.org/documents/131302_wssd_report_reissued.pdf .

[19] COP 7, Decision VII/5, par. 18.

[20] COP 7, Decision VII/5, Annex I. Elaborated programme of work on marine and coastal biological diversity.

[21] COP 7 Decision VII/28, Kuala Lumpur, 9 - 20 February 2004, Protected areas (Articles 8 (a) to (e)); http://www.cbd.int/decisions/?m=COP-07&id=7765&lg=0 .

The programme of work on marine and coastal biological diversity explicitly reconfirms the importance of participation of indigenous and local communities and relevant stakeholders for MPAs[22].

3.4 OSPAR Convention[23] (1992)

In 1992 the regional OSPAR Convention for the Protection of the Marine Environment of the North-East Atlantic was established. The Convention applies to the 'maritime area', that includes the internal waters up to the freshwater limit, the territorial seas, the areas beyond the territorial seas that fall under the jurisdiction of the contracting parties and the high seas, including the bed and the subsoil of all those waters.

The Convention of 1992 was mainly aimed at reducing pollution. Only in 1998 a fifth annex was adopted that specifically dealt with the protection and conservation of the ecosystems and the biological diversity of the maritime area[24]. This Annex V does not contain an explicit obligation for the contracting parties to establish protected areas. Neither does it establish an international list of protected areas. But the contracting parties are urged to take the necessary measures to protect, conserve and restore, where practicable, the ecosystems and the biological diversity of the maritime area (article 2, a, Annex V). The OSPAR Commission is among other things charged with developing means, consistent with international law, for instituting protective, conservation, restorative and precautionary measures related to specific areas or sites or related to particular species or habitats (article 3, b, ii, Annex V). Upon ratification of Annex V the contracting parties also emphasized that it is not the intention to duplicate work. Overlaps with other international measures should be avoided. With regard to fisheries and maritime transport Annex V even states explicitly that under Annex V no measures shall be adopted in this respect (article 4, Annex V).

The actual provisions with regard to MPAs were later developed in ministerial declarations, an OSPAR recommendation and OSPAR guidelines. In the Sintra Statement, made at the Ministerial Meeting of the OSPAR Commission in 1998, the commitment was taken that the Commission will promote the establishment of a network of MPAs, to ensure the sustainable use and the protection of marine biological diversity and its ecosystems. During a following Ministerial Meeting in Bremen in 2003 a more concrete goal was defined, to identify a first set of MPAs by 2006, to establish what gaps then remain and

---

22 COP 7, Decision VII/5, par. 27.
23 Convention on the Protection of the Marine Environment of the North-Eastern Atlantic, Paris, 22 September 1992 (hereafter: OSPAR Convention); in force since 25 March 1998; http://www.ospar.org; ratified by Belgium by the Act of 11 May 1995, Belgian Law Gazette 31 January 1998.
24 Annex V, The Protection and Conservation of the Ecosystems and Biological Diversity of the Maritime Area; ratified by Belgium by the Act of 6 March 2002, Belgian Law Gazette 23 September 2005.

complete by 2010 a joint network of well-managed MPAs that together with Natura 2000 is ecologically coherent (Bremen Statement, 11)[25].

The strategy of the OSPAR Commission (2003) determines that a network of MPAs will be identified based on the guidelines for the identification and the selection of MPAs. This network can also include Special Protection Areas or Special Areas of Conservation, designated under the Birds and Habitat Directives (Strategy, 4.3., c) [26].

In 2003 the Commission laid down criteria for the identification of species and habitats that must be protected[27], and a list was drawn up of endangered species and habitats, which was reviewed in 2004[28], with a description of the habitats in this list[29]. A recommendation of 2003[30] aims at an ecologically coherent network of well-managed MPAs by 2010 (Recommendation 2003/3, 2.1.). An MPA is defined as "*an area within the maritime area for which protective, conservation, restorative or precautionary measures, consistent with international law have been instituted for the purpose of protecting and conserving species, habitats, ecosystems or ecological processes of the marine environment*". The OSPAR Network of MPAs consists of areas that have been reported to the OSPAR Commission by the contracting parties, together with any other area outside the jurisdiction of the contracting parties, which has been included in the network of the OSPAR Commission (Recommendation 2003/3, 1.1.).

The contracting parties should consider which areas within their jurisdiction meet the criteria. They must report to the Commission the areas that they have selected as components of the OSPAR network (recommendation 2003/3, 3.1). For each area a management plan has to be developed and the contracting party must determine which management measures would be appropriate (Recommendation 2003/3, 3.3.). If an area is designated as Special Protection Area or a Special Area of Conservation under the Birds or Habitat Directives, it may also be reported to the OSPAR Commission as a component of the OSPAR network. However, the contracting parties are not obliged to take any action in respect of that area on the basis of this recommendation (Recommendation, 2003/3, 3.5.).

The recommendation with regard to the establishment of a network of protected areas was supported by guidelines for the identification and selection of

---

[25] Bremen Statement, Ministerial Meeting of the OSPAR Commission, Bremen 25 June 2003.

[26] 2003 Strategies of the OSPAR Commission for the Protection of the Marine Environment of the North-East Atlantic (Reference number: 2003-21); http://www.ospar.org/eng/html/ welcome.html.

[27] Criteria for the Identification of Species and Habitats in need of Protection and their Method of Application (The Texel-Faial Criteria), (Ref. nr. 2003-13).

[28] 2004 Initial OSPAR List of Threatened and/or Declining Species and Habitats (Ref. nr. 2004-06).

[29] Descriptions of habitats on the initial OSPAR list of threatened and/or declining species and habitats (Ref.nr. 2004-07).

[30] OSPAR Recommendation 2003/3 on a Network of Marine Protected Areas.

MPAs in the OSPAR Maritime Area[31], as well as guidelines for the management of those areas[32]. In 2006 some additional guidelines were issued to provide support in the development of a network of protected areas[33]. In 2007 a self-assessment checklist was developed as a guideline for the establishment of a network of MPAs[34], as well as a self-assessment scorecard to assess the effectiveness of the management of OSPAR MPAs[35].

From an OSPAR status rapport of 2006 (OSPAR Commission 2007a) about the OSPAR MPA network it appears that 87 areas are designated by six contracting parties, with a total surface area of 26.619 km². The majority of the areas fall within the territorial sea and are already designated as Special Protection Areas or Special Areas of Conservation under the Birds or Habitats Directives. A number of countries, including Belgium, have not yet reported areas to the OSPAR Commission. In Belgium there is an investigation going on as to whether the designated Belgian MPAs qualify for inclusion as OSPAR areas, or whether other areas may qualify for inclusion. For that purpose a report was produced (Haelters *et al.* 2007) from which it appears that the already designated MPAs in the Belgian part of the North Sea do not fully qualify for the criteria for the identification and selection of OSPAR MPAs. With the exception of gravel banks it was not possible to identify areas with endangered habitats or endangered species, as included in the OSPAR list. One new area is proposed: the Westhinder area. This is an area with hard substrata, with a surface area of 119 km² or about 3.4% of the Belgian marine waters. The area is mainly situated within the Belgian EEZ. However, the report does not mention anything about possible designation as MPA under national legislation. But these hard substrata areas do possibly qualify as Special Areas of Conservation under the Habitats Directive.

The OSPAR Convention and the related documents pay little attention to participation. With regard to possible management methods the guidelines about the management of OSPAR MPAs only mention among other things advisory committees, arrangements with private organisations, institutes or individual persons, involved in the implementation and the management of the area. Also the self-assessment scorecard for the management of areas pays attention to participation: one of the questions that have to be answered on the scorecard is whether stakeholders have a meaningful contribution in management decisions. The criteria that were developed for the designation of areas, in-

---

[31] Guidelines for the Identification and Selection of Marine Protected Areas in the OSPAR Maritime Area (Ref. nr. 2003-17).
[32] Guidelines for the Management of Marine Protected Area in the OSPAR Maritime Area (Ref. nr. 2003-18).
[33] Guidance on developing an ecologically coherent network of OSPAR Marine Protected Area (Ref. nr. 2006-3).
[34] Guidance for the design of the OSPAR Network of Marine Protected Areas: a self-assessment checklist, (Reference number: 2007-6).
[35] Guidance to assess the effectiveness of management of OSPAR MPAs: a self-assessment scorecard, (Reference number: 2007-5).

clude mainly ecological criteria. A second set of criteria are practical criteria and considerations. One of those criteria is the degree of acceptance for the inclusion of an area as OSPAR MPA: *"The establishment of the MPA has a comparatively high potential level of support from stakeholders and political acceptability."* The Belgian report (Haelters *et al.* 2007) on the possible designation of Belgian OSPAR MPAs also takes into account practical considerations for the selection of OSPAR MPAs. One of those considerations is public support. The report states the following: *"Particular areas in the coastal area already have a protected status. An additional label like OSPAR MPA requires in practice no other, supplementary measures under OSPAR than the measures (that will be) included in a management plan, and as a consequence this would not attract much attention from the public and the authorities. The designation of the entire coastal zone as a protected area would cause a lot of resistance by the users. The support of policy makers and stakeholders will be all the stronger if well-known key species are proposed for protection, and if protection, and the measures that may be linked to it, have an* [36] *impact on current activities (…)"*. (Haelters *et al.* 2007: 24).

The OSPAR Convention as such does not establish a new category of MPAs. A network of MPAs is proposed in political statements and a non-binding recommendation. The areas reported to the OSPAR Commission are protected on the basis of among other things international or national legislation. Up to now there seems to be an overlap mainly with the Natura 2000 areas. It is not yet clear what the added legal value of the OSPAR areas is, which also fall under national jurisdiction. The OSPAR network may possibly provide added value for the designation of areas on the high seas, but this lies outside the scope of this book. Furthermore, activities in the context of the OSPAR Convention mainly provide support for the contracting parties with regard to the establishment of criteria for designation. The OSPAR network can also play a role in the management of cross-border MPAs (OSPAR 2007b).

4. European Obligations

The growing interest in MPAs also applies to Europe. The European nature conservation Directives and the European Marine Strategy Directive constitute the most important tools for European policy in this regard.

---

[36] There seems to be a mistake in the orginal Dutch text of the report. According to the authors of the report they meant that support will be broader if there is *no* impact on current activities (telephone conversation with Jan Haelters, 13 February 2008).

4.1 European Directives and the Designation of Special Protection Areas or Special Areas of Conservation

The Birds Directive[37] and the Habitats Directive[38] constitute the core of EU nature policy. Both Directives provide the basis for the establishment of protected areas.

4.1.1 Implementation of the Birds and the Habitats Directives at Sea

Both Directives apply to marine areas. Article 4, § 1 of the Birds Directive states that member states designate areas as Special Protection Areas for the species of Annex I, taking into account their protection requirements in the geographical sea and land area where this Directive applies. For species that are not listed in Annex I the member states take similar measures, bearing in mind their need for protection in the geographical sea and land area where this Directive applies (art 4, § 2, Birds Directive). Annex I lists 29 sea bird species for which Special Protection Areas must be designated (European Commission 2005). According to article 1 the Directive relates to the conservation of all species of naturally occurring birds in the wild state in the European territory of the member states to which the EC Treaty applies. This implies that the Directive applies in any case to the territorial sea, since that is part of the territory of a state. Moreover this Directive can also cover areas outside of territorial sea, insofar as the member states have jurisdiction. The area of application of Community Law and the legislation of member states is supposed to coincide. If member states exercise sovereign rights beyond the territorial sea, Community Law may also apply there (IJlstra & Nollkaemper 1990).

Just like the Birds Directive, the Habitats Directive applies to marine areas as well. In the definition of natural habitats the Habitats Directive explicitly speaks of terrestrial and aquatic areas (article 1, b, Habitats Directive). The annexes of the Habitats Directive include marine habitats and marine species: 9 marine habitat types in Annex I (European Commission 2007) and 18 species in Annex II (European Commission 2005). Examples of marine habitats are sandbanks which are slightly covered with sea water all the time (habitat 1110) and estuaries (habitat 1130). The marine and coastal habitat categories mentioned in Annex I of the Directive are broadly defined and may allow for more than one interpretation by member states in the identification of areas to be designated (Mitchell 1998). Marine habitats and species are underrepresented in the annexes of the Directive. However, before the annexes are reviewed in order to add new marine habitats and species, the Commission thinks that

---

[37] Directive 79/409/EEG of 2 April 1979 on the Conservation of Wild Birds, *PB L* 103, 25 April 1979 (hereafter: Birds Directive); text of the Directive, with later amendments, see http://eur-lex.europa.eu/LexUriServ/site/nl/consleg/1979/L/01979L0409-20070101-nl.pdf.

[38] Directive 92/43/EEG of 21 May 1992 on the Conservation of Natural Habitats and of Wild Fauna and Flora, *PB L* 206, 22 July 1992 (hereafter: Habitats Directive); text of the Directive, with later amendments, see http://ec.europa.eu/environment/nature/legislation /habitatsdirective/index_en.htm.

member states should first fully implement the existing obligations, in particular with respect to the Natura 2000 network (O'Brian 1998).

Just as for the Birds Directive, the Habitats Directive, in addition to being applicable in the territorial sea, also applies to the continental shelf and in the EEZ. This is confirmed in scientific literature (among others: Warren 1997; Cliquet 2001; Owen 2001; Backes 2001), in national jurisdiction[39], in jurisdiction by the Court of Justice[40], by the Council of the European Union[41] and the European Commission (European Commission 2007).

4.1.2 The Designation of Special Protection Areas and Special Areas of Conservation

On the basis of article 4 of the Birds Directive, member states have to take special conservation measures for species mentioned in Annex I of the Directive, as well as for regularly occurring migratory species that are not mentioned in Annex I, to ensure their survival and reproduction in their area of distribution. For this purpose the member states shall classify the territories that in number and size are most suitable for the conservation of those species as Special Protection Areas (SPAs), taking into account their protection requirements in the geographical land and sea areas to which this Directive applies. The designation of SPAs should be carried out by a formal decision of designation, which is obligatory for third parties[42]. The designation must also be reported to the Commission. The Court of Justice has produced extensive jurisdiction relating to the designation of SPAs. In essence it results in member states having very little policy margin for designating areas and only being allowed to invoke ecological (ornithological) criteria for the designation of areas. Social or economic criteria must not play a role in the designation or non-designation of an area (see below).

With the Habitats Directive the European Union aims, among other things, to create a European ecological network of Special Areas of Conservation (SACs), the so-called 'Natura 2000' network. The network must maintain the natural habitats and habitats of species of community importance described in Annexes I and II in a favourable conservation status and if necessary restore them. The Natura 2000 network will also include the SPAs of the Birds Directive (article 3, Habitats Directive).

---

[39] R v. Secretary of State for Trade and Industry vs. Greenpeace, Queen's Bench Division (Crown Office List), CO/1336/99, 5 November 1999; http://web.uct.ac.za/depts/pbl/ jgibson/iczm/cases/greenp.htm.

[40] Court of Justice, 20 October 2005, Case 6/04, Commission vs. Great Britain.

[41] Annex to Council Conclusions on the Strategy for the Integration of Environmental Concerns and Sustainable Development into the Common Fisheries Policy, Luxembourg, 25 April 2001, point 15; http://ue.eu.int/ueDocs/cms_Data/docs/pressData/en/agricult /ACF20DE.html.

[42] Court of Justice, 27 February 2003, Case C-415/01, Commission vs. Belgium.

Member states contribute to the establishment of Natura 2000 by designating areas as SACs. The procedure for the establishment of the SACs is described in article 4 and consists of various stages. First of all each member state shall propose a list of sites indicating which natural habitat types in Annex I and which species in Annex II that are native to its territory the site currently hosts. The designation must take place on the basis of the criteria in Annex III (Stage 1) and relevant scientific data. Annex III includes the ecological criteria on which the designation should be based. Just as for the designation of SPAs of the Birds Directive, member states should not take into account economic and social criteria in the designation of SACs either. Normally speaking, these national lists should be transmitted to the European Commission within three years after notification of the Directive (1995). Many member states, including Belgium, did not meet this obligation in time, so that the designation of the network has been delayed.

A second stage in the establishment of the Natura 2000 network consists in the Commission establishing a list of Sites of Community Importance (SCIs), drawn from the Member States' lists identifying those which host one or more priority natural habitat types or priority species and based on the criteria in Annex III (Stage 2). This list of areas should have been established within six years after notification of the Directive. So this should have already been achieved in 1998. But since the establishment of national lists has been delayed, the drawing up of the community list is delayed as well. The decisions of the Commission for the establishment of the list are divided up according to the biogeographical region. The Belgian part of the North Sea falls under the Atlantic Biogeographical Region for which the Community list was drawn up in 2004[43].

Once an area has been declared to be an SCI according to the procedure described above, the member state involved designates that area as soon as possible (and within six years at the most) as an SAC. For certain countries such as Belgium, this term has been theoretically postponed until 2010 due to the delay in the previous stages. Policy decisions have however proposed a different time frame: according to the EU Biological Diversity Plan (European Commission 2006) the network of SPAs ad SACs in the marine environment should be completed by 2008. The necessary management measures should be taken by 2012 and this applies both to the SPAs designated under the Birds Directive and the SACs under the Habitats Directive. For the designation of the Natura 2000 network in the marine environment the Commission has issued guidelines for both the designation and the management of those areas (European Commission 2007).

The Birds and Habitats Directives as such do not provide any obligations with regard to participation in the designation of SPAs and SACs. This is left to the

---

43 http://ec.europa.eu/environment/nature/natura2000/sites_hab/biogeog_regions/index _en.htm.

member states, in accordance with their own administrative systems. The procedures for public consultation differ quite strongly from state to state, from no or little consultation of stakeholders to a detailed discussion with users about management measures (European Commission 2002).

To get an overview of the number of areas that have been designated as SPAs and SACs, we can refer to the Natura 2000 Barometer[44]. This barometer also provides an overview of the areas with a marine component. From the latest version of the barometer (December 2007) it appears that 514 SPAs with a marine component have been designated (total surface area: 59.090 km²) as well as 1.277 SCIs with a marine component (total surface area: 80.818 km²).

4.1.3 The Conservation of Special Protection Areas and Special Areas of Conservation

According to article 4, § 1 and 2 of the Birds Directive member states must take special protection measures to ensure the survival and reproduction of the species listed in Annex I and of regularly occurring migratory birds. According to jurisdiction of the Court of Justice member states must take adequate protection measures (see Commission vs. France with regard to the Seine estuary)[45]. Beside the positive conservation measures member states must also take action to prevent negative effects on the SPAs. The measures were originally included in article 4, § 4, 1st clause. As a consequence of the quite strict interpretation of this provision by the Court of Justice this regime was replaced by article 6, § 2-4 of the Habitats Directive (see below). Finally member states must also strive to prevent pollution and deterioration of habitats outside the protection areas (article 4, § 4, 2nd clause).

For the areas that do qualify to be designated as SPAs, but have not been formally designated by the member states, the Court of Justice has produced far-reaching jurisprudence. In this the Court states that if an area should have been designated, but actually has not, then it is not the regime of article 6 of the Habitats Directive that prevails, but the (stricter) regime of article 4 of the Birds Directive. In concrete this means that it is not allowed to reduce the area for economic reasons. This can only be done for imperative reasons of overriding public importance.

Member states must also take the necessary conservation measures in implementation of the Habitats Directive (on the basis of article 6, § 1). Furthermore member states must take appropriate action for both the SPAs and SACs to avoid the deterioration of natural habitats and of habitats of species and to avoid disturbance of the species for which the areas have been designated (article 6, § 2, Habitats Directive).

---

44 http://ec.europa.eu/environment/nature/natura2000/barometer/index_en.htm.
45 Court of Justice, 18 March 1999, Case C-166/97, Commission vs. France (Seine estuary).

An assessment framework for the implementation of (new) activities is determined in article 6, § 3 and 4: any plan or project that is not directly connected with or necessary to the management of the site, but likely to have a significant effect thereon, shall be subject to appropriate assessment of its implications for the site in view of the site's conservation objectives. The national authorities can only agree to the plan or project after having ascertained that it will not adversely affect the natural features of the site concerned and after having provided opportunities for participation if necessary (article 6, § 3, Habitats Directive). A possible exception is provided for in article 6, § 4 Habitats Directive: a plan or project may nevertheless be carried out, in spite of a negative assessment of the implications for the site, if certain conditions are met. No alternative solutions should be available; it should concern imperative reasons of overriding public importance, including reasons of a social or economic nature; and the member state should take all compensatory measures necessary to ensure that the overall coherence of Natura 2000 is protected. The Commission should be informed of the compensatory measures adopted. If the site concerned hosts a priority natural habitat type and/or a priority species, only considerations relating to human health or public safety, to beneficial consequences of primary importance for the environment or, further to an opinion of the Commission, to other imperative reasons of overriding public interest may be raised. Given the importance of article 6, § 3-4 a further concretization of concepts such as *significant consequence* and *appropriate assessment* will be very important. The Court of Justice has recently made some conclusions about those concepts in answer to prejudicial questions about the cockle fisheries in the Wadden Sea[46].

4.2 Marine Strategy and Future Directive

In October 2005 the European Commission proposed a Marine Strategy Framework Directive (COM (2005) 505)[47]. Meanwhile this proposed Directive has been approved by the European Parliament[48]. The objective of this Directive is to achieve a good environmental status in the marine environment by

---

[46] Court of Justice, 7 September 2004, Case C-127/02, concerning a request for prejudicial decision under article 234 EG, submitted by the Council of State (Netherlands) by decision of 27 March 2002, recorded on 8 April 2002, in the procedure 'Landelijke Vereniging tot Behoud van de Waddenzee' (National Association for the Protection of the Wadden Sea), 'Nederlandse Vereniging tot Bescherming van Vogels' (Dutch Association for the Protection of Birds) against the Secretary of State for Agriculture, Nature Management and Fisheries, in the presence of the Coöperatieve Producentenorganisatie van de Nederlandse Kokkelvisserij (Cooperative Producers' Organisation of the Dutch Cockle Fisheries) UA.

[47] Proposal for a Directive of the European Parliament and of the Council establishing a Framework for Community Action in the field of Marine Environmental Policy (Marine Strategy Directive), 24.10.2005, COM (2005) 505.

[48] Position of the European Parliament adopted at first reading on 11 December 2007 with a view to the adoption of Directive 2008/.../EC of the European Parliament and of the Council establishing a Framework for Community Action in the field of Marine Environmental Policy (Marine Strategy Framework Directive), P6 TC2(COD)2005(0211).

2020. With regard to MPAs the preamble to the Directive states that the establishment of MPAs, including areas designated under the Birds and Habitats Directives and international or regional agreements, is an important contribution to the achievement of good environmental status (Preamble par. 6). Establishing such protected areas will be an important step to fulfil the commitments undertaken at the World Summit on Sustainable Development and in the context of the Convention on Biological Diversity, and to contribute to the creation of a coherent and representative network of protected areas (Preamble par. 7).

Further on the Preamble states that this Directive supports the position taken by the European Community in the context of the Convention on Biological Diversity on halting biodiversity loss, ensuring the conservation and sustainable use of marine biodiversity and on the creation of a global network of MPAs by 2012. Additionally, the Directive should contribute to the achievement of the objectives determined in the programme of work on marine and coastal biological diversity (*see above*), including a number of goals, targets and activities aimed at halting the loss of biological diversity and at securing the capacity of the marine ecosystems to support the provision of 'goods and services'. The Directive should also support the programme of work with regard to protected areas, with the objective of establishing ecologically representative systems of MPAs by 2012. The obligation to designate sites under the Birds Directive and the Habitats Directive is an important contribution to this process (Preamble, par. 18). It is crucial for the achievement of the objectives of this Directive to ensure the integration of conservation objectives, management measures and monitoring activities set up for spatial protection measures such as SPAs, SACs and MPAs (Preamble, par. 21).

Art 13. of the Directive as such deals with protected areas. Programmes of measures should include spatial protection measures contributing to a coherent and representative network of MPAs, such as the SPAs, SACs and MPAs as agreed by the EU or the member states in the context of international or regional agreements. Article 21 establishes the obligation of drawing up a specific progress report on protected areas. On the basis of information provided by the member states by 2013 the Commission shall report by 2014 on progress in the establishment of MPAs.

The Directive thus provides for new legal grounds for commitments already entered into with regard to MPAs. It strongly emphasizes the role of the SPAs and SACs under the Birds and Habitats Directives. Still, it does not add any concrete or new elements to those Directives.

5. National Legislation

5.1 Legal Basis

The legal basis for the designation and management of MPAs in the Belgian part of the North Sea can be found in the Federal Act of 20 January 1999 on the protection of the marine environment (hereafter the Marine Environment Act)[49]. This Act contains a whole set of measures for the protection of the marine environment, which are developed in chapters relating to nature conservation (protection of areas and protection of species), prevention of and dealing with pollution, environmental permits and environmental impact assessment. The chapter on nature conservation of the Marine Environment Act was quite radically amended by the Act of 17 September 2005, among other things to provide a legal basis for the voluntary user agreements (Cliquet and Bogaert 2006). By the amendment of 21 April 2007 some further modifications were made to the Act. Those modifications mainly concern other chapters and are less relevant to this topic.

5.2 Legal Basis for the Fulfilment of International Obligations

The Marine Environment Act is intended to fulfil various international obligations. This appears from article 6: *"In a decision taken in consultation with the Council of Ministers the King may take all measures that are necessary for the implementation of the obligations relating to the protection of the marine environment in the sea areas stemming from international treaties and European regulations or Directives, in particular (...)"*. There then follows an enumeration of some Conventions and Directives, such as the Birds and the Habitats Directives, the Ramsar Convention, the Convention on Biological Diversity and the Convention on the Law of the Sea *(see above)*.

5.3 Legal Basis for the Designation of Marine Protected Areas

Based on this Act, MPAs can be designated by Royal Decree. Article 7, § 1 of the Act determines that the King may establish MPAs and take measures that are necessary for the protection of those areas. The term MPAs is a generic name for the various categories of MPAs that are provided for by the Act. The King can designate the following categories as MPAs: integral marine reserves, specific marine reserves, SPAs or SACs, closed areas and buffer zones (article 7 § 2). Integral marine reserves are to be left in their natural state. In a specific nature reserve appropriate management should strive to maintain or restore the existing situation in a state that their ecological function assigns to them. A third category of MPAs are the SPAs and SACs, intended for the conservation

---

[49] Act of 20 January 1999 on the protection of the marine environment in the marine areas under Belgian jurisdiction, Belgian Law Gazette 12 March 1999, as amended by the Act of 3 May 1999, Belgian Law Gazette 29 May 1999, the Act of 17 September 2005, Belgian Law Gazette 13 October 2005 and the Act of 21 April 2007, Belgian Law Gazette 10 May 2007.

of certain marine habitats or special species. The category of SPAs and SACs implement the Bird Directive and the Habitats Directive. The closed areas are zones in which particular activities are not permitted during the whole year or part of the year. A last category is the buffer zones that are designated for the additional protection of MPAs and in which the restrictions to activities are less strict than in the marine reserves.

The Act does not make any further provisions concerning the procedure for designating the MPAs. For the designation of the SPAs and SACs we have to refer to the Bird and Habitats Directives and the interpretation of those Directives by the European Court of Justice. Belgian legislation provides neither procedural obligations with regard to participation in the designation of the MPAs.

By means of an implementation order the necessary measures must be taken to clearly delimitate the MPAs and if necessary to indicate them on the nautical charts. Moreover the necessary measures should be taken to inform the public about the restrictions that apply to those areas (article 7, § 3, Marine Environment Act).

5.4 Exception for Military Activities

Article 7 of the Marine Environment Act includes a general provision about the MPAs. Paragraph 4 of this article provides for an exception to this provision for military activities: "*The measures referred to in § 1 do not apply to military activities. However, the military command, in consultation with the Minister, shall make every effort to prevent damage and environmental disturbance, without jeopardizing the deployment and readiness of the armed forces*". Due to the amendment of 2005 the following is added "*and taking into account the specific statute of the military domain*". The added value of this insertion is unclear. There was already an exception provided for military activities. It is unclear whether 'military domains' at sea can be accepted according to international law (during times of peace).

5.5 Marine Reserves

The original Act of 1999 is based on a general protection principle in the marine reserves, prohibiting all activities in principle, with the exception of the activities that are permitted by the Act. Activities that are always permitted are supervision and control, monitoring and scientific research and military activities. Navigation and fisheries are activities that are regulated internationally and for which in certain cases international action is required to restrict or prohibit them. Therefore those activities are not automatically prohibited in the Act, but the original text of the Act provided that these may be prohibited by implementation order and if need be after taking the necessary international action. In the amended Act the activities that fall under the jurisdiction of the Flemish Region (fisheries, pilotage services, dredging,) have been added to those exceptions.

The new article 8, § 1, Marine Environment Act now reads as follows:

"In the specific and integral marine reserves all activities are prohibited, except for:
(i) supervision and control;
(ii) monitoring and scientific research (…);
(iii) navigation, unless it is restricted under article 20 of this Act;
(iv) the activities falling under article 6, § 1, V, of the Special Act of 8 August 1988 for the Reform of the Institutions;
(v) the activities falling under the jurisdiction of the Flemish Region as determined in article 6, § 1, X, last section, of the Special Act of 8 August 1988 for the Reform of the Institutions;
(vi) military activities, without prejudice to the provisions of article 7, § 4, second clause."

An important difference compared to the original Act is that there are no provisions to restrict or prohibit those activities. The amendment does not anywhere stipulate that those activities could be restricted or prohibited by Royal Decree. Such a legal ground, by which the Minister is empowered to prohibit those activities, is certainly required if the marine reserves are to be more than an empty shell. The explanatory memorandum to the amendment says that the exception to fisheries is an update of the Act in view of the altered distribution of competences (since fisheries has become a Flemish responsibility). Also according to the explanatory memorandum, article 8, §1, (v) states for reasons of clarity and completeness that the other activities that fall under the competence of the Flemish Region (such as dredging) are not part of this regime. This, however, is contrary to the objective of the original text of the Act, which actually had the intention to prohibit the activities under Flemish competence in marine reserves too. This was in no way contrary to the distribution of competences, since nature conservation at sea is under federal competence. By excluding all these Flemish activities from the prohibitions in the marine reserves, this regime is seriously eroded.

Article 8, § 2 provides an additional possibility of making exceptions for the *special* marine reserves: *"In contravention of article 8, § 1, the King may allow activities that do not adversely affect the existing situation in the special marine reserves when there are sound reasons, by a decision adopted after consultation in the Council of Ministers ".* As such this option of making exceptions does not constitute a problem. Possibly the original act was too rigid, thus hampering the designation of marine reserves. Still this additional possibility of making exceptions only makes sense in case of a general principle of protection, under which basically all activities are prohibited. By adding the important exceptions to § 1 this general protection principle has been so eroded that the additional possibility of making exceptions makes little sense.

A second remark concerns the formulation *"that do not adversely affect the existing situation".* If the marine environment has already been adversely affected, it will be possible to permit many activities. It would be better only to authorize activities taking into account the conservation objectives or the intended protection and restoration of the reserve.

5.6 Special Protection Areas and Special Areas of Conservation

In the amended text of the Act a new paragraph 3 has been added to article 8, including protection measures for the SPAs and SACs. Article 8, § 3, Marine Environment Act states: "*In the Special Protection Areas and the Special Areas of Conservation the King may, by way of a decree adopted in consultation with the Council of Ministers, partly or completely prohibit activities, except for the following activities:*
(i) supervision and control;
(ii) monitoring and scientific research by, by order of or with the consent of the government;
(iii) navigation, unless it is restricted under article 20;
(iv) activities falling under article 6, § 1, V, of the Special Act of 8 August 1988 for the Reform of the Institutions;
(v) activities falling under the jurisdiction of the Flemish Region as stated in article 6, § 1, X, last section, of the Special Act of 8 August 1988 for the Reform of the Institutions;
(vi) military activities, without prejudice to the provisions of article 7, § 4, second clause."

In contrast to the marine reserves it is assumed that for SPAs and SACs all activities are permitted, unless they are prohibited by Royal Decree. This principle is in accordance with the Birds and Habitats Directives. However, the problem lies in the following part of the paragraph, excluding a whole list of activities that therefore cannot be prohibited in those areas. This concerns the same list as the one provided for the marine reserves. This poses a problem if the conservation objectives for these areas cannot be achieved. In that case there is a conflict with the Birds and Habitats Directives. Moreover this is contrary to the 'appropriate assessment' that is provided by the Royal Decree on the Special Protection Areas (*see below*). According to this appropriate assessment, activities that have a significant negative impact on the SPAs or SACs cannot be permitted unless they follow an exceptional and strict regime. But since various activities cannot be prohibited in the Act, there is a conflict between the Act and the Royal Decree (in which case the Act takes precedence over the Royal Decree, but the Act is in conflict with the Birds and Habitats Directives). Just as for the marine reserves, a legal ground has to be provided here as well, by which the Minister acquires competence to prohibit activities, in order to achieve the conservation objectives.

5.7 Legal Basis for User Agreements

Due to the amendment of 2005 an article 8 bis was added to the Act, providing a legal basis for the user agreements. A user agreement is defined in the Act as *"an agreement between the Minister and the users of a Marine Protected Area which supports measures for the protection of those areas"* (article 2, 22°, Marine Environment Act).

Article 8bis, Marine Environment Act says:
"§ 1. For the Marine Protected Areas referred to in article 7, § 2, the Minister can conclude a user agreement for every protected area.
§ 2. A user agreement meets the following minimum requirements:
(i) the user agreement does not replace the statutory legislation or regulations and does not deviate from them by making such regulations less strict;
(ii) the user agreement is an appropriate tool to protect the intended marine area;
(iii) the user agreement is concluded for a particular term, expiring at the latest on the expiry date of the corresponding policy plan, in accordance with article 9 of this Act.
The King decides on the further conditions for concluding user agreements between the Minister and the users of Marine Protected Areas.
§ 3. For every Marine Protected Area the Minister can conclude a user agreement with every user or organisation of users of that Marine Protected Area who are involved, on condition that the latter can prove that:
(i) it has the status of 'legal person' or entity;
(ii) it is sufficiently representative of the users of the Belgian marine areas who are part of the same interest group;
(iii) in accordance with its articles of association it has the power to conclude a user agreement or it has been given a mandate to do so by at least three quarters of its members.
The King shall determine the rules with regard to conclusion, implementation and termination of the user agreement."

Although the principle of voluntary user agreements can certainly have a positive effect on the support for and the chances of success of the protection of MPAs, some remarks should be made. The Act imposes certain minimum requirements on the user agreements:
- *they should not replace the statutory legislation or regulations and should not be less strict.* We think this is a quite obvious and unnecessary provision, considering the hierarchy of legal standards.
- *the user agreement is an appropriate tool to protect an area.* With regard to the SPAs and SACs, this is only correct insofar as the conservation objectives are achieved. However, this guarantee is not built into the Royal Decree on User Agreements and Policy Plans.
- *a user agreement is concluded for a particular term.* In this respect questions may arise concerning the long term objectives of marine reserves. In terrestrial areas long term management is provided particularly in reserves, whereas temporary management agreements apply to the less vulnerable areas of natural interest outside the reserves.

Finally it should be observed that there is no compliance supervision of user agreements. In other words, nobody follows them up and nobody knows whether they are complied with.

5.8 Legal Basis for Policy Plans

In contrast to the original article 9 that only applied to the specific marine reserves, the new article 9 applies to all categories of MPAs. The original article 9 has disappeared, although this article provided a legal basis for taking measures relating to nature conservation, management, restoration and development as well as measures for nature education. Furthermore this article provided for the establishment of a management committee for the specific marine reserves. The new article 9 provides a legal basis for the establishment of policy plans. Article 9 of the Marine Environment Act says: "*For the Marine Protected Areas referred to in article 7, § 2, a policy plan shall be drawn up for every Marine Protected Area in order to assess the applicable protection. The King shall determine the rules relating to the procedure, content, conditions, term and form that these policy plans must comply with.*"

The conditions of the user agreements and the policy plans are concisely developed in a separate Royal Decree of 14 October 2005[50]. This Royal Decree also includes the procedure for the establishment of policy plans (article 8-11, Royal Decree 'User Agreements and Policy Plans'). Such a policy plan should contain information on the protection measures and user agreements that apply to the MPAs. Furthermore it should include the results of the monitoring (assigned to the federal scientific institution 'Management Unit of the North Sea Mathematic Models' – MUMM) as well as an assessment of the effect of both the protection measures and the user agreements. Possibly a policy plan can also contain a review of the protection of the area and proposals on new MPAs to be established and the protection measures that should be taken in those areas (article 7, Royal Decree 'User Agreements and Policy Plans').

This means that the user agreements are assessed and possibly amended in the context of the policy plan. With regard to termination, the Royal Decree stipulates that in case of repeated, accidental or deliberate non-compliance with the agreement, the Minister can unilaterally terminate the user agreement (article 6, Royal Decree 'User Agreements and Policy Plans'). However, this does not guarantee in any way that the conservation objectives of the MPAs will be achieved. No legal ground is provided in case the measures that are based upon voluntary user agreements are not effective (and hence cannot ensure adequate protection) or not respected. It seems highly doubtful to us whether the users will lose any sleep over the fact that the Minister can unilaterally terminate the user agreement (see also the inadequate supervision, above). In addition to the system of voluntary user agreements, it would have been better if the regulation had provided for a legal ground allowing to impose binding

---

[50] Royal Decree of 14 October 2005 relating to the conditions, conclusion, implementation and termination of user agreements and the establishment of policy plans for the Marine Protected Areas in the marine areas under Belgian jurisdiction, Belgian Law Gazette 31 October 2005 (hereafter: Royal Decree 'User Agreements and Policy Plans').

measures in case the protection measures on the basis of voluntary agreements are not adequate or are not respected.

From the user agreements and policy plans it appears that the government wants to make users and stakeholders develop a sense of responsibility by means of consultation and participation. Also the procedure for the establishment of policy plans provides for a public inquiry, a consultation meeting with representatives appointed by the users of the MPA and a public consultation meeting (article 9, Royal Decree 'User Agreements and Policy Plans'). This confirms the choice of a more interactive policy, which was also made in the preparation of the designation (*see next chapter*). The designation of the MPAs was indeed finally preceded by an intensive round of consultations with the various users of the marine environment and the local authorities, even though such consultation is not legally provided for in the Marine Environment Act. Opting for consultation in these phases of the policy process strengthened support for the final establishment of the protected areas. Nevertheless an appeal for stay of execution of the Special Protection Areas Royal Decree was submitted on 30 December 2005 by the NV Electrabel and dredging company NV Ondernemingen Jan De Nul. The occasion for this was the Ministerial Decree of 25 June 2005[51] abolishing a former Ministerial Decree on the granting of an authorization for building a wind turbine park to the north of the 'Vlakte van de Raan'[52]. This case is still pending.

5.9 Restriction of Fishing Activities

The amendment of 2005, due to which it is no longer possible to prohibit or restrict fishing activities in the marine reserves and the SPAs and SACs on the basis of the Marine Environment Act, can seriously hamper an effective nature policy in the Belgian MPAs. From scientific research it appears that (certain) fishing activities such as beam trawling, which is practised by 95% of the Belgian fishing fleet, can have a significant impact on the ecology of benthic ecosystems (see among others Rabaut *et al.*, submitted). The original text of the Act left the possibility open to restrict or prohibit fishing in the MPAs in implementation of the Act. As a consequence of the legal amendment to the Act of 2005, fishing activities cannot be prohibited or restricted on the basis of the Marine Environment Act.

---

[51]   Ministerial Decree of 25 June 2005, Belgian Law Gazette 5 August 2005.
[52]   Ministerial Decree of 25 June 2002 with regard to assignment to the temporary association Electrabel - Ondernemingen Jan De Nul of an authorization to build a park of 50 wind turbines with a nominal capacity of 2 MW for the production of electricity from winds in the sea areas to the north of the 'Vlakte van de Raan' and Ministerial Decree of 25 June 2002 with regard to the assignment to the temporary association Electrabel - Ondernemingen Jan De Nul of an authorization for the exploitation of a park of 50 wind turbines with a nominal capacity of 2 MW for the production of electricity from winds in the sea areas north of the 'Vlakte van de Raan'.

Due to the Belgian federal state structure, the North Sea policy is divided among several institutional levels. The federal government has competence over nature conservation at sea (on the seaward side of the low-water mark). The Flemish Region has competence over nature conservation on land, but also for activities at sea, such as dredging and sea fisheries. If from a nature conservation point of view it is necessary to restrict or prohibit certain fishing activities in the MPAs, this should in our view be within the competence of the federal government on the basis of its powers relating to nature conservation at sea. But due to the amendment to the Act in 2005 the federal government itself has excluded this possibility in the Marine Environment Act, by stipulating that activities that fall within the competence of the Flemish Region cannot be prohibited or restricted in the marine reserves and SPAs and SACs on the basis of this Act. As a consequence, restrictions on fishing activities, if they are desirable, should be imposed on the basis of Flemish legislation. Since there is no structural collaboration in Belgium on nature conservation in the coastal area and the marine environment (Cliquet *et al.* 2004), this may be an additional obstacle to taking necessary measures. If area specific measures were taken at Flemish level, this would not be easy for users in relation to transparency and clarity since the legislation on one and the same area would then be divided between several legal texts, from different levels of decision-making.

An additional difficulty for restricting fishing activities is imposed by the European fisheries policy and legislation. Fisheries is within the exclusive jurisdiction of the European Union, in the framework of the Common Fisheries Policy (CFP). The basic regulation is embodied in Regulation 2371/2002 of 20 December 2002 on the conservation and sustainable exploitation of fisheries resources[53]. Environmental policy however, is a shared jurisdiction between the EU and the member states. Moreover the EC Treaty requires that environmental matters are integrated into other domains such as fisheries policy. The question then is to what extent member states have powers available for restricting fishing activities with a view to achieving nature conservation objectives and whether such measures should be taken within the CFP. In the end there are four possible options:
1. fishing can only be restricted by the EU within the CFP framework;
2. fishing can be restricted by the member states within the CFP framework;
3. the restriction of fishing activities is seen as a nature conservation measure and is taken by the EU;
4. the restriction of fishing activities is seen as a nature conservation measure and is taken by the member states.

The European Commission holds the opinion that fisheries management measures should be taken within the framework of the CFP, since fisheries are in the exclusive jurisdiction of the EU. This also applies to measures regulating fishing activities in view of the conservation of a Natura 2000 site (European

---

[53] Council Regulation (EC) Nr. 2371/2002 on the conservation and sustainable exploitation of fisheries resources under the Common Fisheries Policy, *OJ L* 358, 31 December 2002.

Commission 2007). But it can be argued that the restriction of fishing activities, with the objective of protecting particular habitats or species such as marine mammals, is an environmental measure that can be taken by the EU as well as by member states on the basis of their shared jurisdiction relating to the environment. In the end this will have to be clarified by the Court of Justice. Up to now there is no clear jurisprudence determining the appropriate legal basis for measures for fisheries, as nature conservation measures (Owen 2004a).

If the restriction of fishing activities should actually be introduced within the framework of the CFP, another question is whether member states still dispose of powers to enable them to take such measures. On the basis of the basic regulation on fisheries, the member states have a number of limited powers. These may be too limited in extent and time to meet the requirements of conservation measures imposed by the Birds and Habitats Directives (Owen 2004b).

6. Implementation: Designation and Management of Marine Protected Areas in Belgium

6.1. Designation of Marine Protected Areas

In 2005 five MPAs were designated in the Belgian part of the North Sea, after a difficult policy process (*see next chapter*). The designation was done by Royal Decree of 14 October 2005[54]. It concerns three SPAs that were designated in the context of the Birds Directive. Those areas mainly aim at the protection of some bird species, such as Great Crested Grebe, Common Tern, Sandwich Tern and Little Gull. Moreover two Special Areas of Conservation have been designated in the context of the Habitats Directive: The 'Vlakte van de Raan' and the 'Trapegeer-Stroombank'. Those two areas have a characteristic size and distance from each other so that they are biologically linked (Rabaut *et al.* submitted).

Table 1 gives an overview of the areas, with their size as well as the habitat types and/or species for which the areas have been designated.

---

[54] Royal Decree of 14 October 2005 on the establishment of Special Protection Areas and Special Areas of Conservation in the marine areas under Belgian jurisdiction, Belgian Law Gazette 31 October 2005, amended by the Royal Decree of 5 March 2006, Belgian Law Gazette 27 March 2006 (hereafter: Special Protection Areas Royal Decree).

Name	Size	Habitat types and/or species
SPA 1	110.01 km²	Little Gull (*Larus minutus*), Great
SPA 2	144.80 km²	Crested Grebe (*Podiceps cristatus*),
SPA 3	50.95 km²	Sandwich Tern (*Sterna sandvicensis*), Common Tern (*Sterna hirundo*)
Trapegeer Stroom-bank (SAC1)	181.00 km²	Sandbanks which are slightly covered with sea water all the time (1110) Mudflats and sandflats not covered by sea water at low tide (1140)
Vlakte van de Raan (SAC2)	19.17 km²	Sandbanks which are slightly covered with sea water all the time (1110)

Table 1: overview of the designated SPAs and SACs in Belgium

In the designation of the two Habitats Directive Areas some habitat types are cited as reason for the designation. The Royal Decree did not mention species of Annex II of the Habitats Directive. But the species of Annex II that are found in the Belgian part of the North Sea fall under the Decree for the Protection of Species of 21 December 2001[55]. As a consequence those species are protected in all marine areas that fall under Belgian jurisdiction. It concerns the following species: Bottlenose Dolphin (*Tursiops truncatus*), Harbour Porpoise (*Phocoena phocoena*), Grey Seal (*Halichoerus grypus*), Harbour Seal (*Phoca vitulina*), Sea Lamprey (*Petromyzon marinus*), European River Lamprey (*Lampetra fluviatilis*) and Twaite Shad (*Alosa fallax*) (Decleer 2007). Moreover the Royal Decree of 2001 also protects some other species of Annex II in all Belgian marine areas, but this refers to species that are only found exceptionally: Otter (*Lutra lutra*), Loggerhead Sea Turtle (*Caretta caretta*), Green Sea Turtle (*Chelonia midas*), Sturgeon (*Acipenser sturio*), Allis Shad (*Alosa alosa*) and North Sea Houting (*Coregonus oxyrhynchus*).

In addition to the five MPAs a first, though small (6.76 km²) marine reserve was designated near to the 'Baai van Heist' by the Royal Decree of 5 March 2006[56]. This reserve is situated in one of the three SPAs (SPA 3) and is linked to the existing Flemish nature reserve 'Baai van Heist'.

---

[55] Royal Decree of 21 December 2001 with regard to species protection in the marine areas under Belgian jurisdiction, Belgian Law Gazette 14 February 2002 (hereafter: Species Protection Royal Decree).

[56] Royal Decree of 5 March 2006 for the designation of a specific marine reserve in the marine areas under Belgian jurisdiction and to amend the Royal Decree of 14 October 2005 for the designation of Special Protection Areas and Special Areas of Conservation in the marine areas under Belgian jurisdiction, Belgian Law Gazette 27 March 2006 (hereafter: Marine Reserve Royal Decree).

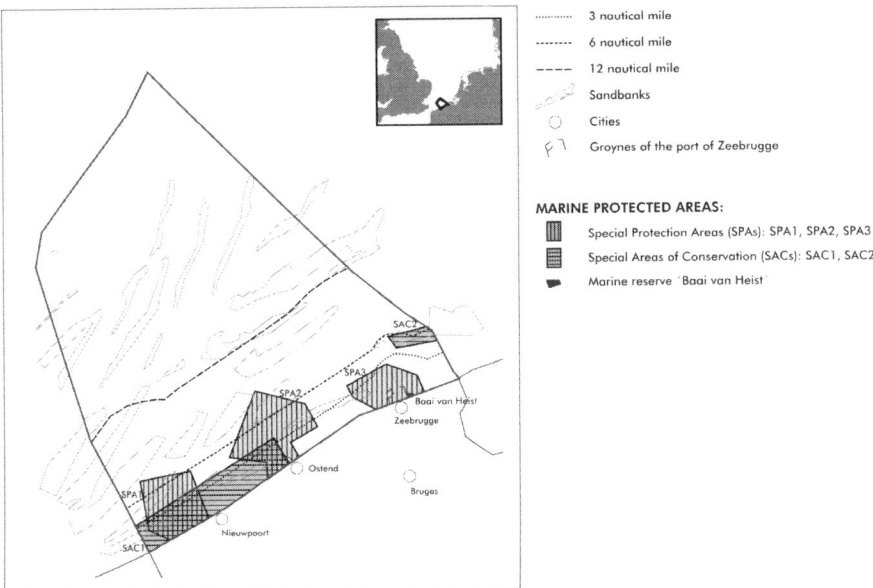

Figure 2: Overview of designated MPAs in Belgium

6.2 Management Measures in the Marine Protected Areas

To get an overview of the measures that apply within the MPAs, we have to look at the Marine Environment Act and the Royal Decrees on the designation of the areas.

As already indicated all activities are permitted in the SPAs and SACs on the basis of the Act, unless they are restricted or prohibited by Royal Decree. On the basis of the Act, however, it is not possible to restrict or exclude supervision and control, monitoring and scientific research, military activities, sea fisheries, pilotage and beaconing services to and from the harbours, rescue, and towing services as well as dredging. Navigation can only be restricted according to a procedure that is provided by the Act and in accordance to international law. Finally in the Royal Decree the following activities are (absolutely) prohibited in the three SPAs and two SACs: civil engineering, industrial activities and activities of advertising or commercial companies (article 5 and article 10, 1°-3°, Special Protection Areas Royal Decree). For the two SACs there is the additional prohibition to deposit dredged material and inert materials of natural origin (article 10, 4°, Special Protection Areas Royal Decree).

For the five areas also the 'appropriate assessment' for plans and projects is obligatory (article 6 and article 11, Special Protection Areas Royal Decree) as provided in article 6 of the Habitats Directive. The appropriate assessment follows the environmental impact assessment procedure as provided in the

Royal Decree of 9 September 2003[57] with regard to the rules on the environmental impact assessment in implementation of the Marine Environment Act.

In SPA 1 and SPA 2 *(see table 1)* species specific measures are imposed in view of the conservation of four bird species for which the areas have been designated. In winter, helicopter exercises at a height of less than 500 ft (152.4 meter) are prohibited, as well as the passage of high-speed vessels and water sports competitions. The Minister of the Environment must consult with the Minister of Defence on the planning of artillery exercises and other military activities off the coast of Lombardsijde (article 7, Special Protection Areas Royal Decree).

Beside these protection measures that are imposed by the Royal Decree, the user agreements and the policy plans also play a crucial role in the policy. It is possible to conclude such agreements with several users such as the water sports enthusiasts (article 12, Special Protection Area Royal Decree), in which the Minister can determine additional conditions after consultation with the users of the MPA. For every area, agreements have already been concluded with organisations of the water sports recreation sector. Those agreements mainly emphasize the distribution of information on the protected areas by the water sports organisations to their members. Moreover they recommend some measures for the protection of the marine environment (e.g. the recommendations not to fish close to wrecks, to avoid damage to the sea bed when dropping anchor, to respect fauna and flora at sea).

For every SPA and SAC a policy plan must be established within three years after the designation of the area (2008) (article 14, Special Protection Area Royal Decree). At present the policy plans are prepared by the Federal Administrative Department for the Environment. The MUMM is charged with monitoring these areas (article 13, Special Protection Areas Royal Decree).

In the specific marine reserve 'Baai van Heist' all activities are prohibited, except for supervision and control, monitoring and scientific research, fisheries, dredging and other Flemish competences at sea, military activities, the laying and maintenance of cables and pipelines, the digging of trenches and the raising of the sea bed and the activities falling within the scope of the user agreements (article 5, Marine Reserve Royal Decree). The Royal Decree also provides for an appropriate assessment of the plans or projects (article 6, Marine Reserve Royal Decree). For the marine reserve a user agreement must be concluded and within three years a policy plan must be established. The Management Unit of the North Sea Mathematical Models is charged with monitoring this area (article 7-9, Marine Reserve Royal Decree).

---

[57] Royal Decree of 9 September 2003 on the rules with regard to environmental impact assessment in implementation of the Act of 20 January 1999 for the protection of the marine environment in the marine areas under Belgian jurisdiction, Belgian Law Gazette 17 September 2003.

It remains to be seen whether the current measures in the MPAs will be sufficient to meet international requirements such as achievement of the conservation objectives for the SPAs and SACs or the obligation to achieve an effective management for existing MPAs (in the context of the Convention on Biological Diversity). The main aim of the legislator was to prevent new activities in those areas. The existing activities can largely be continued.

7. Conclusions

There is an extensive legal framework for the establishment and effective management of MPAs at global and European level. But there is still a lack of clarity about the concept of MPAs, the classification of the existing MPAs, the planning horizons used and the management objectives. Belgium has an explicit legal basis for the designation and the management of MPAs, on the basis of the Marine Environment Act of 1999. An amendment to this Act in 2005 resulted in some important shifts, so that the amended Act is less strict than the initial one.

The management of MPAs in Belgium is legally and technically hampered by the complex governmental and administrative structure. The Marine Environment Act is a federal law but it cannot restrict or prohibit particular activities in the marine reserves and the SPAs and SACs, as those fall within the jurisdiction of the Flemish Region (for example fisheries). This makes the legal situation very complicated.

In implementation of the international and national legal obligations, six MPAs have been designated in Belgium so far. The management measures are restricted and mainly aimed at restricting future activities. Existing activities remain practically untouched. Therefore, the question is whether the current management regime is sufficient to meet international obligations. Monitoring will have to prove whether these MPAs are more than an empty 'shell'.

Attention to the importance of participation in the designation and management of MPAs has grown in the past few years. This is mainly evident at international level. The aspect of participation is almost entirely absent from the Birds and Habitats Directives. Afterwards some attention was certainly given to this, among other things in the Commission guidelines on the establishment of the Natura 2000 network in the marine environment. Initially this aspect was also absent from the Belgian legislation, but this was partly remedied by including the instrument of the user agreements and the procedural obligations in the establishment of the policy plans. Although these user agreements may be useful in making various stakeholders take more responsibility, they do not provide any guarantee for an efficient and effective management of the MPAs.

This indicates an area of tension between, on the one hand, the merely scientific approach during the designation and management of MPAs, as included in some laws, and, on the other hand, a bottom-up approach starting from the input of local communities and stakeholders. Since both approaches have advantages and disadvantages, we would advocate a 'middle-ground approach' between the strictly scientific approach and the bottom-up approach (*see also*: Jones 2002; Jones 2006). With the user agreements and the policy plans, this middle-ground approach is only partly included in the Belgian legislation. From the following chapter it will appear that nonetheless a kind of middle ground was adopted in the designation of the MPAs in Belgium in 2005 and 2006, by combining scientific data with the inclusion of informal consultations. As will appear from that chapter, intense stakeholder involvement from the start of the policy process constitutes an important element in the chances of success for the designation of MPAs. This is advisable for the designation of future MPAs that will be designated on the basis of national legislation or on the basis of international regulations such as the OSPAR MPAs.

References

AGARDY, T., P. BRIDGEWATER, M.P. CROSBY, J. DAY, P.K. DAYTON, R. KENCHINGTON, D. LAFFOLEY, P. MCCONNEY, P.A. MURRAY, J.E. PARKS & L. PEAU (2003). 'Dangerous targets? Unresolved issues and ideological clashes around Marine Protected Areas'. *Aquatic Conservation: Marine and Freshwater Ecosystems* (4): 353-367.

BACKES, C., H. DOTINGA & E.J. MOLENAAR (2001). 'Natuurbescherming in de Noordzee'. *Milieu en Recht*, (6).

CBD (2004). Technical Advice on the Establishment and Management of a National System of Marine and Coastal Protected Areas, SCBD, CBD Technical Series no. 13.

CLIQUET, A. (1996). 'Mogelijkheden in internationaal en nationaal recht voor de bescherming van mariene habitats'. In B. Jadot (Ed.) *Het natuurbeschermingsrecht*. Kluwer: Antwerpen.

CLIQUET, A. (2001). *Natuurbehoud in het mariene en kustzonemilieu. Overzicht en analyse van de juridische mogelijkheden, met bijzondere aandacht voor het mariene en kustzonemilieu van België*. Proefschrift tot het behalen van graad van doctor in de rechten. Universiteit Gent.

CLIQUET, A., F. MAES & J. SCHRIJVERS (2004). 'Towards integration and participation in coastal zone decision making for Belgium'. In D. Green (Ed.), *Delivering Sustainable Coasts: Connecting Science and Policy*. Littoral 2004, Aberdeen, September 2004, Proceedings Volume 1. Cambridge: Cambridge Publications.

CLIQUET, A. & D. BOGAERT (2006). 'Mariene beschermde gebieden in het Belgisch deel van de Noordzee: een eerste stap in de richting van het behoud van de mariene biodiversiteit?'. *Tijdschrift voor Milieurecht*: 165-171.

DECLEER, K. (Ed.) (2007). *Europees beschermde natuur in Vlaanderen en het Belgisch deel van de Noordzee. Habitattypen / Dier en plantensoorten.* Mededelingen van het Instituut voor Natuur- en Bosonderzoek, 2007 (1). Brussel: Instituut voor Natuur- en Bosonderzoek.

EUROPEAN COMMISSION (2002). *Commission Working Document on Natura 2000.* Brussels: European Commission.

EUROPEAN COMMISSION (2005). 'Natura 2000 in the marine environment'. *Natura 2000 Newsletter* (19): 2-5.

EUROPEAN COMMISSION (2006). *EU Action plan to 2010 and beyond, Annex 1 to the Communication from the Commission. Halting the loss of biodiversity by 2010 – and beyond. Sustaining ecosystem services for human well-being.* COM(2006)216 final, 22.05.2006. Brussels: European Commission.

EUROPEAN COMMISSION (2007). *Guidelines for the establishment of the Natura 2000 network in the marine environment. Application of the Habitats and Birds Directives.* Brussels: European Commission.

GUBBAY, S. (1995). 'Marine Protected Areas – past, present and future'. In S. Gubbay (Ed.), *Marine Protected Areas. Principles and techniques for management.* London: Chapman & Hall.

HAELTERS, J., F. KERCKHOF & J.-S. HOUZIAUX (2007). *De aanduiding van mariene beschermde gebieden in de Belgische Noordzee: een mogelijke uitvoering van OSPAR Aanbeveling 2003/3 door België.* Brussel: Federaal Wetenschapsbeleid, Koninklijk Belgisch Instituut voor Natuurwetenschappen, Beheerseenheid Mathematisch Model Noordzee.

IJLSTRA, T. & A. NOLLKAEMPER (1990). *Gebiedsbescherming op de Noordzee. Een analyse van de juridische mogelijkheden en beperkingen.* Utrecht: NILOS/Ministerie van Landbouw, Natuurbeheer en Visserij.

IUCN (1994). *Guidelines for Protected Area Management Categories, CNPPA with the assistance of WCMC.* (http://app.iucn.org/dbtw-wpd/edocs/1994-007-En.pdf).

IUCN (2007). *IUCN Categories – Their Application in Marine Protected Areas.* (http://groups.google.com/group/wcpamarine-summit/web/preparing-for-the-iucn-categories-summit).

JONES, P.J. (2002). 'Marine Protected Areas strategies: issues, divergences and the search for middle ground'. *Reviews in Fish Biology and Fisheries* (11): 197-216.

JONES, P.J. (2006). 'Collective action problems posed by no-take zones'. *Marine Policy* (30): 143-156.

KELLEHER G. (1999). *Guidelines for Marine Protected Areas. World commission on protected areas of IUCN.* Best Practice Protected Area Guidelines Series 3.

MITCHELL, K. (1998). 'European Seminar on Implementing the Habitats Directive in Marine and Coastal Areas: Background Paper'. In C. Coffey (Ed.), *Implementing the Habitats Directive in Marine and Coastal Areas.* Proceedings of a Seminar Held at Morecambe Bay, England, 22 - 24 June 1997. Luxemburg: Office for Official Publications of the European Communities.

MPA NEWS (2005). 'Global Targets for MPA Designations Will Not Be Met; Experts Respond'. *MPA News,* 7(5): 1-2.

MPA NEWS (2007). 'Do We Really Need 50 Ways to Say "Marine Protected Area"? Views on MPA Terminology, and Efforts to Categorize MPAs'. *MPA News*, 8(10): 1-3.

O'BRIAN, M. (1998). 'Update on the Habitats Directive and its Implementation in Marine and Coastal Areas'. In C. Coffey (Ed.), *Implementing the Habitats Directive in Marine and Coastal Areas*. Proceedings of a Seminar Held at Morecambe Bay, England, 22 - 24 June 1997. Luxemburg: Office for Official Publications of the European Communities.

OSPAR (2007a). *2006 Report on the Status of the OSPAR Netwerk of Marine Protected Areas*. publication nr. 319. OSPAR Commission.

OSPAR (2007b). *The legal basis for managing Transboundary Marine Protected Areas*. publication nr. 321. OSPAR Commission.

OWEN, D. (2001). 'The application of the wild Birds Directive beyond the territorial sea of European Community member states'. *Journal of Environmental Law* 13(1): 39-78.

OWEN, D. (2004a). *Interaction between the EU common fisheries policy and the Habitats and Birds Directives*. IEEP Policy Briefing. London: Institute for European Environmental Policy.

OWEN, D. (2004b). 'Protecting marine SAC's and SPA's from fishing activities: who has the power to impose restrictions?'. In J. Ritterhoff, S. Gubbay & C. Zucco (Eds.), *Marine Protected Areas and fisheries*. Proceedings of the International Expert Workshop held at the International Academy for Nature Conservation, Isle of Vilm, Germany 28 June – 2 July, 2004. Bonn: BfN – Skripten.

RABAUT, M., S. DEGRAER, J. SCHRIJVERS, S. DEROUS, F. MAES, D. BOGAERT, M. VINCX & A. CLIQUET. Accepted. Policy Analysis of the 'MPA-process' in Temperate Continental Shelf Areas. *Aquatic Conservation: Marine and Freshwater Ecosystems.*

RAMSAR (2007a). *Wetland CEPA: The Convention's Programme on communication, education and public awareness (CEPA), 2003-2008*. Ramsar handbooks for the wise use of wetlands, 3rd edition, vol. 4. Gland: Ramsar Convention Secretariat.

RAMSAR (2007b). *Participatory skills: establishing and strengthening local communities' and indigenous people's participation in the management of wetlands*. Ramsar handbooks for the wise use of wetlands, 3rd edition, vol. 5. Gland: Ramsar Convention Secretariat.

WARREN, L. (1997). 'Legal boundaries and the Scope for Effective Marine Nature Conservation in offshore Areas'. In R. Earl (ed.), *Marine environmental Management. Review of Events in 1997 and Future Trend.*, Kempley: Candle Cottage.

WELLS, S. & J. Day (2004). *Application of the IUCN protected area management categories in the marine environment*. Parks, Vol. 14, no 3. Gland: IUCN.

WOOD, L.J. (2006). *Summary Report of the Current Status of the Global Marine Protected Area Network, and of Progress Monitoring Capabilities.* UNEP/CBD/COP/8/INF/4. (www.cbd.int/doc/meetings/cop/cop-08/information/cop-08-inf-04-en.doc).

WOOD, L. J. (2007). *MPA Global: A database of the world's Marine Protected Areas.* Sea Around Us Project, UNEP-WCMC & WWF. (www.mpaglobal.org).

The Designation of Marine Protected Areas in Belgium.
An Analysis of the Decision Making Process

Dirk Bogaert, An Cliquet, Dino De Waen and Frank Maes

1. Introduction

After the legal-technical analysis of the instrument of Marine Protected Areas (MPAs) in the previous chapter, we will describe in this chapter the results of the analysis of the policy process of the designation of MPAs in Belgium. The description of the analysis results pays attention to the dimensions distinguished in the Policy Arrangement Approach (PAA): discourse, actors, rules of the game and power (*see chapter 1*). In the analysis we distinguish three periods: the first designation proposal (1999), the second designation proposal (1999-2003) and the third designation proposal (2003-2006).

2. The First Designation Proposal. A Classic Top-down Approach? (1999)

After the necessary parliamentary preparations, the Act on the protection of the marine environment in the marine areas under Belgian jurisdiction was approved on 20 January 1999, the so-called Marine Environment Act. Starting from an international legal context and a number of relevant international principles, the Act provided for the possibility of the designation of MPAs (*see chapter 2*).

Before we reconstruct the first designation proposal, and analyse it in relation to four perspectives that are set out in the PAA (actors, resources, discourses and informal and formal rules), we shall consider the initiators and the definition of the objective.

2.1 The Initiator(s)

During the in-depth interviews the respondents were asked who they consider to be the initiator for the establishment of MPAs in Belgium. The opinions of the respondents on this issue are divided. Three actors are indicated as possible initiator: the then Secretary of State for the Environment Jan Peeters, the conservation movement and the 'administration'.

What is remarkable is that respondents from civil society (the midfield) choose the Secretary of State, whereas the governmental actors consider the conservation movement to be the initiator. Where the conservation movement is concerned, there is mention of the 'Kustwerkgroep' (Coastal Working Group), Greenpeace and Birdlife International. The 'Kustwerkgroep' is a working group of the non-profit organisation 'Natuurpunt' (the former 'Natuurreservaten vzw') in which both academics and civil servants are involved. It is seen as a *think tank* that also would have passed on ideas relating to MPAs to the authorities. Finally, only two respondents consider 'the administration' to be the real initiator. The mayor of one coastal municipality talks about the Flemish nature conservation administration (ANB, then AMINAL - nature section) in this connection, although designation of such areas is a federal matter. One federal official insists that the initiator is the MUMM (Management Unit of the North Sea Mathematical Models and the Scheldt estuary), which as the federal administration prepared the whole issue under the then Secretary of State Peeters. Other respondents also attribute an important role to the 'administration' for the first period, and within this the trigger role for MUMM. According to some respondents the MUMM clearly had its own agenda, and this agenda was not totally in tune with that of Secretary of State Peeters who was politically responsible for the issue (*see below*).

One respondent states that a study day organised in 1994 by the international nature conservation organisation WWF was the real start of thinking about MPAs in Belgium. On this study day, it is said, the idea of integrated coastal zone management with particular attention to integral coastal nature reserves was launched in Belgium.

In summary we can put that the civil society actors, in particular the nature conservation movement, played a role in the agenda setting phase. Prepared by the federal administration MUMM, a first attempt was made to translate this into policy by the then Secretary of State Jan Peeters.

2.2 The Definition of Objectives. The Double Problem for which a Solution Was Required

From analysis of the documents it appears that two problems were outlined, which would be solved by the designation of MPAs: the protection of sites of special marine ecological interest on the one hand and the fulfilment of international obligations on the other. In policy documents we find a discourse based on scientific knowledge and insights. The setting up of MPAs is seen as an important resource for the protection of marine species and habitats. At the same time it is argued that the setting up of these areas is required to fulfil international obligations.

During the in-depth interviews, the respondents were also asked about the problem that had to be resolved by the setting up of MPAs. All respondents refer to the protection of areas of special ecological interest in the North Sea for species and habitats. Other arguments are: the protection of heritage sites (sandbanks), the uniqueness (sandbanks are only found along the Belgian and French coastlines), the geomorphologic importance, to the protection of the fish stocks. Two representatives of the authorities point out that limiting economic and recreational activities with the intention of protecting the North Sea, is an important objective. One respondent point out that originally the idea was to set up integral coastal reserves that are particularly concerned with the land-sea interface.

In addition to scientific arguments legal arguments are also put forward during the in-depth interviews. Reference is made by the authorities and a scientist in this case to obligations that arise from the international (e.g. Ramsar, OSPAR) and European regulations (e.g. Birds and Habitats Directives). It is notable that the respondents usually have an incomplete picture of international obligations. It is also striking that this likewise applies to the officials and politicians interviewed. Guidelines, treaties and conventions are confused with each other. However, the dominant feeling is that international obligations were the reason for designating MPAs in Belgium.

> 'Nevertheless something had to be done because being the worst pupil in the class is certainly not recommended and Belgium was in danger of becoming just that. The EU was the most important factor.'

We can then also conclude that on the basis of scientific insights and international legal obligations the nature conservation movement and the federal government felt the need to designate MPAs in Belgium.

2.3 Approval and Growing Disapproval: the First Challenging Coalitions

In the agenda setting phase, according to various respondents, the conservation movement in Belgium played an important role by organising a study day (*see above WWF*) but also by earlier informal consultation with civil servants and people in the academic world, such as the 'Kustwerkgroep' of 'Natuurpunt', for instance. In the beginning there is a supporting coalition put together from people in the conservation movement, the authorities (civil servants) and the academic world. Although it appears there are no supporting coalitions at that time in addition to the conservation movement, a local politician refers to the importance of (socialist) networks. This network theory is not confirmed by other respondents. From within the environmental movement it is pointed out that the socialist party (sp.a) at that time was seen as the most important political advocate of the idea of MPAs. The Marine Environment Act was, for example, supported by this part of the political spectrum. In their opinion it should surprise nobody that the first initiative for the setting up of MPAs came about under a socialist Secretary of State (Jan Peeters).

Shortly after the approval of the Marine Environment Act, and even before its publication in the 'Belgisch Staatsblad' (the Belgian official law gazette of 12 March 1999), the first articles appear in some Flemish newspapers in which reference is made to possible negative consequences of this new Act and decisions relative to its implementation. On 6 February 1999 the Flemish daily newspaper 'Het Nieuwsblad' carries the headline *'Zeilen verboden, schieten mag wel'* (Sailing forbidden, shootings allowed), with reference to the prohibition of the organisation of a Sailing Week in Nieuwpoort. The 'Vlaamse Vereniging voor Watersport Nieuwpoort' (VVW) (Flemish Association for Water Sports – Nieuwpoort) makes first critical noises about the new (planned) policy regulations:

> *"'We were not consulted at all on the whole environmental area and the cancella-*
> *tion of our sailing week, in which 750 boats from Belgium and abroad take part is a*
> *direct attack on the economic impetus that we, together with other associations and*
> *local authorities, want to give to the Westhoek*', says Steven Desloovere, manag-*
> *ing director of 'Vlaamse Vereniging voor Watersport Nieuwpoort vzw' (VVW). In*
> *Brussels they are working assiduously on further restrictions that will do damage*
> *to the economy of the whole Flemish coast. And what are we to think then of the*
> *military target practice, with light and heavy ammunition being shot at airplanes,*
> *that continues undisturbed in the military domain of Lombardsijde?"*

(*The Westhoek is the most western corner of Belgium in the angle between the coast and the French border)

The direct cause of this press article was VVW Nieuwpoort's request for per-mission to organise an F1-race at sea. When seeking information about how this should be done it was learned from the federal administration MUMM that the Marine Environment Act existed and what would be the likely impli-cations of this. The latter were described in the draft implementation orders (Royal Decrees) that were prepared at that time, but as yet had no force of law. Before these draft implementation orders had passed through a process of serious political discussion, they leaked out and, to a great extent, predeter-mined the incipient public debate.

> *'If you read the text literally then it was certainly the case that you could do noth-*
> *ing anymore.'*
> *'It was really the case that the landlubbers are going to tell us what and what not*
> *to do. How is it possible that the North Sea can be handed over to the 'King'?'*

The first press articles about the MPAs appear, before the government circu-lated information about the Marine Environment Act and the first designation proposal and they have a distinctly negative drift. Various respondents from civil society, authorities and science, see this as being the start of a challenging coalition against the - largely unknown - MPAs designation proposal. 'VVW Nieuwpoort' subsequently mobilised others involved in water sports and fish-ing as well as local politicians and so got protest under way.

Only on 9 March 1999, and in reaction to growing protest, is clarification pro-vided for the mayors of coastal municipalities and a press conference was given by Jan Peeters, the then Secretary of State for Pensions, Security, Social Integration and Environment (Letter Peeters 1999). The press release starts from the international legal grounds of the Act and emphasises that the new Act is a framework Act that *'mainly gives execution to a series of international agreements, treaties and obligations that were ratified by the countries around the North Sea.'* (Letter Peeters 1999: 1). During the meeting with the press a first proposal is formulated for the designation of three MPAs: the 'Broersbank', the 'Baland- and Stroombank' and the 'Baai van Heist'. Proposals were also formu-lated for six shipwrecks. The press release describes likewise that it is the "*Act that determines what can and cannot be done in these specific marine reserves*", and announces that there will be regulations to execute other provisions of the law. The press release also contained five annexes with the draft Royal Decrees and outline maps. The media coverage that followed is focused on the protection of fauna and flora (De Morgen, 10.03.1999) and the setting up of three marine reserves (Het Nieuwsblad, 10.03.1999). At the same time attention is given to what and what is not permitted in the areas to be designated.

The designation proposal was prepared by the administration, without consultation with the stakeholders on the coast. However the press release reports forms of official consultation for those involved in the fishing industry (in cooperation with the Minister of Agriculture) and for the shipping industry (with the competent authorities). The first designation proposal can in this sense be seen as a classic top-down approach, in which information for non-governmental actors is only provided because there was growing protest.

This lack of consultation forms an important point of criticism by coast users and especially among local politicians *(see below)*. According to various respondents from the authorities, civil society and science, this was the main reason why the mayors of the coastal municipalities seem to have played an important role in the protest against the designation proposal.

'They are all special characters (whatever the political colour). They are mayors of coastal municipalities and are rather allergic to everything that comes from above.'

The Secretary of State, Jan Peeters organised a meeting with the mayors of the coastal municipalities in reaction to the growing protest (Minutes 1999a). This meeting was under the chairmanship of the Governor of the Province of West Flanders. The lack of consultation that the mayors complained of is parried by the Secretary of State with the fact that *"there was full parliamentary agreement on the new Act that will generate restrictions; otherwise it would make no sense to approve an Act for the protection of the marine environment."* (Minutes 1999a). At the same time the Secretary of State attempted to quieten down the mayors of the coastal municipalities by saying that decisions will only be taken when all the sectors involved have been heard. The Governor of West Flanders, who chaired this meeting, repeated the importance of this (Minutes 1999a).

In the weeks after the consultation with the mayors and the associated press conference, the protest against the first designation proposal is growing, with outspoken newspaper headlines as a result:

- *"Bescherming zeemilieu houdt geen rekening met toerisme en economie"* ('Marine environment protection doesn't take tourism and the economy into account') (Het Nieuwsblad, 11.03.1999);
- *"Noordzeewet zorgt voor deining bij zeilers"* ('North Sea Act is upsetting the yachtsmen') (Het Laatste Nieuws, 11.03.1999);

- *"Vissers op straat tegen 'broodroof'"* ('*Fishermen on the streets against 'bread snatching'*) (Het Nieuwsblad, 17.03.1999);
- *"Doodsteek voor Nieuwpoort"*('*Kiss of death for Nieuwpoort'*) (Het Nieuwsblad, 19.03.1999);
- *"Algemene mobilisatie tegen mariene reservaten"* ('*General mobilisation against marine reserves'*) (Het Nieuwsblad, 20.03.1999);
- *"Vissers en hengelaars betogen tegen 'groen fundamentalisme"* ('*Fisherfolk and anglers demonstrate against 'green fundamentalism'*) (Het Nieuwsblad, 22.03.1999).

The mayor of Koksijde, the VVW Nieuwpoort and Heist, the Shipowners' Association, the mayor of Nieuwpoort and a coalition of fishing industry, trade unions, shipowners' associations, anglers' federations (boat anglers' federation, angling sports federation and the federation of beach anglers) are quoted. In short, in this period there is talk of a growing challenging coalition against the authorities' plans for the setting up of MPAs. In interviews the various involved respondents signal that this is a new coalition. They state that before this the users of the North Sea had almost no contact with each other. In a certain sense we can conclude that the MPAs had an exceptionally mobilising effect.

The new coalition is made up of local users (water sports, fishing, shipowners) and local politicians. The protest is at its high point on 20 March 1999 when about 150 fishermen, beach fishermen and water sports enthusiasts hold a demonstration in Oostende. The demonstrators threaten to blockade the harbours. The words used become harsher ('*Nature reserves at sea are unacceptable to us*') and it is clearly dead-set against the proposed policy that is perceived as a policy created by a 'green lobby':

> *"Jan Peeters' department is manipulated by the green lobby consisting of Walloon scientists from the North Sea Mathematical Model Control Unit."* (Chairman of the Shipowners' Association, in: Het Nieuwsblad, 22.03.1999).

As protest continued to grow against designation of the MPAs the Secretary of State had to freeze the designation procedure rather quickly. The Governor of West Flanders was asked to start consultation with different users of the North Sea in various working groups (*see below*). From his position, the Governor was seen as a neutral and objective person who could depolarise a polarised dossier. Yet, some respondents think that this consultation also had a mainly political and strategic function with the intention of calming down public debate as federal elections were to take place in the same year. The conclusion that almost nothing happened with the results of the consultation in the subsequent period strengthened this suspicion (*see below*).

2.4 Coalitions of Opinion and the Discourses Employed

Before now we have stated that in the conservation movement and the federal authorities the need was felt to designate MPAs on the basis of scientific insights and legal obligations.

From an analysis of newspaper articles from the beginning of this period it appears that the opponents' declarations illustrated the NIMBY syndrome. Not surprisingly, the protest started in the coastal municipalities where there was a suggestion of designating marine reserves. Important elements in the opponents' discourse as reproduced in the media reports were, among others:

- problems with enforced restrictions and prohibitions: e.g. off-shore activities;
- the expected damage to tourism, recreation and water sports;
- the expected damage to the economy (harbour, shipping, fisheries);.
- perception of unequal treatment of different sectors: military activities are clearly still permitted;
- perception of inequality between countries: in France (e.g. Brayes-Dunes) and the Netherlands there are no similar restrictions and prohibitions;
- the lack of involvement in the policy process;
- the problem of subsidiarity.

The discourses used by the objectors at first focussed mainly on prohibitions that would result from the designation of the MPAs and the consequences of this for economic activities. *'Nothing more will be possible, we shall not be able to pursue our economic activity any more, tourism will decline ...'* or *'do we have to give up our existence for a few birds?'* were continual refrains. The fishing sector spoke about 'snatching the bread out of our mouths'. There was certainly a coalition of water sports and fishing enthusiasts together with ship owners, that expressed itself in the form of a similar message ... all 'sea users' who feared for the future of their activities.

In the perception of the objectors and in the discourses that they used, there was, in addition, also a question of discrimination. For one thing no restrictions seemed to be placed on certain sectors such as the military. The fact that military activities at sea could be continued and their own activities (surfing, sailing, fishing ...) would cause too much disturbance provoked a great deal of incomprehension. On the other hand there was also talk of unevenness of treatment between countries. The North Sea users pointed out that neither in the Netherlands nor in France did similar prohibitions apply, and this would result in unfair competition.

Through an inadequate or deficient government communication in the initial phase there was from the outset a fundamental problem of mistrust between the initiators and other actors. The discourses of the initiators did not mesh with that of the North Sea users. This was partly because of the arguments used, which did not tally with the experience of the North Sea users and for them indicated a lack of knowledge.

> 'The official said that if a group of surfers – windsurfers are never in a group – surf through a flock of birds, the birds will be stressed. The whole hall was rolling on the floor with laughter and they were wondering what they were dealing with.'

Besides the arguments they used, the North Sea users also took umbrage at the authoritarian style that was used by the authorities. As a result the feeling was fostered that MPAs were a Brussels phenomenon, or the so-called 'landlubbers' intended to reduce the autonomy of the real coast users. The fact that the official responsible for communication at the federal administration MUMM is a French speaker by origin, only strengthened this feeling. During interviews local politicians in particular refer to what was called interference from above by people who lacked the necessary know-how.

> 'A Brussels civil servant who did not know [the area], made designations without asking himself what the consequences were. It's often what happens. By people who don't have the necessary local knowledge.'
> 'It's the same with the 'RUPs' and the 'PRUPs' (Spatial Implementation Plans (RUPs) and Provincial Spatial Implementation Plans (PRUPs), note of the editor), that are drawn up by civil servants and they are the people who are most out of touch with reality.'

In addition, the fact that the initiators referred to obligations in international and above all European regulations forms an important point of criticism in the discourses of the challenging coalition. During the interviews water sports enthusiasts, among others, point out that Europe is misused by the authorities in this discourse and that this is encouraged by 'the Greens'.

> 'They said that it came from Europe, but that is faulty information ... When they do not dare to say something themselves, they say 'Europe obliges us to (...).' Everyone understood this as 'the Greens are out to get us again'.'

Among the objectors to the MPAs there was also a perception of a discourse coalition between 'the Greens' and 'the Authorities'. What precisely is meant by 'the Greens' varies from respondent to respondent. Some of them mainly or exclusively focus on the environmental movement, and so reduced this movement to a single conservation organisation ('Natuurpunt'). Other respondents talk of an amalgam of environmental organisations ('Natuurpunt', WWF, Greenpeace ...). Yet other respondents speak of a coalition between the environmental movement and political parties that are considered to be towards the left of the political spectrum such as sp.a (the Flemish socialist party) and/or 'Groen!' (formerly 'Agalev', the Flemish Green Party). When the authorities are being discussed, it is striking that it includes both politicians and administration. Among these the federal administration MUMM is the principle target.

It is clear that there are different discourses and discourse coalitions relating to the setting up of MPAs. The lack of communication and information from the initiators fed all sorts of speculation and disinformation by the rapidly growing challenging coalition and led to an adjustment of the informal and formal rules.

2.5 Power and Resources: Legislation and Knowledge as the Most Important Resources

The most important resource at the disposal of the initiators, is said, by most actors, to be legislation and regulations. Based on a new legal framework, the Marine Environment Act, the MPAs were to be designated. Where the initiators use (international) law and regulations as arguments of power, we see that, on the contrary, legal instruments were seen in a very negative light by opponents of the designation process.

> 'Regulations? They have become a weapon for people who want to force something through'.

A second important resource that the respondents mention when replying, is scientific knowledge. On the basis of scientific knowledge and insight, sites were proposed for designation as MPAs by the federal administration MUMM. At the beginning scientific knowledge counts as a conclusive argument in the initiators' discourses. During the interviews (2006-2007) scientists actually state that in the first designation proposal the scientific knowledge was inadequate in fact.

> 'The scientific foundation for the designation was not strong enough and could easily be challenged.'

The fact that progress was made with the proposals for designation is attributed to international obligations and these came principally through Europe. The European Authorities had anyway formulated obligations in various directives which the member states had to fulfil. In these, certain criteria such as timing were laid down (see chapter 2).

It is clear that the resources employed met with great resistance from the North Sea users. The failure of the first attempt at designation can really not be attributed to this alone. Certain respondents attribute the failure to the fact that the initiators did not have sufficient means and to the lack of clarity as to who could bring which means into action. A federal official who was involved with the designation process at that time express it in the in-depth interview as follows:

> 'Nobody was prepared to invest in it.'

Among other things, the lack of clarity resulted from the fact that the Marine Environment Act was a new Act which was being applied for the first time. On the other hand it was also because of a lack of political priority, which, for example, resulted in no measures being prepared for the (economic) compensation of users who would be negatively affected by the designation. No financial means were provided.

> '*I think that they provided insufficient social and economic instruments for compensation and this was detrimental.*'

Respondents point out that this was not necessarily with malicious intent but rather as a result of a lack of personnel and insufficient capacity.

> '*I saw that they didn't consult the stakeholders, but this was not necessarily a sign of ill will. Perhaps they didn't have the staff.*'
> '*Earlier there were certainly too few people and means, and they also had the wrong profile. Primarily a scientific and legal profile.*'

The opposition, developed by the above described challenging coalition, contributed in large measure to the failure of the process. Above all the (political) power of the mayors of the coastal municipalities should not be underestimated here, according to the politicians who were interviewed. On the other hand several North Sea users complain about a lack of interest and involvement of local politicians and mayors. From the opponents' perception of power in this period, it seems that they especially attributed a lot of power to '*the administration*', followed by '*the Greens*' (*see above*).

As resources the opponents used know-how (as North Sea users), a variety of people (mobilising capacity) *and* the media. Via mediagenic activities (protest marches, open public meetings...) the pressure was put on the decision makers. The blockade of a harbour was even threatened (*see above*).

2.6 Informal and Formal Rules: the Dominating Dimension

In their evaluation of the start of the designation process, supporters and opponents of the MPAs pay a lot of attention to the role of regulations in general and in particular to the issuing of laws and regulations. Legislation and regulations were the government's dominant policy instruments in the first attempt at designation of MPAs, with the Marine Environment Act as the most important Act. Economic and social instruments were not brought into application or only late or inadequately. The informal and formal rules that were followed in which the initiator made no provision for participation, initially not even for the provision of information, formed the breeding ground for disinformation. Opponents considered the Act and the announced implementation orders above all as a typical example of government with all sorts of restrictions being imposed from Brussels without consultation with local actors and administrations. In the interviews, legislation and regulations are an important target of criticism in the initial phase of the designation process. All the actors make comments on the *'precision of prescription'*, *'formality'* and *'authority'* (*see chapter 1 analytical framework*).

The Marine Environment Act and the possibilities of issuing prohibitions it provided for, were seen as being 'severe' to 'very severe' by the North Sea users. The perception existed that the regulations were drawn up in a very strict manner, so that they would greatly reduce the freedom of action of the North Sea users. The draft royal decree of Secretary of State Jan Peeters strengthened this interpretation, as in various versions of the draft for the designation of MPAs there was indeed provision for all sorts of prohibitions, without any prior consultation or discussion with the users involved. One shipowner put it as follows:

> *'Peeters intended to forbid fishing. (...) The whole 'Stroombank' is going to be protected, and fishing and pleasure cruising will be forbidden.'*

But politicians who were interviewed also recognise the problem:

> *'Yes, but that was because they thought that the way they went fishing would be rigorously dealt with. (...) If you read the text literally then it was indeed the case that you would not be permitted to do anything any more.'*

Other respondents (authorities and market) on the other hand point out that precisely the lack of *'precision of prescription'* constituted an important problem in the first proposals for designation. After all, in the Marine Environment Act it was not precisely prescribed which regulations would apply in the MPAs. An official phrases it as follows:

> *'In the first attempts one of the fundamental mistakes is that it is not precisely specified in the federal regulations which rules apply in the MPAs, in contrast to the Flemish regulations on the environment (we know what that contains). At federal level they first wanted to go ahead with designating and then would say which rules are applicable by a separate royal decree. That fed uncertainty.'*

This is confirmed by a member of staff in a ministry and a representative of the harbour administration, who respectively state:

> *'My feeling and perception is that they wanted to designate the areas without really knowing what the precise regulations would be.'*
> *'Moreover, we had so many questions. We asked if we could dredge. They said that would be permitted, but they didn't know the conditions.'*

In the first stage the intention was first to propose a designation and present it for approval without its being clear what consequences the designation would have for the users. During the interviews, local politicians mention in relation to this that in the past there have already been negative experiences and refer among other instances to the designation of the Birds Directive Special Protection Areas where just years after the designation prohibitions and obligations were linked to the status of protection.

> 'Oh European Birds Directive Areas? We must protect the birds. Everyone says: 'That's magnificent'. But if they then go on to say what it means: that you can no longer go on the beach in winter, that you can no longer collect shells, that you can no longer go for a walk, that you can no longer put up beach tents, that you can no longer do this and that...'
> 'Birds Directive Areas, set up in 1988, I remember that Dupré was then the Flemish Minister of the Environment. And before the meeting he produced a batch of plans and said that the Flemish Government had to designate Birds Directive Areas. But he said that that had no importance and no effect at all. We simply had to send it on to Europe. Do I need to show you where these areas are? Oh no we answered, it's just fine...In this way the areas were designated by the Flemish Government. Now you can see what later came along in terms of regulations. The consequences are serious.'

The distrust felt by the users and local politicians that grew out of these experiences formed for various actors at that time a breeding ground for loathing of any additional form of legislation and regulations.

Formality and *authority* are less spoken about by the respondents in the evaluation of the first attempt at designation. It was clear that it was a matter of legislative instruments (Act, draft Royal Decrees). It was less clear what the possible consequences of non-compliance would be.

2.7 A Classic Top-down Approach

To a large extent there was unanimity among the respondents about the management style used by the authorities during the first attempt at designating the MPAs. All actors speak about a closed authoritarian style that meant that local people were not involved in any way.

> 'They thought: 'we will promulgate protection, and everything will be OK'.'
> 'They made regulations and then presented them. 'We draw something up and you can say what is wrong.' That was the model and that meant that everyone was against it.'
> 'The first plan went completely wrong. They came to explain how it was going to be. Due to protest it was then removed.'

The North Sea users saw the first attempt at designation as an example of *fait accompli* politics, where everything was prepared and decided internally. The North Sea users were unexpectedly and suddenly confronted with what was seen as decisions from Brussels.

'The people in Brussels presented it in a totally wrong way. They wanted to get it through quietly, at least that is how it came across.'

The officials of the federal administration MUMM who were involved, state that the reason for the management style used is mainly due to the lack of personnel. They had neither enough people or resources nor the necessary experience. The fact that the royal decrees prepared by the administration (MUMM), without the foreknowledge of the responsible Secretary of State, leaked out in advance due to the request for authorisation to organise the International Sailing Week in Nieuwpoort, is seen as an illustration of this.

The total lack of participation and, initially, even of information dissemination and communication from the government, led, from the very beginning, to a fundamental distrust on the part of the North Sea users. The meeting with the mayors and the press conference of 9 March 1999 (*see above*; Minutes 1999a) organised by the Secretary of State, could not avoid that the distrust led to growing protest and major problems of implementation. The Marine Environment Act was indeed approved, but the implementation orders were 'put on the back burner' out of sheer necessity. The mayors of the coastal municipalities did not feel involved or only too late and urged postponement of the designation of the marine reserves.

In a letter to the Governor of the Province of West Flanders (20.04.1999), the Secretary of State refers to the consultation with the mayors of the coastal municipalities, when he states to understand that many of those involved are asking themselves questions about the designation process. The Secretary of State also proposes to steer the policy process by providing consultation with all stakeholders, organised by the Governor of the Province of West Flanders:

> "*It seems right to us that before concrete and definitive implementation provisions are decided, a broad consultation will be organised with all interested parties so that a report can be drawn up on the nature and meaning of the activities that could be subject to the above-mentioned provisions. You have promised to organise this consultation and to draw up a report about it. The deadline will be about next 15 September.*"

The Secretary of State suggested working with a phased consultation, so that in the first phase all interested parties would be inventoried, "*together with their activities and concerns*". On the basis of this inventory the departments and collaborators of the Secretary of State would propose new provisions for the implementation of the Marine Environment Act.

> "*By means of the above-mentioned inventory and proposals for implementation orders the second phase can then follow, making possible – on the basis of a new consultation – the drawing up of a final report of the consultation meetings by about 15 September 1999.*"

On the initiative of the Governor a study day was subsequently organised on 25 June 1999 with the objective of making an inventory of the activities that take place in the areas of special ecological interest and of the importance attached to them (Minutes 1999b). In the working groups they wanted to identify the possible conflicts and list proposals for sustainable conservation of the marine areas. The following working groups were set up: energy distribution and communication, harbour activities and shipping, water sports, professional and recreational fisheries. During the discussions in the various working groups both procedural and content related objections were expressed. As far as content is concerned the scientific (ecological) knowledge on which the designation proposals were based, 'was seriously doubted' (among others by the Water Sports and Recreational Fishing Working Groups). Moreover, the working groups stated that the designation proposals were based on a one-sided (ecological) approach without taking into account other sectors. On the procedural side, the lack of consultation and participation in earlier phases of the policy process were criticised by all working groups (Minutes 1999b).

Where the working groups initially had the objective of making an inventory of the marine activities and the interests of the various sectors, they rapidly appeared to be already fora for consultation and debate. After this first round it was clear that there was a need for thorough consultation with all the stakeholders and not least with the local authorities. On issues of content it was clear that there were all sorts of objections against the proposals that had been formulated for the designation and that these came from various sectors and some public administrations (mainly from the Ministry of Agriculture in relation to fisheries).

The time for consultation with the various North Sea users, 25 June 1999, not only came late in the designation process but also late in the legislative life of the federal government led by Dehaene (Dehaene II – as it is known, 23 June 1995-12 July 1999). After the composition of a new federal government in the summer of 1999 a new Minister (for the first time a 'Green') with responsibility for the environment, was charged with following up the North Sea policy.

In conclusion it can be said that the first attempt at designation of MPAs can be seen as an example of the classic top-down policy, which had little ambition with regard to participation and this only in reaction to protest.

3. The Second Designation Proposal. Continuation of Policy? (1999-2003)

With the coming to power of the Verhofstadt I government (12 July 1999-12 July 2003), Magda Aelvoet, the Deputy Prime Minister and Minister of Consumer Affairs, Health and Environment, became responsible for the North Sea. On 26 August 2002 Magda Aelvoet resigned after the controversial Belgian armaments sales to Nepal and was replaced by Jef Tavernier, a member of the same party. Thus in a period of 3 years the responsibility for the North Sea passed through the hands of the same number of policy makers at federal level.

3.1 Two Ministers and a Lack of Supporting Coalitions

After the first designation proposal ran up against growing opposition from the users of the North Sea because of content and procedure (lack of participation), new initiatives were developed in this period.

The Governor of the Province of West Flanders presented a report of the consultations with the various users of the North Sea to Minister Aelvoet, with the question whether she could agree with the consultation procedure that had been introduced by her predecessor (Minutes 1999c). After her agreement additional rounds of consultation were planned with new actors: the environmental organisations and the local authorities. In both consultations an historical sketch was given with particular attention to the protest that the first designation proposals had provoked and the need for consultation that was felt as a result. Three important groups of actors were identified for the subsequent designation process of MPAs: users of the North Sea (the sectors), the environmental organisations and local authorities (Minutes 1999c). After a first consultation, the proposed process, which was intended to arrive at a consensus between the various actors, came to a halt.

Minister Aelvoet, and later Minister Tavernier, launched almost no further initiatives. When asked for an explanation for this, the respondents stated in their interviews that this was to be attributed, to a large extent, to the fact that the protest during the first period had been so extensive that the designation of the MPAs was politically very difficult in this period. In addition to the importance of challenging coalitions (water sports enthusiasts, fishermen, ship-owners, members of local authorities...) respondents referred in their interviews to the lack of explicit supporting coalitions. When politicians were interviewed it appears that the initiatives of both 'green' Ministers lacked political support at federal government level. But a change of attitude could also be seen among earlier allies during this period. The nature conservation movement, for example, manifested itself considerably less about MPAs during this legislature than in the preceding period. Representatives of the nature conservation movement gave three possible explanations for this: the great fuss that arose as a result of the first attempt, the shift of political responsibility from a socialist secretary of state to 'green' Ministers with whom there was less 'tradition' and not least the linking to the offshore wind turbine dossier. Above all, the first proposals for the establishment of wind turbine parks (see below) and the intended link between wind turbine parks and MPAs could, among other things, gain little support from 'Natuurpunt' and certain scientists. Anyway, in the wind turbine dossier the environmental movement showed a lack of cohesion. Whereas 'Natuurpunt' and the 'Stichting Noordzee' (North Sea Foundation) did not support the proposed areas for establishing wind turbines, the Flemish umbrella environmental movement, Bond Beter Leef-milieu (federation of the Flemish environmental movement) certainly did.

Finally, one other actor ought to be mentioned in relation to this period: Prince Laurent. Minister Tavernier, in dialogue with Vera Dua, the Flemish Environmental Minister, and a member of the same party, undertook yet one more attempt to launch the idea of 'integral coastal nature parks'. This initiative enjoyed the support of Prince Laurent, who first heard the idea from Edgar Kesteloot, former board member of the nature conservation movement BNVR (Belgian Nature and Ornithological Reserves). The idea gained insufficient support and so went no further.

3.2 Discourse: Silence Falls on the Marine Reserves

There was hardly mention of marine reserves or MPAs in this period. Environmental organisations and public authorities had the opportunity to put questions for clarification and to formulate comments during their respective consultative meetings (Minutes 1999c; Minutes 1999d), but later the debate quietened down and attention shifted to wind turbine parks at sea.

During the consultation meetings a shift could be detected in the government's discourse. In addition to basing themselves on scientific insights and international legal obligations, the representative of MUMM dwelt on a short history of the situation during the introduction to the meeting. What was striking was that attention was especially given to the 'sea of protest' that the first designation proposals had provoked among various actors.

> "A proposal of a total ban on commercial fishing could not be considered by the Ministry of Agriculture, possibilities of taking protective measures within the sites could not be further investigated because of discussion that arose among various users. At the meeting of the mayors of coastal municipalities (early March 1999) the same proposals were put forward, with a sea of protest as a result. Until the present time, no Royal Decree has been adopted."(Minutes 1999d)

In the opening speech the federal government referred to three elements. Firstly, the necessity for thorough consultation, prior to taking definitive decisions. Secondly, the objective of the framework Act that should be respected. Thirdly, from analysis of the documents it appeared that the federal government tailored its arguments to the target group. For nature conservation organisations it was stated:

> "The fact that ecological thinking must not and may not be lost sight of"
> (Minutes 1999d)

For local authorities it said:

"The vision of municipality councils and local authority departments is very important"
(Minutes 1999c)

From the discourse analysis it appears that the federal government was anxious as a result of the fierce protests that the first designation proposal had provoked. The many questions, comments and criticisms that were formulated during the consultation with the local authorities only added to this, notwithstanding the fact that various authorities had not declared themselves against marine reserves as such. The most important point of criticism was the lack of involvement.

From the nature conservation movement there were calls for nature and area protection, tackling environmental pollution and integrated coastal management and the implementation of international regulations in this area. Furthermore, the nature conservation movement's discourse also showed interest in institutional problems (fragmentation of jurisdictions) and in the style of administration used. There was a plea for more to be done in the areas of information and participation:

"The implementation orders need to be announced to the public by the Minister with the message that the measures taken are permanent and represent added value for nature, tourism, recreation and fishing. The various users (among others, yachtsmen/women, people fishing as a sport...) should be included in this information campaign." (Minutes 1999d)

It is clear that in this period the discourse of various actors shifted from the definition of problems in the direction of (first initiatives towards) the solution of problems. Through lack of political priority the debate about MPAs really quietened down during Minister Aelvoet's period of office. In this time an important link was made with developments in the related energy policy area. Minister Aelvoet linked the discourse concerning the MPAs with the new discourse relating to the wind turbine parks. The fuss that really arose in this period in relation to the first proposals for the establishment of offshore wind turbine parks and the expected visual nuisance that would be experienced by the municipalities along the coast, contributed to the halting of the MPAs designation process. A scientist expresses it as follows:

'The communication about the wind turbines was not so very well received either. To then push through MPAs in such a phase is impossible.'

On the subject of the MPAs it became fairly quiet until the moment when Minister Tavernier appeared to develop a number of initiatives in 2003. What is noticeable is that there is hardly a single respondent who refers to this initiative. Minister Tavernier and the Flemish Minister Vera Dua, supported by Prince Laurent, made a plea for 'integral coastal nature parks'. With respect to contents this meant an important change of discourse given that this con-

75

cerned both an integral approach to sea *and* land. Still the idea found very little response and was not followed up (*see below*).

At the end of the legislature (spring 2003), 'Natuurpunt' ('Kustwerkgroep') argued for the designation of MPAs in its election statement issued for the federal elections of 2003. In this way, the nature conservation movement sought to keep the subject on the political agenda. The socialist party sp.a took this up during the discussions for the formation of a new government and urged the appointment of a Minister for the North Sea, who would indeed be in place in the next legislature.

3.3 A Problem of (Political) Power

As the most important explanation for the fact that it was not possible to des-ignate MPAs in Belgium in the period 1999-2003, the respondents gave not only the considerable powers of obstruction developed by users of the North Sea and local politicians, but above all the lack of (political) power of those who were newly responsible for policy. One respondent put it as follows:

'Presumably the Greens were not then strong enough to get it through.'

The lack of experience of the new Ministers (Aelvoet and Tavernier) and their ministerial offices, were mentioned as possible explanations. It was, after all, not only the first policy in-put of the politicians concerned, but also the Green Party's first contribution to federal policy in Belgium.

According to the politicians interviewed, party political relationships seem to have lain at the basis of the lack of policy in this period. Designation was no longer within the jurisdiction of a socialist party (sp.a) Minister, but was within that of a Minister from 'Groen!' ('Green!'at that time still called Agalev). Various actors point to the fact that at that moment there was a struggle going on between the two parties for the left wing of the electorate. The ecological theme that was traditionally *the* theme of the green party was an area where the socialist party wanted to develop a better profile for itself. It was therefore not so evident that the socialist political family would unconditionally support initiatives relating to designation, a subject on which they themselves had failed in the previous period. This uncertainty also made it less easy for the nature conservation movement, seen as the force behind this dossier, to sup-port the new policy.

'At that moment we knew at once how that little political world was structured. Because even if the Greens were in favour, the Reds would oppose. They had their own think tank and strategies.'

The nature conservation movement put much less effort into the MPAs dossier in this period. The most important resource for the nature conservation movement was reference to international legislation and regulations, and scientific knowledge. During consultation with the Minister, for example, a lot of weight was given to a study of the then 'Insituut voor Natuurbehoud' (IN - Institute for Nature Conservation), the present INBO (Research Institute for Nature and Forest), on the ornithological importance of the Belgian marine waters (Seys *et al.* 1999).

The follow-up of other more urgent policy dossiers really demanded all the energy from the Minister(s) in charge and as a result there were also fewer resources mobilised from that side also and the designation process almost came to a standstill. The designation of MPAs disappeared from the political agenda in this period. In the interviews, a former Minister put it as follows:

'In the first years there was no time, appetite or opportunities.'

3.4 Informal and Formal Rules: Marine Reserves a Struggle Against Wind Turbines?

As already stated, the political (and public) attention shifted in this period from the MPAs to the wind turbine parks at sea. In the nature conservation movement this shift in policy focus was experienced as very fundamental.

'Wind turbines must be set up; there was no mention of MPAs.'

With the near shore wind energy parks that were now being prepared, new users appeared in the North Sea area. It was soon clear that these wind turbine parks not only required new space but also new informal and formal rules relating to zoning and adjustment to other sorts of use. At the time of the first proposals (at the end of 1999-spring 2000) for the setting up of wind turbine parks at sea, there was no clarity about the rules of the game that would apply here. In parliamentary debates the then Secretary of State for Energy and Sustainable Development, Olivier Deleuze, answered[1]:

'(...) as stated in point a) the site(s) of the parks will be proposed by the companies. The government will not decide on these sites a priori.'

The lack of formal rules and 'precision of prescription' in the answers produced by the policy makers in this period, led not only to uncertainty among the market players involved but also among coastal dwellers and local politicians.

On 20 December 2000, a Royal Decree was issued concerning the conditions and the procedure for the granting of the area concessions for the construction and exploitation of installations for the production of electricity from water, sea currents or wind, in Belgian marine waters in accordance with the law of

---

[1]   Request for explanation by LETERME, Y., d.d. 27 March 2000, about the building of an offshore windmillpark, Kamer, 1999-2000, nr9 p. 3338.

the sea (Belgian Law Gazette, 30 December 2000), and official applications could be submitted. Two project proposals received the required area concessions: the temporary association 'Electrabel-Ondernemingen Jan de Nul' (27.03.2002) on the 'Vlakte van de Raan' and the project proposal of 'C-Power' (05.07.2002) on the 'Wenduinebank'. Only the temporary association finally obtained the required environmental permit. 'C-Power' had to suspend its project as a result of failing to obtain the necessary permits and subsequently had to wait until 2003 (27.06.2003) before it gained an area concession for the construction of a far shore wind turbine park on Thornton Bank, 27 to 30 kilometres distant from the coast.

The fact that it was planned to place the proposed wind turbines close to the Belgian coast, met with complaints mainly from the coastal population and local municipality councils, respectively of De Haan and Knokke, because of a feared visual pollution. In addition, during the consultation procedures objections also arose relating to shipping and security, morphology and geography, ecological values, spatial planning and fisheries (*for a detailed survey see*: http://www.mumm.ac.be/NL/Management/Sea-based/ windmills.php). Various actors (inhabitants, local administrations, action groups ...) resorted to legal means in order to thwart the planned near shore wind turbine parks off the Belgian coast. The dossier on wind turbine parks off the Belgian coast, polarised opinion, with Minister Aelvoet as supporter and an amalgam of opponents, among who were now also to be found a part of the environmental movement (*see below*).

The fact that a mixed group of actors was undertaking legal steps against the proposed projects off the Belgian coast illustrates the polarised character of this dossier. Coastal dwellers, municipality councils, the Province of West Flanders, the 'Zeevisserijfonds' (Sea Fisheries Fund), nature conservation organisations ('Stichting Noordzee') *and* Dutch municipality councils all contested the extended area concession and the environmental permit. Finally a petition launched by an inhabitant of Knokke, Mrs Soete, and the Knokke district council, led to an Order of 25 March 2003 (Order of the Council of State, number 117.482) that ordered the suspension of the environmental permit that had already been issued for the construction of a wind turbine park only a few kilometres from the coast at Knokke.

During the interviews various respondents referred to developments in the related policy area of energy, for the designation process of the MPAs. The wind turbine dossier was seen as a priority in this period, but ran into trouble as a result of growing protest. The linking that Minister Aelvoet formerly made between the wind turbine dossier and the designation of the MPAs, immediately meant that during this legislature no progress was made on this issue either. From the wind turbine dossier it was very clear that citizens not only become more articulate but, above all, draw power from legal resources too. The complaint before the Council of State brought by an inhabitant of Knokke had a sort of catalyst function for the policy.

'Mrs Soete's complaint led to a tendency towards more transparency and support.'

3.5 A Donkey Bumps into the Same Stone Twice Anyway: Top-down

After the MPAs designation dossier almost came to a halt under Minister Aelvoet, at the end of 2002 reports appeared in Flemish daily newspapers about the new plans of her successor, Minister Tavernier:

> *"Minister wants to designate three areas in the sea for the protection of birds"* (Het Laatste Nieuws, 11.12.2002)

What was noticeable in the policy was that no account seemed to be taken of the insights and recommendations ensuing from the consultative meetings at the beginning of the legislature. In this sense it certainly seems as if the policy makers had learned nothing from the earlier unsuccessful attempts at designation. Now once again the policy had been prepared by officials (MUMM) with little transparency and federal politicians, without prior consultation with the users of the North Sea. Once again the designation proposals were based on scientific knowledge. And once again they wanted to proceed to designation of the MPAs without clarity about the potential consequences for the users of the North Sea... A local politician put it as follows:

> *'Minister Aelvoet did not do much, in all honesty. Tavernier has certainly made an attempt but he once again made the mistake of designating the areas without knowing what the regulations would be. They would come later...'*

Lack of participation and of 'precision of prescription' resulted in the fact that the plans that were prepared top-down soon ran into fierce protest. At the request of the Mayor of De Panne (a coastal muncipality) the Minister was asked to give clarification on the subject of the plans that had been announced in the press, at a consultation with the mayors of the coastal municipalities (Minutes 2003a). During the clarification by officials from the Ministry and MUMM, the importance of implementing the European Bird and Habitat Directives was especially emphasised:

> *"This must take place according to a European directive. Only scientific arguments may be used for this designation. The socio-economic concerns will be dealt with in a later phase. (...) During the designation process only ecological factors may be taken into account according to the Directive and no participation is possible."* (Minutes 2003a)

In reaction to the lack of participation and the perceived threats, the mayors of the coastal municipalities subsequently convened a press conference in order to express their anxiety about the policy. The newspaper headlines spoke for themselves:

> *"Kustburgemeesters tegen bescherming marien milieu"* (Mayors of the coastal municipalities against protection of the marine environment) (De Standaard, 14.01.2003);
> *"Kustburgemeesters boos op Vlaams Minister van Milieu Jef Tavernier"* (Mayors of the coastal municipalities angry with Jef Tavernier, Flemish Minister for the Environment) (Het Laatste Nieuws, 14.01.2003);
> *"Wij willen inspraak over milieugebieden in zee."* (We want a say on environmental areas in the sea) (Het Laatste Nieuws, 14.01.2003);
> *"Mogen we nog zwemmen in zee?"* (Can we still swim in the sea?) (Het Nieuwsblad, 14.01.2003).

In a consultative meeting with the Minister that followed this (Minutes 2003b), the mayors' grievances and questions were scrutinized and the Minister held out the prospect of representation of the mayors of the coastal municipalities in the advisory committees that would be established to draw up management plans for the marine reserves. This was confirmed once again at the launching of the idea of 'integral coastal nature parks', when the Minister declared that he would provide structural consultation via an advisory committee, that would represent on equal terms both the involved government departments and other interested parties from professional, academic or environmental circles (VLIZ 2003).

After the launching of the idea of 'integral coastal nature parks' (*see above*) by Jef Tavernier, the Federal Minister, and Vera Dua, the Flemish Minister, supported by Prince Laurent, protest nevertheless arose again among the local mayors who once more declared that they had not been involved in the preparation of the policy.

> *"Kustburgemeesters voelen zich opnieuw buitenspel gezet"* (Mayors of coastal municipalities feel that they have been excluded from the game again) (Het Laatste Nieuws, 14.03.2003)

The idea of 'integral coastal nature parks' was not followed up at all and, with the prospect of new federal elections, the designation process related to MPAs went quiet again. There was hardly any continuity in the MPAs designation process in the first years after the Marine Environment Act. Changing jurisdictions, changing discourses and changing informal and formal rules made the designation process thus far a discontinuity process. For the time being, the only continuity seemed to lie in the fact that the management style used could predominantly be described as top-down and that none of the designation proposals led to an effective designation of MPAs.

4. The Third Designation Proposal. A Successful Designation? (2003-2006)

With the coming to power of the new federal government (Verhofstadt II, 12 July 2003-21 December 2007) a specific paragraph on the North Sea was included in the governmental agreement. For its implementation, important new resources (people and means) were provided, for example by the creation of a Minister for the North Sea. This Minister would have the right to take initiative in the coordination of all matters relating to the North Sea policy at Ministerial level. For the first time Belgium got a Minister for the North Sea, in the person of Johan Vande Lanotte. On 15 October 2005 Johan Vande Lanotte resigned and was replaced as Minister of the North Sea by Renaat Landuyt.

4.1 A First Belgian Minister for the North Sea as the Most Important Shift of Power?

The most important shift relating to resources and power took place in this period according to many respondents in the creation of the function of a Minister of the North Sea. The fact that the ministerial portfolio was taken up in the new legislature by Johan Vande Lanotte – considered to be a power politician by many – generated authority.

> 'For sure, anyone other than Vande Lanotte would never have gotten things done with that approach.'

Respondents point to the political past of the Minister as the reason for this; he built up an image of himself by his involvement in important dossiers on coastal matters such as the 'Duinendecreet' (Dunes Decree), but also by the fact that the Minister himself is from the coast and at that time represented a large part of electorate of the area. The Minister himself also refers to this as a strong point during the interview:

> 'I am also from the area, with 30% of the votes in my pocket, so I cannot run the risk of having large groups against me. My greatest strength is also my greatest weakness.'

Moreover, the Minister of the North Sea recruited people to his ministerial office, who were exempt from other tasks to work towards the designation of the MPAs as a priority. In the interviews, respondents from government, civil society, market as well as scientists state that the role of those people working in the ministerial office should not be underestimated.

The linking together of the responsibility for North Sea issues with the responsibility for the budget *and* the deputy-premiership produced a concentration of political power, in the opinion of many respondents.

'The power of Vande Lanotte as deputy prime Minister was crucial.'
*'A political heavyweight, who could play the part of Minister for the North Sea.
His portfolio was not so wide but he clearly had great political power. And if such
a person feels that the sea is important then it gets on the political agenda.'*

The fragmented competences that result from the complex structure of the
Belgian state, resulted, on the other hand, in the fact that there was no mention
of total concentration of power. The federal government, for example, could
not impose restrictions on fisheries, since this is within the competence of the
Flemish Region. But it could impose restrictions on shipping. The division of
competences, according to some civil servants, was used by the then Minister
as an alibi in order to avoid certain sticking points, perhaps for pragmatic
reasons.

*'They have got round a tricky point: commercial fisheries. Whereas the economic
aspects are regional the ecological aspects are federal. They could have integrated
this perfectly into an approach in consultation with the regions. But this didn't
happen. (…) it is a missed opportunity, but on the other hand if it was a breaking
point for the establishment of the MPAs then perhaps they would not even have
come into existence by now.'*

The then Minister and his staff declared that, given the fragmentation of competences during the designation procedure, a great deal of effort was put into
consultation. With the federal partners this took place in a special Task Force
set up for the purpose. With lower levels of competences such as Flemish Region, the Province and the mayors of coastal municipalities there was consultation. Whereas in the first period the mayors were perceived as powerful
actors where resistance was concerned, we see that in this period they did not
really count as an opposition. Consultation in the early stages and linking to
other dossiers (among others, wind turbines, *see below*) were seen as an explanation for this by the policy makers who were involved. Yet this consultation
was not able to solve the problem of fragmentation of competences. Various
people involved explained that the division of competences constituted not
only an administrative problem but also caused a lack of involvement of, for
example, port authorities (under Flemish competence).

What is remarkable is that also for the third and successful attempt at designation, respondents do not point to economic means as important resources.
Even now no provision was made for financial means of compensation for
adversely effected users, for example. Respondents give two possible explanations for this. The first – and possibly most important explanation – is that the
respondents state that no restrictions were placed on users of the North Sea. A
second explanation is that agreements were concluded with important economic actors. So clarity was first established about exploitation zones for sand,
gravel and wind *(see below)* and, during the negotiations the fishing community got the promise that opportunities would be created for aquaculture in
the offshore wind turbine parks that were to be set up. It is noticeable that

almost all respondents state that they have no idea how the arrangements were made. However, they *do* point to the fact that the power of certain economic sectors (dredgers, sand and gravel extractors, energy…) in the MPAs designation dossier must certainly not be underestimated.

> *'These men dictate to the Minister, see. Even if he's called Vande Lanotte. If they say that it has to be like this or that, well …'*

Whereas during the first attempt at designation scientific knowledge, alongside legislation and regulations were considered as the most important resources, this was far less the case in the third attempt. During this attempt it was no longer exclusively about scientific knowledge but just as much about layman's or users' know-how or knowledge.

> *'It is not possible to explain things to these people that cannot be explained. Their knowledge is considerable and shouldn't be underestimated; they came up with suggestions themselves! About shipwrecks too - the greatest defenders of shipwrecks are divers. Also because it has happened that one of them was caught on a hook (fish hook, editorial note) …'*

Besides, the scientific knowledge used, differed in various respects from that used in the first attempt. This was partly as a result of new insights, more data but also more as a result of a difference in emphasis. A federal civil servant explains it as follows:

> *'What changed on our side is that a very precise scientific basis was asked for, and I have to confess that this on certain points it differed from our first proposals.'*

The new insights confronted scientists with strategic questions anyway. For instance, how could they argue for the great scientific value of 'Vlakte van de Raan', after they had recommended this area as a potential site for the setting up of wind turbines in an earlier period (*see above*)? Various respondents from the scientific and policy sector state that there is still a lack of scientific knowledge now and that this is certainly so with regard to monitoring and evaluation of the MPAs which have been designated in the meantime.

On the subject of power and resources, respondents finally point out that the impact of Europe on the final designation cannot be underestimated. The threat of a conviction for late, incomplete or wrong implementation of European Directives weighed in the advantage of those who argued in favour of designation. Policy makers therefore used Europe as an argument of power, and this was often greeted by the initial opponents with disbelief.

> *'They used the argument that it came from Europe, but in our opinion that is not true. But it is also the case that Europe should get involved in the issue at some time.'*

4.2 Informal and Formal Rules. A Phased Approach and Spatial Planning

At the end of 2003, the new Minister for the North Sea announced plans for the 'Sustainable Management of the North Sea'. The following extract from the Minister's press release (Communiqué 2003) makes clear that, among other things, a phased approach was envisaged for this:

"On Friday 19 December 2003, the Minister for Economy and Energy, Fientje Moerman, and the Minister of the North Sea, Johan Vande Lanotte, have received the green light from the government for the execution of the first stage in the Sustainable Management of the North Sea. As a result, there will be a review of the present designation of the zones for the exploration and exploitation of sea sand and sea gravel and of the permit policy and the zone for the establishment of wind turbines in the sea will be designated. Both Ministers will submit the necessary Royal Decrees to the Council of Ministers for approval in the course of the following months.
Minister Johan Vande Lanotte plans to present the second stage, with among other things concrete measures for the designation of MPAs, to the government in the spring of 2004, after consultation with all parties involved." (Communiqué 2003)

Crucial for this period is the conclusion that the informal and formal rules relating to MPAs have been adapted to rules for other uses of the North Sea. No longer the Marine Environment Act alone, but rather the overall spatial planning and development of the North Sea were now considered priority. A spatial planning, in which the protection of the marine environment was provided for, after there was first clarification about the zoning of important economic activities such as offshore wind turbine parks and sand and gravel extraction. Various respondents call the idea of spatial planning for the North Sea a new idea, inspired by the fact that new users (wind energy) showed up, who claimed a part of the sea. A scientist expresses it as follows:

'On the one hand we were not aware until then what had happened at sea, we were little interested in that. Until suddenly a new player arrived and claimed an area on which other users were already established. Suddenly it became more important to put those uses on the map and to see where everyone was. Spatial planning at sea was suddenly something necessary.'

The market considered the lack of planning by the government as the most important cause of failure for the earlier attempts at establishing offshore wind turbine parks.

'We have always said that spatial planning must be done by policy makers, as that is not something for a private company. That is also what went wrong in the first procedure for nearshore parks where we had to do a lot of guesswork as a result of the absence of a functional spatial planning policy.'

According to most respondents it would never have been possible to designate MPAs without the link to the dossier of wind turbines and sand and gravel extraction, due to which things were made clear in advance for the 'heavy' economic activities. A representative of the market answered the question as to whether MPAs would have been designated without clarity about the zoning of wind energy and sand and gravel extraction:

'Very difficult.'

According to respondents from government, civil society, market and science, the on-going legal procedures for the wind turbine parks constituted a catalyst for the global zoning process. The then Minister for the North Sea states in an interview:

'We had to move forward. We couldn't do anything else. Because the process was already up and running; we were stuck with the problem of the procedure for the 'Vlakte van de Raan', and four years soon pass.'

Changing informal and formal rules concerning the wind turbine parks therefore had important consequences for the designation process of the MPAs. By cancelling the earlier attributed permit for the exploitation of wind turbines near to the Belgian coast, Minister Vande Lanotte created a lot of goodwill among members of local authorities who had emphatically opposed the establishment of the wind turbine parks before, because they expected that it would create an eyesore when looking out to sea from the coastal holiday resorts. Partly due to this, the protest of the mayors of the coastal municipalities in the subsequent designation process was significantly smaller than during earlier attempts.

4.3 Rules of the Game. Shifts in Formality, Authority and Precision of Prescription

In addition to the adaptation to the informal and formal rules for other uses in the North Sea and the choice of a phased approach, another important shift took place concerning the informal and formal rules. The existing Marine Environment Act was amended on various points. According to the then Minister, among others earlier problems concerning *precision of prescription* were encountered with these amendments.

'The Act allowed for little flexibility. The classifications were not good, it was everything of nothing. You get something started without saying what it contains. It didn't allow for consultation first and then designation. A very bothersome Act.'

The amendments really implied changes especially concerning *formality* and *authority* (*see also chapter 2*). So, for example, provision was made for voluntary user agreements that were based on a voluntary character, shared responsibility and trust rather than on strict prohibitions set down in formal legislation and regulations.

In contrast to the first attempt in which designation was proposed without its being clear what the consequences of this would be for users, in this attempt clarity was created at the same time about possible prohibitions and injunctions, so that the confidence of the users was to a large extent restored. All respondents state that the instrument of voluntary user agreements played a crucial role in this. In total six user agreements were concluded between the Minister for the North Sea and the users of the three Special Protection Areas, the two Special Areas for Conservation 'Trapegeer Stroombank' and 'Vlakte van de Raan', and for the specific marine reserve 'Baai van Heist' (*see figure 3 for a general outline map*). For the users the signatories were as follows: 'Stichting Watersport- en Recreatie' (Watersports and Recreation Foundation), 'Nautibel' (Federation of Belgian Nautical Companies), 'Nautiv' (Federation of Flemish Nautical Companies), de V.V.H.V. ('Vlaamse Vereniging Hengelsport Verbonden' – Flemish Association for Angling Unions) and a representative for 'Zeehengelsport' (Sea Fishing Sport). For the 'Baai van Heist' this was enlarged to include V.V.W. ('Verbond van Vlaamse Watersportverenigingen' – Union of Flemish Watersports Associations) and the V.Y.F. ('Vlaamse Yachting Federatie' – Flemish Yachting Federation).

The user agreements are concluded for a period of 3 years and contain the legal framework, the coordinates, the objective, a reference to the policy plan and an overview of the agreements concluded (*see chapter 2*). On top of the existing legal obligations the users contract to keep disturbance in the protected areas to a minimum during specified periods. The Minister for the North Sea intended to responsibilise the users by permitting them to make an active contribution via communication about the MPAs to their own supporters and clients. To support this the federal government undertakes to provide, among other things, current and user friendly information on its website www.de-noordzee.be (user agreements). In addition to an active contribution on the communication front, there is also provision for involving the signatories in the drawing up of the policy plans in which the management of the MPAs will be set out. The rough draft of the policy plan will be presented to the signatories and discussed in a consultative manner.

Nevertheless the respondents during the interviews are not undividedly positive about the voluntary user agreements. Respondents from market, civil society, government and science reported both advantages and disadvantages during the interviews.

The following advantages were seen in the user agreements:
* The voluntary approach creates support and increases the chances of respecting the commitments.
  '*It was a way to mobilise them, to let them think positively and cooperatively what we can do, instead of negatively of how we can prevent it.*'

'The feeling that it isn't a rule or an ultimatum from above. The perception of the actors is that it is something of their own. They could work with it and feel that they will have an advantage if it appears to work well.'
- Responsibility now lies with the users.
'Possession in the sense of ownership, people feel themselves involved and responsible.'
- New networks are created between users.
- It leads to win-win situations.
- It is a flexible instrument.

The instrumental argument 'to create support' is the most cited argument by respondents and certainly by policy makers.

The following disadvantages were seen in the user agreements:

- The lack of compulsory character as a result of which the question if raised whether the objectives can be realised.
'I think that this again leaves some doors open…'
'And if you really look at it then they are empty boxes. 'I'm not going to restrict you and then you will go along with me and you have to communicate this to your supporters.'
- Creating vagueness for those not involved. People have no perception, or an unsatisfactory one, of other users and the contents of other user agreements. One ship-owner states that he is not aware of the existence of these agreements.
'I hadn't realised that before now, but we have no knowledge of what other sectors have agreed. (…) We have our own agreements, but we have no idea of the rest.'
- Noting is provided for in maintenance and supervision.
- Users could get the feeling that no further protection measures are called for.
- The progress of the process is slower (consultation, involvement…).
- Creation of lack of clarity about regulations.
- Creation of differences between various areas.
- Lack of clarity about the fact whether the signatories effectively represent the sectors.
'The agreements do not really exist for the users. I don't hear anything about them.'
- The temporary character of the agreements doesn't give sufficient certainty.
'User agreements can be concluded with users and the administration. So if those people change their minds then you've had it.'
- There is no agreement with 'hard users'.
'Yes but, just have a look at who these user agreements have been concluded with.'

Where the voluntary nature of the instrument is seen as an important advantage with regard to creating support, the respondents see it at the same time as being the most important disadvantage. A key concept in the analysis by respondents seems to be lack of clarity. Lack of clarity for those not involved but also about the representative nature of the signatories and the familiarity with the instrument among real users. Although it is efficient, the question is whether it is also an effective instrument for the realisation of the objectives.

Various actors from administration, science and civil society speak about 'toning down' of the Marine Environment Act and/or a minimum transposition of the European Directive in this light, and wonder if the present Act and the designation of MPAs is still adequate to the initial objective: the protection of the marine environment.

> 'They opted for the easiest and probably the only feasible method. Then it would seem they opted to get some areas on paper (for the EU) without hitting the present users too hard. This was probably the only solution, even with such a political heavyweight.'
> 'Some progress was made, but among the supporters the suspicion is growing that it is an empty box. That finally nothing will happen!'
> 'It can't be any other way because there is not a single regulation that supervises the users or changes anything related to their activities.'

The last point is also recognised by the users of the North Sea themselves. The users point out that after the designation of the MPAs nothing changed in reality for them and that this is also the reason why they no longer fought designation.

> 'They made it less rigid (the legislation, editorial note) and defined the boundaries. We are suddenly permitted to enter the area again and the sailers as well, and that is the main thing. If they want us out tomorrow then they'd have a trouble. Those zones are too vast.'
> 'It doesn't have many repercussions. We are not damaged in our interests. We didn't go fishing there anyway.'
> 'We have agreed not to hold any motor boat races between November and March. But just tell me what idiot goes racing in that period on the North Sea? No, to be honest, we have no restrictions, we don't know either why we should get any.'

Particularly the market judge the change in the informal and formal rules rather positively. An important explanation, besides the fact that no additional prohibitions were imposed, is that after a period of uncertainly, at last clarity and certainty were created.

> 'Positive because something has happened. There was clarity. A decision had been taken and it was designated. We now knew what we had to adhere to.'

4.4 New Rules of the Game, New Discourses

It is clear that, after the issue of the designation of the MPAs quietened down during the previous legislature, the Minister for the North Sea launched a revived discourse during this period.

The government discourse in this period was strongly adjusted in comparison with the earlier attempt(s). Attention was now mainly directed towards routes that could lead to solutions for all those involved, rather than towards definition of problems and objectives. More attention was given to the grievances and expectations of the users of the North Sea, who were consulted through bilateral deliberations. This implied not only an important shift in the management methods, but especially also in discourses. The most important shift that took place was that in this period the government discourse was not exclusively based on scientific opinion but also on opinion presented by the users of the North Sea. The government discourse thus coincided better with that of the users. The figure of the Minister for the North Sea was not an unimportant factor in this. The fact that the then Minister is originally from the coast (Ostend), and personally committed himself to leading these bilateral talks with the users, re-established confidence.

'Typical of him, he was talking in the local Ostend dialect in the meetings! It amazed me that he was so personally involved in all of this. He was then still Deputy Prime Minister and this was happening on a Saturday morning. I had a feeling that this man is really going for it. And this man, you have to admit, could explain things in a really simple way.'

In contrast to the earlier periods the government discourse was not lead by a 'landlubber'.

At the same time, in the discourse used the objectives were clearly formulated from the beginning: the regulation of the use of the North Sea and the designation of the MPAs (source: press reports). The emphasis lay on the discourse, in comparison with the first attempts, far less on prohibitions and much more on shared responsibility (*see for example* User agreement 2006). Therefore no respondent refers to prohibitions for this period, and this in contrast to the earlier designation proposals.

4.5 From Challenging to Supporting Coalitions?

For the third attempt at designation of MPAs the Minister for the North Sea and his office staff were described as initiators and leaders and not the nature conservation movements or the administration as was the case during the first designation proposals (*see above*).

An important shift in comparison with earlier periods was, according to policy makers, especially the changed attitude of local politicians (mayors of the coastal municipalities), in addition to the growing support among former opponents such as water sports enthusiasts and anglers. The shift in attitude among local politicians is partly to be explained by another approach (with consultation and involvement) but also by the linking to the offshore wind turbine parks dossier.

The designation procedure led not only to shifting positions of actors but also to mutually changing relations between actors. The shifting positions are probably seen most in the support that among others water sports enthusiasts and fishermen in this period gave to the designation proposals. At the time of the first designation proposals both actors were still driving forces within the challenging coalitions. Among leisure time anglers, the support for MPAs led to a number of internal tensions, with the result, among others, of the publication of a critical article on the role of the 'Vlaamse Hengelverbond' (Flemish Anglers' Union) in a sea angling periodical ('Zeehengelsport'). In the interview a representative of the (leisure time) anglers suggested nevertheless:

> 'At the moment there is no problem at all within the angling sport world. We can live with the situation. If I have to ask an angler why he is losing sleep at night it will not be anything to do with this.'

The mutually changing relationships resulted mainly in new forms of consultation. So, for example, in this period consultations arose between nature conservationists and sea anglers (relating to the placing of gill nets) but also between sea anglers and commercial fishermen and between nature conservationists, commercial fishermen and the promoters of wind turbine parks at sea. The latter were thinking then about combining aquaculture for mussel cultivation with building offshore wind turbine parks or of ways of cooperation with nature conservation associations.

> 'We see that we will get further together than apart. There are for example plans to use cameras placed on the tern island to film the building of the wind turbine parks.'

What is noticeable is that a number of officials answer that they do not know if there is ultimately support for the designation of the MPAs. As the explanation for this they conjecture that few people are aware of the existence of these areas. Yet they observe that in this phase there is no public resistance or protest any more.

As explanation for the ebbing away of protest, policy makers point to the approach taken by the Minister for the North Sea, who addressed himself to that part of the population that considered themselves to be opponents or challenging coalitions in earlier periods.

> 'They were all against, but they knew that it would then (subject to consultation, editorial note) also be good for them.'

The Minister for the North Sea and his office staff set up bilateral talks with the most important opponents and put a great deal of effort into consultation with the mayors of the coastal municipalities. The opponents in the important parallel wind turbine dossier played an important role too. Concretely this was about, among other things, individual citizens and local municipality councils that had started legal procedures against the proposed sites for the establishment of offshore wind turbine parks. Via a Master Plan for the North Sea, the Minister and his office staff gave priority to consultation and concluded agreements with the important economic actors such as sand and gravel extractors and the wind energy sector, important absentees during the earlier attempts at designation. At no time did these players intervene in the public debate about the designation of the MPAs. Various respondents see the explanation for this to be found in the huge economic interests and the political influence of the sectors associated with them.

'(…) They deal with that on other levels, you see. Ministerial offices…'

On the political front, certain respondents from government and civil society mention a 'challenging coalition' around the figure of the federal Minister Verwilghen who especially defended the particular interests of the water sports enthusiasts in the so-called inter-departmental working group (Task Force North Sea) and in this way attempted to slow down the designation process. The support of the Federal Government for the policy of the Minister for the North Sea was not unanimous.

4.6 Bilateral Consultation as the Key to a Successful Designation?

In contrast to earlier attempts the majority of those interviewed, actors from science, civil society and market, state that they were informed and consulted by the Minister for the North Sea, with the exception of *one* port authority.

The Minister for the North Sea clearly opted for consultation in an early stage of the designation process. It is interesting that in addition to official consultation, bilateral consultation was also selected with, as a priority, all actors who had shown themselves to be trendsetters or key figures in the debate, the users of the North Sea, civil society…

'They organised more informal consultation opportunities with civil society and organisations for those involved in water sports, fishing… people who have declared themselves to be users. They got them directly involved.'

The fact that this consultation was conducted on a bilateral basis between the ministerial office staff and the various actors, meant that there was little transparency for the other actors and specialised administrative offices. The actors had no way of seeing the progress and content of the other bilateral talks, certainly not the actors who were not consulted such as the port authorities.

'Information about others' needs was not provided. You could only put forward your own needs. We asked for the whole sea, of course. Everyone did that probably.'

> *'This has not been an open process, and it was very centralised. You have no idea of the concerns of the other stakeholders and neither do you know how they have proceeded.'*

In parts of the market and civil society sectors there was the fear that the closed bilateral consultations had led to a form of backroom politics in certain cases.

> *'The fear that agreements were made with certain sectors behind closed doors of which in the end the costs will be higher than the benefits. There is distrust.'*

On the other hand it certainly repaired and/or created a relationship of confidence between the government and the parties consulted, who especially appreciated the openness and accuracy of the Minister and his office staff.

> *'We never came out with the feeling that they were busy behind the scenes. It was an open process. They were always looking for solutions. It was give and take, but we did not only have to make compromises.'*
> *'We saw that we could speak about certain problems in a very relaxed way. There was regular feedback. We received reports and we were kept informed. This produced trust.'*

The bilateral consultation did not only represent a change in style from earlier designation attempts, but also a fundamental shift in content. Whereas in earlier attempts policy was prepared top-down and was subsequently (in the best case) communicated to those involved, those involved were now approached with a question.

> *'We now asked questions to the various actors: 'You didn't want it to happen like that, but what did you want then? How far can we go?''*

In other words: the consultation was used in order to gather information (experiences, knowledge…) from the various actors and to explore boundaries. This new approach was clearly communicated to the various parties involved.

At the same time, the Minister used the opportunities to spread information about ecological values and legal obligations, as a result of which misunderstandings and vagueness from the past could be corrected. In addition, it was clearly indicated what was negotiable *and* that decisions needed to be taken. Some respondents therefore make reference to an authoritarian style.

> *'Yes, but he (the Minister, editorial note) has pushed through his own ideas and his own vision. He certainly listened and he consulted, but in each talk he said clearly where the line was. The 'Vlakte van de Raan', for example was not on the table.'*

All actors saw the choice of bilateral consultation as a logical and necessary choice. From the experiences with the earlier attempts everyone was now convinced that bringing the various actors together was too sensitive and unlikely to lead to positive outcomes.

After the bilateral consultations the consultation went on with various actors from the same sector. In this way, for example, collective consultation took place with 'Natuurpunt', 'Bond Beter Leefmilieu' (federation of the Flemish environmental movement) and 'Vogelbescherming Vlaanderen' (Bird Protection Flanders) as representatives of the environmental movement (Minutes 2004a). With the users of the North Sea similar consultations led to the drawing up of user agreements (*see above*). With scientists the consultation took place in a so-called expert group (*see for example* Minutes 2004b). It was important that the participants of the consultation were explicitly asked to respect the confidentiality of meetings and the documents relating to them so that the process should not be harmed. The federal administration MUMM was asked to gather all information and to formulate initial designation proposals. The information to be gathered concerned both data relating to ecological values as well as information about (potential) conflicts and possible positive actions for the avoidance of these conflicts. From the consultation and from a note from 'Dienst voor Zeevisserij' - (Sea Fisheries Service) it actually appeared that the designation of MPAs was still a very sensitive subject for the fishing industry and in certain cases even unacceptable (Minutes 2004b). For these reasons the Minister decided to visit the fishing industry for a consultation:

'In this manner we hoped to get to know the fishing fleet and win back their trust. The aim was to create support in the fishing industry (protect breeding grounds = an added value for fishermen).'

In the months that followed the Minister and his office also put a great deal of effort into consultation with local policy makers (*see for example* Minutes 2004c). The following passage from the report (Minutes 2004c) illustrates the Minister for the North Sea's approach:

"Minister Vande Lanotte immediately reassures the Governor and the mayors of the coastal municipalities who are present: 'In order to manage the North Sea in a sustainable fashion (2nd phase), 5 special protection areas (3 for birds and 2 for habitats) be designated once the concrete protection measures are fully known by all sectors and interested parties. (...) The new protection measures (general and species specific) shall be taken by arrangement with the various sectors."

The proposals from the discussions with the mayors were, according to the report, taken into consideration in the draft amendment to the Act, for drawing up of the user agreements and for drawing up two Royal Decrees. Before discussing this in Parliament, the Minister for the North Sea checked this once more in talks with members of local authorities (Minutes 2005). This approach obliged former opponents such as the Mayor of Knokke, and others also, to express their respect:

> *"Mayor Lippens of Knokke-Heist congratulated the Minister on his manner of approaching and pointed out the contrast with earlier when the Birds Directive areas were approved by our Ministers without being really aware that very heavy protection measures were attached to this. With this methodology the mayors of the coastal municipalities know precisely which measures are attached to the MPAs (...)"*. (Minutes 2005)

It is striking that the respondents, when they compare the various designation attempts with each other, have diverging perceptions of shifts in the government's management style (top-down) towards more governance (bottom-up and participation). The water sports enthusiasts and anglers describe the management style in this period as delegating and cooperative. Scientists likewise speak about delegating, cooperative and even facilitating management style. Civil society (nature conservation and a ship owner) and market (wind turbines) speak of a consultative management style. The difference in evaluation is probably explained by the difference in involvement.

5. The Ultimate Effects of a Long Designation Process

Only with the third designation proposal MPAs were actually designated. Under the previous designation proposals (1999-2003) the designation process got prematurely stuck, or got hardly started or carried forward.

Six years after the Marine Environment Act (2005) five MPAs were designated in the Belgian part of the North Sea (Royal Decree of 14 October 2005). It concerned three areas that were designated in the framework of the European Birds Directive (Special Protection Areas) and were particularly aiming at the protection of certain species of birds such as Great Crested Grebe, Common Tern, Sandwich Tern and Little Gull. Moreover, two areas were designated in the framework of the Habitats Directive (Special Areas of Conservation): the 'Vlakte van de Raan' and the 'Trapegeer Stroombank'. Subsequently, in 2006, the first marine reserve was designated near to the 'Baai van Heist' (Royal Decree of 5 March 2006).

Figure 3: Belgian MPAs, locations for sand and gravel, and offshore wind energy production

Opinion is divided over whether or not the present designation has led to the stated objectives being reached. Although on paper international obligations have been fulfilled, respondents from state, market, civil society and science have asked questions as to the management and enforcement of the MPAs. In this connection, certain people talk of the (wrong) perception that everything has already been done for the protection of the marine ecosystems.

> *'The question is whether they have done more than just designate?'*
> *'Designation has certainly taken place, but as far as the protection itself is concerned nothing has been done.'*

The central question is whether the marine environment in the affected areas was adequately protected? At the present time (2007) it is not obvious to answer this question. This is because of the lack of clearly formulated conservation objectives, among other things, but likewise as a result of lack of monitoring data and the recent character of the designation, which makes comparisons over time difficult. However, it is noticeable that in the interviews (2006-2007) serious questions were formulated by actors from state, civil society, market as well as science about the effects of the present designation. A ship owner states:

> *'Protect fauna and flora on that basis alone? No. Perhaps a little.'*

Respondents from nature conservation movements formulate it as follows:

'Nothing has changed yet except a few lines on the map.'

A scientist confirms to this in passing:

'Because you must honestly admit that nothing has changed now in the MPAs.'

Someone from the market puts it as follows:

'No, it isn't because you designate an area that it then means that it is protected! No active instruments have been added.'

Certain users such as the fishing community resigned themselves to the designation because few – or no – restrictions or negative effects resulted that had an impact on their use of the areas (*see above*).

'Has the objective been reached? You'll have to ask 'the greens'. That is not our problem. As Vande Lanotte said, he protects the fishermen. (...) We don't know where they are and can still fish everywhere. These areas haven't been plotted out you see, so you can just as well make MPAs of the whole sea as long as they do not trouble us.'

However, within this group of users there is also uneasiness that is partly based on experiences from the past, when after a while additional restrictions were linked to an earlier designation. As the most important negative experience they referred to all sorts of protection statutes (e.g. Special Protection Areas and Special Areas of Conservation) on the mainland.

'I don't really know what the objectives were. And certainly not with regard to the future. I don't know what the hidden agenda is? This might just be a first step, you see.'

Other respondents state they are not able to evaluate the effects, since they are not aware of what was agreed exactly with the various actors in the so-called user agreements.

A representative of a port authority conjectures that the designation will reach the objectives, referring to recent experiences on the mainland.

'If you look at the 'Baai van Heist' you can see that after the designation of the area, it clearly began to recover. I can imagine that it will be the same in the marine environment.'

Despite the criticism and often negative judgement of the effects of the designation a majority of the respondents feel that the designation is nevertheless progress. In this they do not only focus on effective protection, but mainly on the numerous side effects that the whole process has brought along, and among these not least the restored trust between the various parties involved. In this connection a fisherman states:

'We've made a good step forward.'

When asked for an evaluation of the results of the designation process, the respondents refer to the importance of other unintentional effects or side effects, in addition to restored trust between government and users and among various actors on the coast. So the Belgian part of the North Sea is put on the map by the designation process, and the discussions that were linked to this. It has become clear for all actors that the use of the North Sea can no longer be unlimited. In any case, the users of the North Sea have now realised that they were not the only users.

'The fact that we recognised that there were many players. The fact that you met each other, got to know each other.'

In the course of the designation process the users of the North Sea consulted with each other. The government and 'the Greens' were considered as the common enemies at first. As the designation process moved forward the government developed into more of a facilitator. The protest had, after all, led to the insight that designation processes can no longer be initiated top-down, but require a more interactive management style with more attention to be paid to consultation, participation and shared responsibility. Some users state that the process led to a change of mentality:

'I am also anti-Green, but I started to think differently.'

Possibly the most important side effect was that the initial protest made it clear that the designation of MPAs should be fitted into a total vision of the use of the North Sea. People understood the necessity of spatial planning and a policy framework for the North Sea with consideration to all users.

6. Conclusions

For the analysis of the MPAs' designation process in Belgium we have defined three periods: 1999, 1999-2003 and 2003-2006. The first MPAs' designation proposal followed shortly after the new Marine Environment Act in 1999 and was not successful. The second designation proposal in the period 1999-2003 was just as unsuccessful. We had to wait until 2005 before the first MPAs in the Belgian part of the North Sea were designated. In this concluding section we consider the main explanations for this. For this reason we refer back to the central question of our survey: 'How did the process for the designation of the MPAs work out and what was the role of participation?'

The First Designation Proposal. A Classic Top-down Approach (1999)

Starting from an international legal context and a number of internationally applicable principles, the federal legislator for the first time provided the necessary informal and formal rules for the designation of MPAs in the Marine Environment Act of 1999. The establishment of MPAs was seen by the federal authorities as an important resource for tackling two problems: the protection of marine ecological values on the one hand and the fulfilment of international obligations on the other. These were also the two most important arguments in the discourse of the nature conservation movement, which tried to put the theme of MPAs on the political agenda in this period and in the period prior to this.

At the setting up of the proposals for MPAs there was talk of a supporting coalition made up of a limited number of actors from the nature conservation movement, the authorities (civil servants) and the academic world. A number of these supporters met each other in rather informal consultative structures such as Natuurpunt's Coastal Working Group. The first designation proposal fairly soon ran up against protest by all sorts of North Sea users (water sports enthusiasts, fishermen, ship owners...) and local politicians. Even before the official launch of the idea of MPAs there was talk of a growing challenging coalition and this on the basis of both content-related as well as procedural difficulties. At the beginning, the discourse used by the opponents focussed mainly on the prohibitions and restrictions that the setting up of MPAs would bring along them. The designation process was from the start already seen as an example of a top-down policy by which the 'landlubbers' (Brussels and the 'Greens') would erode the autonomy of the true inhabitants of the coast. This problem of basic mistrust and lack of legitimacy, was particularly fed by the authoritarian style used by the government, in which initially, during the preparation of policy *and* in the later phases of the designation process, no form of consultation (not even in information) was provided at all. Moreover, the ultimate discourse used by the authorities, based mainly on scientific opinion, didn't mesh with the discourse of the local actors. Nevertheless the authorities (Secretary of State and the administration) used scientific knowledge as an argument of power.

The explanation for the government style used seems to lie, to a large extent, in the then government's capacity problems to carry out the work. They neither had sufficient resources such as the necessary people and means, nor sufficient experience. Only in reaction to the protest was consultation provided for with users and local government officials. The Governor of the Province of West Flanders played an important role here as intermediary, with the necessary authority, but especially legitimacy and trust. Two things that the federal government lacked at that time.

In the first designation proposal the informal and formal rules were *the* dominant dimension. Economic and social instruments were not deployed or were deployed late. All actors formulated their objections relating to the 'precision of prescription' of these informal and formal rules. There was the perception that the rules were drawn up in a very strict way, so that they would greatly reduce the freedom of action of the users of the North Sea. At the same time, under the first designation proposal, it was not clear what consequences the designation would have for the users. In other words, they wanted to present the designation proposal for approval without clarity over possible measures or consequences. Analogous experience from the past with, for example, the designation of the European Birds Directive (also on land) – to which, frequently years after the approval, regulations were added – served for various users and local politicians as a breeding ground for loathing for all additional forms of legislation and regulation. The referral to European obligations with regard to MPAs by the government was perceived by users of the North Sea and local politicians no so much as an argument of power, but rather as an alibi for pushing through the policy of their own choice.

The first designation proposal made it clear that local actors wished to be involved in the policy process relating to the designation of MPAs, and this in an early stage. The top-down approach used created questions of legitimacy (those who lived inland versus the coast), distrust of the federal authorities and the concept of MPAs. The designation process got bogged down without producing the result that the federal authorities had intended.

The Second Designation Proposal. Lack of Policy Continuity (1999-2003)

After the coming to power of the new federal government it was the Governor of the Province of West Flanders who asked the new federal Minister whether the consultation – started up in response to the protest – should be continued. Despite the fact that this was indeed decided on, the designation process came almost to a halt in the period 1999-2002. The principal explanation for this was the huge protest that had been produced by the first designation proposal, as was the lack of explicit supporting coalitions at this time. The initiatives of the new 'Green' Ministers lacked not only local political support but also support at the level of colleagues in the federal government. It was not so clear, for example, that the socialist political family would unconditionally support initiatives relating to designation, since they themselves had failed in the preceding period. Among former supporters such as the nature conservation movement, a changing attitude was also evident. The big rumpus that arose in relation to the first attempt, the shift of political responsibility from the socialist secretary of state to 'Green' Ministers, with whom there was less of a tradition of cooperation, *and* not least the link with the offshore wind turbine dossier were also given as explanations for this.

The impact of developments in the energy policy area with the first plans for the development of nearshore wind turbine parks at sea, should not be underestimated. After all, the 'Green' Ministers linked this dossier to the MPAs dossier. Rather rapidly, this linking appeared to be disastrous in terms of political strategy. The first proposals for the establishment of wind turbine parks in the North Sea brought about yet more consternation, if that is possible, among local actors, local population and politicians than the first proposals for MPAs and this was because of the expected eyesore on the horizon. From the wind turbine dossier it was clear that the population was becoming not only more articulate but in addition were also drawing power from legal resources. Various actors (local inhabitants and authorities, action groups...) searched for legal means to thwart the planned wind turbine parks in the sea off the Belgian coast. The wind turbine parks dossier caused polarisation with Minister Aelvoet as supporter and an amalgam of opponents, among whom was now also a part of the environmental movement.

As the principle explanation for the fact that it had not been possible to designate marine reserves in Belgium between 1999 and 2003, respondents cite not only the considerable blocking power displayed by the North Sea users and local politicians, but also especially the lack of political power and experience of those newly invested with responsibility for policy and a similar lack among the staff in their ministerial offices.

The lack of political priority led to a reduction in resources mobilised. The discourse on the issue of MPAs, with a number of exceptions, also almost came to a halt. During the occasional instances of consultation at the beginning of this government term, the federal government no longer limited itself to scientific expertise and international legal obligations. In the discourse we see a prudent shift from exclusive focus on definition of problems (relating to scientific opinion, international law) towards finding solutions (need for consultation). From the environmental movement more effort was also put into distributing information and into participation. These pleas were not really translated into policy practices.

At the end of that government term (2003), the federal Minister, with the support of Prince Laurent, launched a new initiative for the setting up of 'integral coastal nature parks'. What is striking is that in the pursuance of policy no lessons were drawn from the earlier failed attempts at designation. Once again the policy was not prepared in a very transparent manner by federal civil servants (MUMM) and politicians without prior consultation with users of the North Sea and local politicians. Once again the designation proposals were based on scientific opinion. And once again the federal government wanted to go ahead with the designation of MPAs, without clarity over the possible consequences for the users of the North Sea. The idea of 'integral coastal nature parks' was not followed up and with the prospect of new federal elections the designation process ground to a halt again.

Changing competences, changing discourses and changing informal and formal rules made the designation process thus far into a discontinuous policy process. The only continuity seemed so far to be found in the fact that the style of governance can be overwhelmingly described as top-down and that none of the designation proposals led to an effective designation of MPAs.

The Third Designation Proposal. Governance and a Successful Designation? (2003-2006)

The third designation proposal is characterised by important shifts and this in all dimensions that were investigated: power and resources, rules of the game, discourses and coalitions. The new federal government provided the North Sea with its 'own Minister' who had the right to take the initiative in coordinating all matters relating to North Sea policy at ministerial level. The ministerial portfolio was taken over by an experienced politician who originally came from the coast and who had strong electoral support at that moment. The fact that the responsibility for the North Sea was linked to responsibility for the budget and the post of deputy prime Minister gave it political clout. There was also investment in people, ministerial office staff with the focus on the realisation of a North Sea policy *and* the designation of the MPAs. Since fisheries remained under Flemish jurisdiction, there was, however, no talk of total concentration of power.

We can also see an important shift in relation to the resource of knowledge in this period. No longer exclusively scientific opinion, but also non-professional know-how and laymens knowledge were deployed in preparing policy. To this aim the federal government invested in bilateral consultation principally with the users of the North Sea, the environmental movement and local officials at an early stage of the policy process. The majority of the respondents from the scientific world, civil society and market stated – in contrast to the earlier attempts – that the federal government (the Minister) gave them information and consulted them. The bilateral consultation marked not only a change of style from earlier designation attempts, but also an important shift in content. Whereas in earlier attempts policy was prepared top-down so that it could then (in the best case) be communicated to those involved, the latter were now approached with a question. The bilateral consultation rebuilt trust to a large extent. However, a section of the market and civil society fear that the closed bilateral consultation in certain cases led to a form of backroom politics. In connection with this there is talk of a lack of transparency, also for the specialised administration and the actors who were not consulted, such as the port authorities.

The lack of transparency was also mentioned with regard to the agreements that were made earlier with the sand, gravel and wind sector. The North Sea policy had a phased structure at this time and the informal and formal rules for the designation of the MPAs were linked to those of other forms of use of the North Sea. By way of a master plan, spatial planning of the Belgian part of the North Sea was opted for, and clarity was first created about 'heavy' economic exploitation zones for sand and gravel extraction and wind turbine parks in the sea. The on-going legal procedures against earlier proposals and decisions relating to off shore wind turbine parks formed a catalyst in a real sense. Changing informal and formal rules in this area – the rescinding of earlier concessions – resulted in actors changing positions. Those who had, at the beginning, been opponents of MPAs, such as certain local officials, now positioned themselves as more moderate. Yet other actors such as water sports enthusiasts and fishermen now became more moderate mainly as a result of the consultation process. To a certain extent there was talk of a move from challenging to supporting coalitions, in which the most important opponents suspended their obstructive action.

This was also related to another important change in the informal and formal rules. The existing Marine Environment Act was amended at this time and provision was made for voluntary user agreements. The changes in the Marine Environment Act were related to 'precision of prescription' but contained mainly changes relating to 'formality and authority'. Rather than strict prohibitions based on formal legislation and regulations, informal rules were now favoured (e.g. user agreements) and elements such as a voluntary approach, shared responsibility and trust. Besides it was made clear from the start which consequences a potential designation would have and what measures were involved. Where the voluntary nature was seen as an important advantage with an eye to creating support, respondents at the same time saw it as the greatest disadvantage. A key concept in the respondents' analysis seems to be the lack of clarity. Lack of clarity for those not involved but also about the representativeness of the signatories and familiarity with the instrument among real users. Even though efficient, the question is whether it is also an effective instrument for the realisation of the objectives.

Various actors from the administration, science and civil society speak about a 'watering down' of the Marine Environment Act and/or a minimum transposition of the European Directives, and wonder if the present Act and the designation of MPAs is sufficient for the initial objective: the protection of the marine environment? The latter was also acknowledged by the users of the North Sea themselves who point to the fact that the designation of the MPAs has changed nothing for them in reality and that this is also why they are no longer fighting designation. Principally the actors from the market assess the changes in the informal and formal rules rather positively. A major explanation for this, together with the fact that no additional prohibitions have been imposed, is that finally clarity and certainty have been created after a period of uncertainty.

Opinions are divided over whether the objectives have been reached with the present designation. Even though the international obligations have been fulfilled on paper, respondents from state, market, civil society and science place a question mark over the management and enforcement of the MPAs. Despite this the majority of the respondents feel that the designation is an improvement. In this connection they refer to the numerous knock-on effects that the full process has had, such as re-established trust between various parties involved, the insight that the North Sea cannot be used without limit and that designation should fit in a total vision for the use of the North Sea. From the process side the most important insight was undoubtedly the fact that designation processes can no longer be initiated top-down, but require a more interactive style of governance. It is striking that the respondents, when they compare the various designation attempts with each other, have a divergent perception of shifts in the government's management style (top-down) towards more governance (bottom-up and participation). Water sports enthusiasts and anglers describe the management style in the third period as delegating and cooperative. Scientists likewise talk about a delegating, cooperative and even facilitating management style. Civil society (the environmental movement and a ship owner) and the market (wind turbines) talk of a consultative management style. The difference in assessment can probably be explained by the difference in involvement.

With the present designation of MPAs, the federal government fulfilled its international obligations. The only thing that is not yet clear is whether the more interactive approach used, did any harm to the initial purpose of the designation of the MPAs: sustainable protection of the marine ecosystems in the Belgian part of the North Sea.

References

COMMUNIQUÉ (2003). *Duurzaam beheer van de Noordzee.* Persbericht van 30 december 2003. Brussel: persbericht van het kabinet van de Minister van de Noordzee Johan Vande Lanotte en van het kabinet van de Minister van economie en energie Fientje Moerman.

LETTER PEETERS (1999). *Uitvoering van de wet van 20 januari 1999 ter bescherming van het mariene milieu in de zeegebieden onder de rechtsbevoegdheid van België.* Brief van 20 april 1999 aan de gouverneur van West-Vlaanderen Paul Breyne, LM/DM/15/88629. Brussel: Brief van de Staatssecretaris voor Veiligheid, Maatschappelijke Integratie en Leefmilieu Jan Peeters.

MINUTES (1999a). *Beknopt verslag van de vergadering van de kustburgemeesters.* Verslag van het overleg op 9 maart 1999. Brugge: interne nota van het kabinet van de gouverneur van West-Vlaanderen.

MINUTES (1999b). *Studiedag 25 juni 1999 inzake de toepassing van de wet ter bescherming van het mariene milieu in de zeegebieden onder de rechtsbevoegdheid van België en de instelling van de beschermde mariene gebieden in de Noordzee.* Rapportering van de werkgroepen van de vergadering van 25 juni 1999. Brussel: interne nota van de Beheerseenheid van het Mathematisch Model van de Noordzee en het Schelde-estuarium.

MINUTES (1999c). *Verslag van de overlegvergadering met de openbare besturen van 23 november 1999 inzake strandconstructies (stand van zaken) en de toepassing van de wet ter bescherming van het mariene milieu in de zeegebieden onder de rechtsbevoegdheid van België en de instelling van de beschermde mariene gebieden in de Noordzee*. Verslag van het overleg op 23 november 1999. Brugge: interne nota van het kabinet van de gouverneur van West-Vlaanderen.

MINUTES (1999d). *Verslag van de overlegvergadering met de milieuorganisaties van 16 november 1999 inzake de toepassing van de wet ter bescherming van het mariene milieu in de zeegebieden onder de rechtsbevoegdheid van België en de instelling van de beschermde mariene gebieden in de Noordzee*. Verslag van het overleg op 16 november 1999. Brugge: interne nota van het kabinet van de gouverneur van West-Vlaanderen.

MINUTES (2003a). *Beknopt verslag van de vergadering van de kustburgemeesters*. Verslag van het overleg op 10 januari 2003. Brugge: interne nota van het kabinet van de gouverneur van West-Vlaanderen.

MINUTES (2003b). *Beknopt verslag van de ontvangst van gouverneur Breyne en de kustburgemeesters door Minister Tavernier, Beschermde mariene gebieden in de Belgische Noordzee*. Verslag van het overleg op 22 januari 2003. Brugge: interne nota van het kabinet van de gouverneur van West-Vlaanderen.

MINUTES (2004a). *Afbakening beschermde mariene gebieden, Overleg groen middenveld 07/02/04*. Verslag van het overleg op 7 februari 2004. Brussel: interne nota van het kabinet van de Minister van de Noordzee Johan Vande Lanotte.

MINUTES (2004b). *Vertrouwelijk overleg met de Minister 11.02.2004 afbakening beschermde mariene gebieden, Gemengd overleg met wetenschappers en ambtenaren*. Verslag van het overleg op 11 februari 2004. Brussel: interne nota van het kabinet van de Minister van de Noordzee Johan Vande Lanotte.

MINUTES (2004c). *Beknopt verslag van de vergadering inzake het duurzaam beheer van de Noordzee met Minister Vande Lanotte in aanwezigheid van zijn kabinetsmedewerkers, de gouverneur en zijn medewerkers, de kustburgemeesters of gedelegeerden, de bestendige deputatie van het provinciebestuur van West-Vlaanderen en vertegenwoordigers van het Directoraat-Generaal Leefmilieu*. Verslag van het overleg op 17 oktober 2004. Brugge: interne nota van het kabinet van de gouverneur van West-Vlaanderen.

MINUTES (2005). *Beknopt verslag van de vergadering inzake het duurzaam beheer van de Noordzee met Minister Vande Lanotte in aanwezigheid van zijn kabinetsmedewerkers, de gouverneur en zijn medewerkers, de kustburgemeesters of gedelegeerden*. Verslag van het overleg op 24 mei 2005. Brugge: interne nota van het kabinet van de gouverneur van West-Vlaanderen.

SEYS, J., OFFRINGA, H., VAN WAEYENBERGHE, J., MEIRE, P. & KUIJKEN, E. (1999). Ornithologisch belang van de Belgische maritieme wateren: naar een aanduiding van kensoorten en sleutelgebieden. Brussel: Nota Instituut voor Natuurbehoud IN 99/74.

USER AGREEMENTS (2006). *Gebruikersovereenkomsten tussen de Minister bevoegd voor het mariene milieu, Johan Vande Lanotte en de gebruikers van de speciale beschermingszone 'SBZ1' vertegenwoordigd door dhrn. Annicq en Desloovere voor de Stichting Watersport en –recreatie –in oprichting, drh. Rooms voor Nautibel, de Federatie van Belgische Nautische Bedrijven; dhr Monsieur voor Nautiv, de Federatie van de Vlaamse Nautische Bedrijven; dhr Coussement voor V.V.H.V., de Vlaamse Vereniging Hengelsport Verbonden; dhr. Guillaume voor de Zeehengel-*

sport. Overeenkomst van 6 juli 2006. Brussel: overeenkomst gesloten met de Minister van de Noordzee Johan Vande Lanotte.

VLIZ (2003). *Nood aan maatschappelijk gedragen mariene beschermde gebieden.* Werkdocument naar aanleiding van het werkbezoek van ZKH Prins Laurent en Ministers Vera Dua en Jef Tavernier aan het VLIZ en het Coördinatiepunt Geïntegreerd Beheer van Kustgebieden op 7 maart 2003. Oostende: interne nota van het Vlaams Instituut voor de Zee.

CHAPTER 4

The Provincial RUP for Beaches and Dikes.
A Legal Technical Analysis

Pieter-Jan Defoort and Dirk Bogaert

1. Introduction – Legal Setting

In Belgium federal legislation and regulations for spatial planning and urban development started on 29 March 1962 [1]. This so-called 'Urban Development Act' introduced land use plans, which were called 'plannen van aanleg' (zoning plans). There were zoning plans at four levels: a supra regional plan, regional plans, general municipal zoning plans ('Algemeen Plan van Aanleg' or APA) and specific sub-municipal zoning plans plans ('Bijzonder Plan van Aanleg' or BPA). The supraregional plan (at the national level) has never been developed, but there were 48 regional plans covering the whole territory and containing a 'general' description of land use. Some dozens of municipal zoning plans or APAs were made, but (apart from a few exceptions) these are no longer valid. More important were the numerous specific sub-municipal zoning plans or BPAs, which contain a detailed allocation and layout of a part of the municipal territory.

Three regional plans apply to the coastal region: 'Veurne-Westkust' (west coast), 'Oostende-Middenkust' (central coast) and 'Brugge-Oostkust' (east coast). With regard to our topic, it should be noticed that the regional plans basically did not include the beach as such, but only extended to the dike and/or the dunes. Deficiencies in colouring which were among other things due to the impractical, too little detailed scale of the regional plans on the one hand and the dynamics of beach and dunes on the other, created exceptions to this rule. In exceptional cases the sea dikes and even the beaches were at least partly attributed a use, as in the case of 'Brugge-Oostkust', where a part of the beach was coloured in as a nature area of scientific interest.

Due to the constitutional reform of 1980 the competence for legislation concerning spatial planning was transferred from the Belgian State to the Regions. Since then the Flemish authority has the competence to change regional plans on the territory of the Flemish Region. That competence of the Flemish Region reaches up to the average low-tide mark, also called the base-line. Seawards, beyond the baseline, is a ratio loci competence of the federal government (*see also* legal analysis MPAs).

In 1996 the so-called Planning Decree [2] introduced a new instrument for spatial planning: the structure plans. Structure plans are not land use plans but 'only' policy plans that indicate the desired spatial development of the area concerned. The Planning Decree provided for structure plans at three levels: the Flemish Region, the provinces and the municipalities. In implementation

---

[1] Act of 29 March 1962 with regard to the organisation of spatial planning and urban development.

[2] Decree of 24 July 1996 with regard to spatial planning, *Belgian Law Gazette*, 27 July 1996.

of this decree, the Flemish Spatial Structure Plan[3] ('Ruimtelijk Structuurplan Vlaanderen' - RSV) was enacted. Thanks to the Planning Decree the provinces got planning powers of their own for the first time: they could draw up a Provincial Spatial Structure Plan (PRS W-VL). The existing system of zoning plans was maintained. The Flemish Region remained competent for changing the regional plans, the municipality for drawing up APAs and BPAs. The province could not draw up land use plans itself, but it could ask the Flemish Region to draw up or review regional plans in implementation of the Provincial Spatial Structure Plan and of that part of the RSV of which implementation was assigned to the province.

By Decree of 18 May 1999 with regard to the organisation of spatial planning (Decreet houdende de organisatie van de ruimtelijke ordening - hereafter: DRO) the former Urban Development Act and the Planning Decree were replaced by a completely new decree. The DRO took over the system of structure plans of the Planning Decree in its entirety, except for some terminological changes. However, the DRO replaced the system of zoning plans by a new system of spatial implementation plans: from the moment that a public body has a structure plan, that authority does not make zoning plans any longer, but spatial implementation plans ('ruimtelijke uitvoeringsplannen' - RUPS) in implementation of the structure plans.

The Provincial RUP for Beaches and Dikes ('Strand en Dijk') is an example of an RUP, which was drawn up by the provincial authorities of West Flanders. We should not underestimate the practical importance of this RUP, for example for granting the so-called 'beach concessions'[4]. Although the beach is part of the public domain, it is possible that concessions are granted on the beach, for example to coastal municipalities or for private use. This private use of the beach can be allowed, insofar as it does not affect the designated use of the area or the power of the authorities to regulate and change the use of the area according to the needs and interests of the general public. Beach concessions are preferably granted to coastal municipalities. This is done for example for placing bathing-cabins on the beach. The proposal concerning the area for bathing-cabins must be submitted for approval to the Flemish Agency for Maritime and Coastal Services ('Vlaams Agentschap voor Maritieme Dienstverlening en Kust' – MD&K). On the parts of the beach that are under concession it is not allowed to put up other buildings or constructions, not even temporary or transportable, without prior permission of the Flemish Minister in charge of public works. Since an RUP has regulatory power, the provincial RUP for Beaches and Dikes obliges concessionaires and the public body granting the concessions to respect the urban development regulations.

---

[3] 'Ruimtelijk Structuurplan Vlaanderen' (Flemish Spatial Structure Plan), to be consulted at www.ruimtelijkeordening.be.

[4] Decision of the Flemish Government of 26 April 1995 concerning beach concessions.

In the following part of the text we will deal with two aspects concerning the development of the provincial RUP for Beaches and Dikes that are important for the survey: the procedure of an RUP, where we will focus on the opportunities for advice and consultation on the one hand and the distribution of competences for drawing up an RUP on the other hand. In a next chapter the findings from this legal-technical analysis will be checked on the basis of interviews with privileged witnesses.

2. The Procedure of a Provincial RUP

The procedure of an RUP is more or less the same at the three levels of planning. Considering the topic we are dealing with, we pay attention to the procedure of a provincial RUP, as it is described in articles 44-47 of the DRO.

2.1 Preliminary Draft and Plenary Meetings

The procedure is introduced by a preparatory study phase, during which the Provincial Executive first of all has to appoint a certified spatial planner (article 40 DRO). The preparatory study results in a preliminary draft that is adopted by the Provincial Executive and that is delivered to the civil servant in charge of planning, the benches of Mayor and Aldermen of the municipalities involved and the consultative departments[5]. This preliminary draft is the object of political consultation and consultation among civil servants by means of one or more 'plenary meetings', where the various authorities and administrative departments involved make their positions known. In accordance with case law the organisation of a plenary meeting is not an essential formal requirement or under penalty of nullity required practice, but a practice that is only imposed to ensure the proper functioning of the administration[6]. This implies among other things that an amendment of the preliminary draft due to remarks formulated during the plenary meeting(s), does not mean that the preliminary consultation procedure has to be repeated[7].

2.2 Draft, Preliminary Adoption and Public Inquiry

Once the preparatory study is finished, a draft provincial RUP is provisionally adopted by the Provincial Council.

Within 30 days after the preliminary adoption the draft plan is submitted to a public inquiry for consultation. It is available for public consultation for 60 days at the town hall of all the municipalities involved in the plan. This is announced by means of posters displayed in the municipality, by means of a

---

5   See the Decision of the Flemish Government of 11 May 2001 concerning the designation of institutions and administrations that advise about preliminary drafts of spatial implementation plans.
6   Council of State., n.v. Schelfhout, n° 130.212, 9 April 2004.
7   Council of State, Van Vynckt, n° 173.961, 13 August 2007.

notice in the Belgian law gazette and by means of a notice in three newspapers with provincial circulation. During the public inquiry anybody may address written objections to the Provincial Commission for Spatial Planning (PROCORO), a provincial public advisory council composed of a number of experts and representatives of various interest groups.

During the public inquiry several opinions have to be obtained as well: the advice of the local councils of the municipalities involved and of the Flemish Government – the last one only about the compatibility of the draft with the RSV and a (draft) regional RUP if this exists. Also the local council and the provincial council of the neighbouring municipality/municipalities and province can give an opinion.

The complete dossier is subsequently examined by the PROCORO, which has to formulate an opinion to the Provincial Council within a period of 90 days, counted from the last day of the public inquiry. The PROCORO can ask the Provincial Executive to extend this term by 30 days. If the opinion comes too late, the Provincial Council may ignore it. In other words, the PROCORO takes care of examining and dealing with the objections and opinions and can also give an opinion of its own.

It should be noticed that a public inquiry is considered as a real practice by established case law, which implies among other things that the PROCORO is obliged to examine and reply to all objections and opinions that have been submitted[8]. If the PROCORO has not dealt with certain objections, this should be done by the authority that is adopting the plan[9]. This does not mean that the PROCORO or, if need be, the Provincial Executive must reply to every individual objection in an individual way, but that the text of the opinion or of the decision of the Provincial Executive should give a clear and understandable explanation so that the person who lodged the objection can understand why his/her objection was deemed valid or not[10]. It can be noted here that the people who lodge an objection are not informed individually about the results of the examination of the objections.

The public inquiry is essential because the draft RUP can only be changed by the Provincial Council insofar as those changes are based on or result from the objections of the public inquiry or the opinions given (article 45, § 6 DRO). Moreover there should be a logical relationship between the objection or opinion submitted and the change, and according to recent case law there should even be a specific and explicit will to change in a certain direction[11]. Legal doctrine observes that article 45, § 6 DRO does not affect the existing case law with regard to the earlier regional plans. A 'fundamental', 'substantial' or 'im-

---

8   Annex. Council of State, bvba Golf Practice Club, n° 79.083, 3 March 1999.
9   Council of State, sa Swiss Hotel Leasing Company, n° 160.170, 15 June 2006.
10 Council of State, bvba Pomphuis, n°. 173.287, 6 July 2007; Council of State, sa Swiss Hotel Leasing Company, n) 160.170, 15 June 2006.
11 Council of State, De Braekeleer, n° 160.169, 15 June 2006.

portant' change of the draft plan should be submitted to a new public inquiry, because the public inquiry cannot just be considered as an 'obligatory act', but aims at a useful result (De Waele 2007; Verhoeven 2007).

It may be noted that as a result of those strict requirements an authority will not be easily inclined to amend its draft plan radically as a consequence of the remarks and opinions of the public inquiry, since this would imply that a new public inquiry had to be organised. In that sense one might say that the quoted case law is counterproductive in view of the intended objective of the public inquiry to achieve a useful outcome. But another position might lead to a situation in which the definitive plan strongly deviates from the draft plan that was submitted to the public inquiry. This would mean that citizens would not have had the opportunity to give their opinion about the main principles of the finally adopted plan.

2.3 Definitive Adoption and Approval

The provincial RUP is definitively adopted by decision of the Provincial Council within a term of 180 days from the end of the public inquiry. At the request of the Provincial Executive the Provincial Council can grant an extension of this term by 60 days. If the plan is not adopted within these terms, the whole procedure lapses (article 45, § 7 DRO).

Immediately after the definitive adoption the RUP is presented for approval to the Flemish Government together with the decision of the Provincial Council and the opinion of the PROCORO (article 46 DRO). The Flemish Government, which acts here as supervisory authority, can make no changes to the content of the decision that is submitted for approval, but can only approve the RUP (if necessary only partially) or withhold the approval. The Flemish Government has delegated the competence to approve RUPs to the Minister competent for spatial planning. The Council of State has decided that delegating the power of approval supervision from the Government to the Minister of Spatial Planning is permitted[12] (see in this respect Defoort & Goedertier in press). The decision in this respect has to be taken within a period of 60 days from receipt of the dossier. If this term expires, the Provincial Executive can take the initiative to 'remind' the government within a term of 30 days from the end of the afore-mentioned term. If the Executive does not send a reminder, the draft lapses. If a reminder is sent and the government does not send any decision within a period of 35 days, counted from the day of dispatch of the reminder, the plan is considered to have received tacit approval (with the exception of the expropriation plan, if any there be).

The provincial RUP only becomes binding on citizens after publication of the text of the approval in the Belgian law gazette and after sending a copy of the

---

[12]   Council of State, de Muynck, n° 167.032, 24 January 2007.

plan, of the opinion of the PROCORO and of the adoption and approval to the municipalities, where they are made available for inspection.

To sum up it may be stated that the legislating authority provides for a rather strict procedure with various stages that offer opportunities for official and political consultation. As to the public consultation the PROCORO plays an important role. The individual citizen has the possibility of participating in the procedure in the form of a public inquiry, which takes place after the preliminary adoption of the PRUP by the Provincial Council.

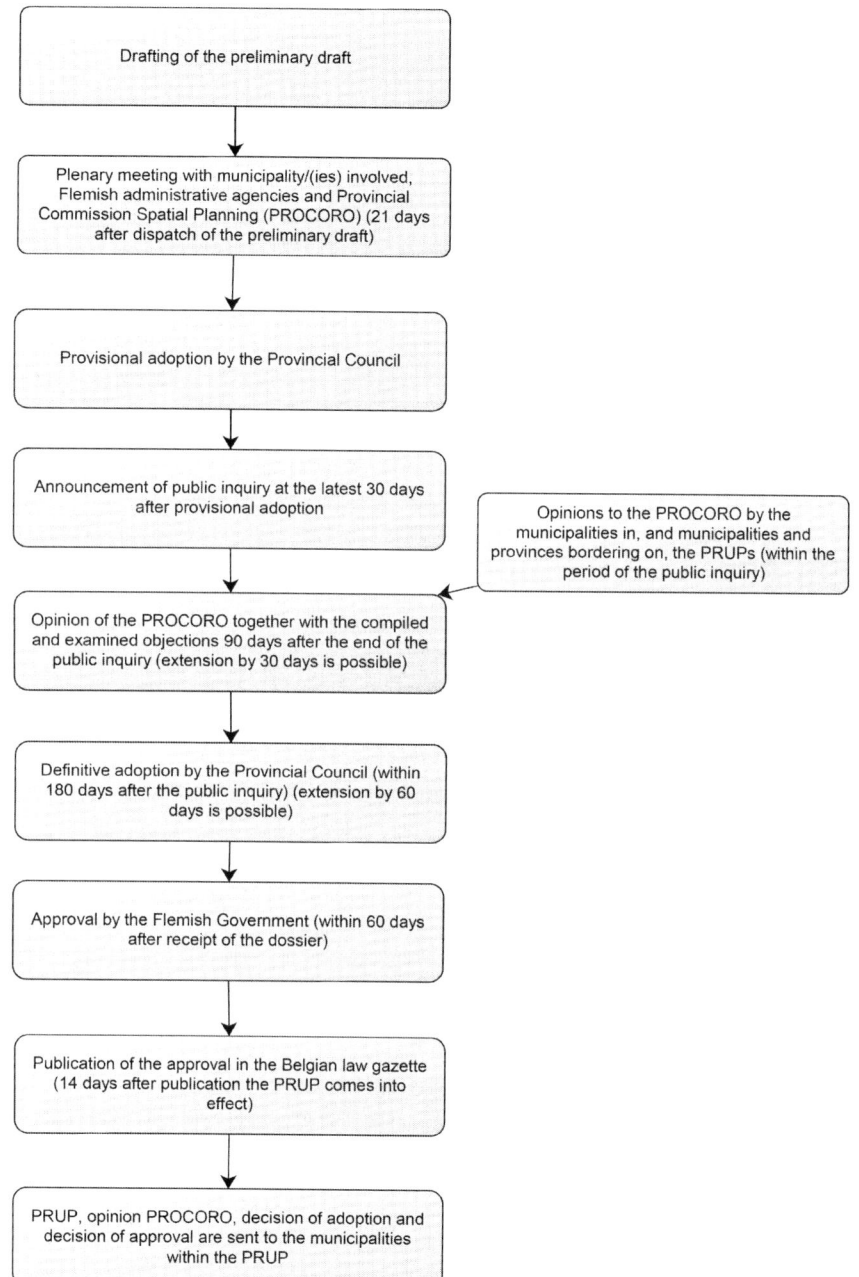

Figure 4: The formal PRUP procedure

3. The Competence to Draw up an RUP: General Principles[13]

As described above, RUPs can be drawn up by three levels of government: the municipality, the province and the Flemish Region. Therefore the question raises of who is competent to draw up an RUP to settle a particular spatial planning situation. After all, a plan that has been drawn up contrary to the rules governing the competences is considered to be null and void, since the rules governing the competences are considered to be rules of public order.

From the DRO we may deduce that the competence to draw up an RUP is linked to the rules on competences of and relating to structure plans: on the one hand a structure plan can contain an explicit instruction to an authority to perform the task of drawing up RUPs for a particular issue, on the other hand every authority has the competence to implement its own spatial structure plan.

Considering this link, and more especially the fact that the distribution of competences for drawing up RUPs depends on the rules governing the competences for the structure plans, we will first deal with the latter, and then we will further examine the specific rules governing the competences relating to RUPs.

3.1 Rules Governing the Competences with regard to Spatial Structure Plans: Subsidiarity and Hierarchy

The rules governing the competences with regard to spatial structure plans are a translation of the principle of subsidiarity on the one hand and the principle of hierarchy on the other.

3.1.1 Subsidiarity

Although the principle of subsidiarity is not mentioned explicitly anywhere in the DRO, nor in the above-mentioned Planning Decree of 1996, nearly all observers assume that the principle of subsidiarity determines the distribution of competences between the various levels of government. The reason why the subsidiarity principle is only implicitly included in the DRO can be deduced

---

[13]   This chapter is an adaptation of a number of extracts from the article by P.-J. DEFOORT, 'Bevoegdheidsverdeling in de ruimtelijke planning. Subsidiariteit: feit of fictie?' (Distribution of competences in spatial planning. Subsidiarity: fact or fiction?), *T.R.O.S.*, 2005, 281-335. For a more comprehensive version and for the numerous acknowledgements, see q.v.

from the parliamentary documents of the Decree[14], which conspicuously lack consistency in content relating to this concept[15].

Although the principle of subsidiarity is not explicitly mentioned in the DRO, article 18 DRO does provide a formal legal translation of this principle. Indeed, this article states that the spatial structure plans of the respective levels deal with the structure determining elements of the level concerned and that they can contain instructions to carry out tasks for implementation for that level and for the lower levels. The third section of article 18 gives a 'definition' of the concept of 'structure determining elements': these are *"the elements that describe the main lines of the spatial structure at the level in question"*. In legal doctrine this definition is described completely justly as "somewhat tautological" or as a "meaningless circular reasoning". To put it briefly, article 18 DRO determines that *"everything has to be regulated at the appropriate level"*, but it is not so clear what this means in concrete terms. Yet the explanatory memorandum of the Planning Decree and of the DRO provides indications for a concrete distribution of topics to be dealt with in the structure plans of the various levels[16]. This is an informative, non-exhaustive enumeration of structure determining elements that are important at regional, provincial and municipal level.

In contrast with the DRO the Flemish Spatial Structure Plan (RSV) specifically mentions the 'subsidiarity principle'. The definition in the RSV reads as follows: *"The subsidiarity principle implies that any authority that is competent for spatial planning deals with those matters that are appropriate to be regulated at the level in question. Decisions have to be taken at the most appropriate level. A decision at a higher level can be justified if the significance and/or the scope clearly surpass the lower level. A higher level only takes action insofar as the objectives of the considered action cannot be achieved adequately by the lower level"*. A footnote stipulates that *"the definition is partly based upon the definition of the subsidiarity principle in article 3B of the Treaty on the Establishment of the European Community (amended by the Treaty of Maastricht)"*[17].

Moreover the RSV provides for a number of indications as to the implementation of the principle[18]. The directive part of the RSV (p. 522) stipulates that structural consultation and collaboration of all government levels is an essential condition for enabling the principle of subsidiarity to function in an optimal way, as well as support in various areas (logistic, technical, information exchange, etc.). Furthermore the RSV explicitly admits that proper guidance and support of municipalities is indispensable in drawing up and implement-

---

[14] See: *Printed Doc.* Fl. Parl., 1998-1999, doc. 1332/1, 22 en 28-29; *Printed Doc.*, Fl. Parl., 1998-1999, 1332/8, 8-10 and 28-30; *Printed Doc.*, Fl. Parl., 1998-1999, 1332/8, 21-27.

[15] *Printed Doc.*, Fl. Parl., 1998-1999, 1332/8, for example p. 46 (article 18), p. 47 (article 19), p. 55 (article 30), p. 58-59 (article 38).

[16] Explanatory Memorandum, *Printed Doc.*, Fl. Parl., 1995-1996, 360/1, 6-7; Minutes, *Printed Doc.*, Fl. Parl., 1998-1999, n° 1332/8, 47.

[17] RSV, p. 311.

[18] RSV, 310-312 list of concepts RSV p. 569.

ing municipal structure plans, in particular for municipalities in rural areas that only dispose of limited resources. Some pages further on the necessity of adequate official expertise at every level of the administration and of a reliable logistic system is stressed once again (p. 524-525).

In practice however it has to be observed that so-called 'subsidiarity' did not lead to the intended decentralisation, or that this is at least not experienced as such by many observers and by the municipalities. In comments we find remarks to the effect that the level of the Flemish Region tends to take over anything that is materially possible and controllable and that due to this municipalities and provinces only have very little room for manoeuvre. As an example of centralisation we can refer to the Flemish competence to designate the natural and agricultural structure. As a matter of fact this means that, in the future, the Flemish Region will also determine indirectly where a municipality will be able (or at least will *not* be able) to provide a football pitch, a local business park or additional houses.

If subsidiarity leads to more competences for lower levels of government, this seems to be the case for 'difficult' dossiers, that is at least how the provinces see it. In practice it can be noticed that the Flemish Region passes on politically 'sensitive dossiers', such as dossiers relating to weekend cottages, sewage water purification plants, golf courses, manure processing, ... to the provinces, even though for some of those matters the RSV explicitly empowers the Flemish authorities [19].

3.1.2 Hierarchy

Article 18 DRO is not only a translation of the subsidiarity principle, but at the same time also expresses the principle of hierarchy between the various levels of planning, more specifically by providing for the possibility of "passing on tasks" to the lower level by the higher level. In a structure plan any government can also set tasks for itself (article 18, second section, 1° and 2° DRO). The distribution of tasks in implementation of a structure plan may concern both tasks that have to be executed in the lower structure plans as well as tasks for the drawing up of RUPs by the same or a lower level.

The principle of hierarchy is also considered in article 19, § 1-4 DRO, dealing with the legal force of various sections of the spatial structure plans (binding, indicative, directive). From these sections it appears clearly that there is a hierarchical relationship between the spatial structure plans of the three levels, in which the lower structure plans have to follow the content of a higher plan [20]. The hierarchy among structure plans is confirmed in articles 24 and 31 DRO, stipulating that lower structure plans harmonise with the higher ones.

---

[19] RSV, p. 421.
[20] Report, *Printed Doc.*, Fl. Parl., 1998-1999, 1332/8, 9.

This hierarchy is highlighted even more by means of article 23, section 2 and article 30, section 2 DRO stipulating that the higher authority can act instead of the lower authority if the lower authority does not implement the tasks that have been assigned to it by a higher structure plan. It should be noted that these provisions apply to all tasks assigned by a higher structure plan, i.e. both for tasks with regard to structure plans and for tasks with regard to implementation plans.

Also the RSV says something about the principle of hierarchy. The RSV states explicitly that the principle of subsidiarity does not affect the hierarchy between the three levels. A lower plan should fit into a higher plan, which may contain imperative instructions about the content of that lower plan (directive p. 310-312).

3.2 Rules Governing the Competences with regard to Spatial Implementation Plans: Linking the Competence to the Distribution of Tasks for Structure Plans

From the DRO – in particular from a combined reading of article 18, second section, 1° and 2°, article 19, § 5 and the articles 41, § 2, 44, § 2 and 48, § 2 DRO – one may conclude that RUPs are drawn up either in implementation of the structure plan of the same level, or in implementation of a higher structure plan that has given an explicit instruction to carry out a task in relation to this.

This principle of linking between structure plans and implementation plans can also be found in the RSV: "2) *The subsidiarity principle is determining for the distribution of tasks with respect to the implementation of spatial structure plans. This means among other things that the authority that has drawn up a spatial structure plan, may possibly assign the implementation of parts of it to lower authorities*" directive section, p. 311); and further down it reads as follows: "*The effect of subsidiarity also implies that any of the three levels is responsible for the implementation of the spatial structure plan in question. Every level then also monitors the implementation assigned to other institutions or lower authorities*" (directive section, p. 312).

Since the distribution of competences for structure plans has its effect on the implementation plans, this means that the authority that provides a regulation in its structure plan, without assigning a task to another level, is itself competent to draw up the implementation plans for the matter concerned. Through a commitment in the structure plan a particular level of planning acquires, as it were, a right of initiative to tackle a spatial issue by means of drawing up a spatial implementation plan. As we will see below, the RSV does not provide any specific task distribution for the issue of beach and dike constructions and finally the provincial authority of West Flanders has regulated this in the provincial structure plan. In the end a provincial RUP has been drawn upon the basis of this structure plan (*see below*).

In this context it is essential to draw attention to the fact that an authority cannot just regulate any matter in its structure plan, but only those matters for which it is competent in accordance with the rules of subsidiarity and (especially) hierarchy described above.

It is observed here that in case of a strict interpretation of the principle of linking between the structure plan at the same level and the competence for drawing up RUPs there may be considerable risk of unwelcome situations arising. For if a structure plan formulates a number of general development perspectives for a particular issue without linking this with an explicit instruction to carry out a task, the strict implementation of the principle of linking between structure plans and implementation plans implies that the level that has formulated the development perspectives is also competent for drawing up the implementation plans for that issue. Such development perspectives however, are not always meant to be 'realized' or 'executed', but rather to 'have their effect' in implementation plans at whatever level. Therefore the principle of linking of competences should not be interpreted too strictly. Still, neither the Decree nor the RSV indicates where the line between linking implementation plans and structure plans must be drawn. The possible uncertainty is even stimulated by the lack of coherence between the distribution of tasks. All through the substantive statements by the RSV the assignment of tasks is formulated in a fragmented and scattered way. Formal aspects are mixed together with the material aspects, so that it is not always clear whether and to what extent substantive elements are actually linked with the distribution of tasks.

3.3 The Relationship Between RUPs and that Between RUPs and Regional Plans

In addition to the relationship between structure plans and implementation plans, the principle of hierarchy also applies to spatial implementation plans. The classical legal hierarchy of standards is explicitly established by decree through article 44, § 2, second section and article 48, § 3 DRO stipulating that the lower implementation plan must not differ from the higher implementation plan[21]. This is an absolute hierarchy: no deviations are possible. With regard to the impossibility of a lower implementation plan deviating from a higher implementation plan, the Minister stated during the discussion in the parliamentary commission that in principle there should be no need for deviation, precisely because the Regions and – mutatis mutandis – the provinces firstly act selectively as to the issue, secondly do not always act in a detailed or "determining" way and finally do not (immediately) act covering the whole area. According to the Minister one level only acts insofar as the matter in question has to be regulated at that specific level and in that case there is basi-

---

[21]   Report, *Printed doc.*, Fl. Parl., 1998-1999, 1332/8, 9.

cally no reason to deviate from that[22]. In practice however things turn out to be different.

The mutual hierarchy between RUPs is also clear from article 38, § 3 DRO, which stipulates that the regulations of a higher spatial implementation plan legally cancel regulations of a lower implementation plan that are contrary to the higher plan. Thus the theory of the 'Steeno judgment' [23], stating that a later regional plan automatically cancels the regulations of an existing BPA that are contrary to the regional plan, is formalized by decree.

The principle of hierarchy does *not* apply to the relationship between regional plans and RUPs. Article 201 DRO states that the regulations of a spatial implementation plan replace the regulations of a zoning plan for the territory to which they relate.

3.4 Distribution of Tasks: Exclusive, Competing and Parallel Competences

The RSV assigns the implementing power for many matters to one or more administrative levels (the so-called 'distribution of tasks'). The distribution of tasks or assignments of competence may take on various forms. By analogy with the distribution of competences in constitutional law, we can distinguish exclusive, competing and parallel competences in the RSV.

From the stipulations of the DRO and from the formulation of the subsidiarity principle in the RSV it appears that the distribution of competences is fundamentally based upon 'exclusive competences', i.e. the competence of one authority in principle excludes the competence of the other. If a particular issue has several points of departure, we might say – by analogy with the jurisprudence of the Constitutional Court on the distribution of competences between the federal state and the Regions and Communities – that it is necessary to examine with which concept of competence the issue to be regulated has the strongest link (Defoort 2007b).

Just like constitutional law the RSV also contains a number of exceptions to the exclusive competences, in particular a number of 'limited or illegitimate competing competences' and 'parallel competences'.

- In case of limited or illegitimate competing competences, one authority establishes the basic rules and other authorities can apply or complete the basic rules, however without their being allowed to erode them. Thus for example the Flemish Region as well as the provinces and the municipalities are competent to provide space for the layout of recreational forests and

---

[22] Report, *Printed doc.*, Fl. Parl., 1998-1999, 1332/8, 10.
[23] Council of State., nr. 23.832, 20 December 1983, later frequently confirmed by the Council of State and the Court of Cassation.

parks in green zones on the outskirts of towns. This should be done how-ever on the basis of a vision for the urban area (RSV, p. 372). Thus Nature Corridor Areas ('Natuurverbindingsgebieden' or NVG) are designated in provincial RUPs, but this should be done on the basis of the Flemish desig-nation of the Natural Structure and by means of "guidelines" established at Flemish regional level (RSV, p. 392) (for an application with regard to beaches and dikes, *see below*).

- In case of parallel competences the policy within one and the same area of competence is implemented in a cumulative way and next to each other by and at different government levels. Thus for example it is possible to select characteristic elements and components of a landscape, intact landscapes and corridors between open spaces and to define specific development perspectives for these elements and components at the three levels of plan-ning. Selection takes place in the respective structure plans, whereas the designation occurs in the RUPs (RSV, p. 415).

3.5 Administrative Supervision: Important Influence on the Exercise of Competences

In order to keep everything coherent, lower plans are subject to supervision of the approval process. The Flemish Government has the power to carry out supervision of the approval process with regard to provincial structure plans (article 27, § 7 DRO) and provincial RUPs (article 46 DRO). The Provincial Executives have the power to carry out approval supervision of municipal structure plans (article 33, § 9 DRO) and municipal RUPs (article 50 DRO). In certain cases the approval supervision implies a wide power of discretion. In this way approval supervision may largely influence or limit the competences of lower authorities.

With regard to the approval of spatial implementation plans the DRO does not state any condition. In accordance with the general rules of the extraordinary administrative control this means that the supervision of spatial implementa-tion plans both concerns a control of legality and a control of public interest. The supervisory authority may for example test provincial and municipal RUPs against the objectives stated in article 4 DRO, which stipulates that spa-tial planning only aims at protecting the public interest. Provincial and mu-nicipal RUPs may for example also be tested against the so-called 'general principles of good governance' – such as the principle of reasonableness, the principle of care, the principle of legal certainty, the principle of legitimate expectation, the principle of proportionality, the principle of equality – since those principles have either constitutional or legal value and hence concern the test of legality. In fact it would be better to talk about a 'legitimacy test' instead of a mere legality test.

The supervision of the structure plans is either limited to a test against the RSV for provincial structure plans (*see* article 27, § 7, first section) or against the

RSV and the provincial structure plan for municipal structure plans (*see* article 33, § 9, last section). Although the approval supervision of municipal and provincial structure plans is limited to conformity (both in form and in content) with the directive and binding sections of the higher plans, this represents a fairly broad scope of discretion for the supervisory authority, in a sense that it is possible to keep an eye on 'proper spatial planning' in general as well. Indeed the RSV contains the principles of 'sustainable development', 'spatial strength' and 'spatial quality' (p. 315-317), concepts that admit of a broad interpretation and furthermore presuppose a subjective assessment.

It is important, however, that the supervisory authority is not able to introduce changes to the decision that is submitted for approval. If the lower authority is not prepared to make amendments, the supervisory authority can partially approve the plan (and hence delete certain passages), on condition that the partial approval does not affect the coherence of the plan in question nor the content that is required by decree. Although the Decree only explicitly mentions the possibility of partial approval for structure plans[24], it should be assumed that this is also possible for RUPs. These two principles will appear to be relevant for the case of the provincial RUP for Beaches and Dikes.

4. *Some Comments on the Rules Governing the Competences* [25]

4.1 The Subsidiarity Principle is an Ideologically Charged Concept

The principle of subsidiarity – which according to the DRO and the RSV would be the basic rule for the distribution of competences – is not just a neutral technical principle. It is on the contrary ideologically charged, as appeared for example during the discussions of the DRO in the parliamentary commission on spatial planning[26]. Due to its vagueness the principle also provides ample opportunity for divergent, often politically inspired interpretations by advocates and opponents of decentralised government. Among other things, due to the fact that the principle covers different and often contradictory opinions and traditions, the question arises whether it is a useful principle for in-

---

[24] Article 27, § 7, first section (provincial structure plan); article 33, § 9, last section (municipal structure plan).

[25] This chapter is an adaptation of a number of extracts from the article by P.-J. DEFOORT, 'Bevoegdheidsverdeling in de ruimtelijke planning. Subsidiariteit: feit of fictie?' (Distribution of competences in spatial planning. Subsidiarity: fact or fiction?), *T.R.O.S.*, 2005, 281-335. For a more comprehensive version and for the numerous acknowledgements, see q.v.

[26] See the position of the Christian Democratic Party (*Printed Doc.*, Fl. Parl. 1998-1999, 1332/8, 22), the Socialist Party (*Printed Doc.*, Fl. Parl. 1998-1999, 1332/8, 22), the Flemish Nationalist Party (*Printed Doc.*, Fl. Parl. 1998-1999, 1332/8, 23-24), the Liberal Party (*Printed Doc.*, Fl. Parl. 1998-1999, 1332/8, 24 and 25) and the Green Party (*Printed Doc.*, Fl. Parl. 1998-1999, 1332/8, 26) respectively.

terpreting the distribution of competences between various levels of government.

According to some commentators the introduction of the subsidiarity principle into spatial planning is used to argue for the widest jurisdiction for local authorities. In this way the subsidiarity principle is used to provide a respectable foundation for the myth 'nearby and hence automatically good', particularly because municipalities have a thorough practical knowledge and because they can achieve "more finely tuned objectives" than linear measures from the higher level.

Others however, ask themselves out loud why the municipality should necessarily be the best qualified or most efficient level of government with regard to spatial planning. They point out that decision making at local level runs the risk of being based upon personal considerations, rather than on legal arguments or that the closest level sometimes can keep too little distance to be able to decide in an objective way. Often decentralisation evokes the image of 'village politics', in which particularism, clientelism, political favours and strict party interests would be an obstacle to spatial planning that tries to serve the public interest. Moreover capacity problems (people and resources) make local authorities – and certainly small municipalities – not necessarily a more appropriate level than higher levels of government.

4.2 The Subsidiarity Principle Applies at Two Levels

Although the subsidiarity principle is first of all a political, social and maybe even a moral principle, it may in certain cases also be a legal standard. That is the case if the principle appears in the text of a law (in a material sense). There are no known judgements in which the Belgian jurisprudence recognizes the subsidiarity principle as an (unwritten) general legal principle.

In this context the principle of subsidiarity can apply at two different levels. On the one hand the subsidiarity principle can be the basic assumption for the *assignment* of competences. In this case the subsidiarity principle applies in a more or less 'pre-legal phase', since it inspires the legal rule (or is supposed to inspire it). On the other hand the subsidiarity principle can serve as an independent testing standard for the *exercise* of (non-exclusive) competences. In this case the subsidiarity principle is an independent legal standard, which applies in a 'legal phase'. We will examine both aspects in more detail below.

4.2.1 The Subsidiarity Principle in the Pre-legal Phase

The question that matters here is to what degree the subsidiarity principle plays or can play a role in determining the rules governing the competences, for example in the distribution of tasks in the RSV. The distribution of competences in the RSV seems to be primarily characterized by the protection of interests. Custers *et al.* (2003) refer for example to the unbalanced distribution of tasks with regard to the designation of the natural and agricultural structure and argue that this can be essentially explained by the Flemish authorities' distrust of the provincial and municipal planning levels to guarantee room for nature and an absolute trust in its own capacities in this respect. In other words, it is a matter of acquiring power or giving up power already acquired, in which the existing power relations will determine whether there will be centralisation or decentralisation.

In the end the distribution of competences is quite arbitrary and for many issues arguments can be found for a different distribution of competences than those laid down by the RSV. Cabus and Saey (2000) conclude that the concrete assignment of tasks surely does *not* show that this is based upon the philosophy that the decision has to be taken at the most appropriate level, but that it is more a matter of things that cannot be done at the Flemish regional level because, for example, the implementation plan is too detailed.

4.2.2 The Subsidiarity Principle in the Legal Phase

In the exercise of non-exclusive competences the subsidiarity principle applies – or should apply – as a legal rule, which means that it can be subject to judicial inspection.

We should note here that the authorities that have to decide in a concrete case, who is competent, are first of all both judge of and party to the matter. The judge may test this decision later as to its legality. There are however a number of reasons why the subsidiarity principle appears to be a (legal) principle that is very difficult to deal with before a judge, not least because of its vagueness and the complete lack of criteria for testing it.

Anyhow, the Council of State is of the opinion that the subsidiarity principle is not a 'legal rule' as such, but that a violation of the subsidiarity principle can be invoked as a means of cancellation insofar as it can be proved that the directive regulations of the RSV have been violated[27].

4.3 To What Extent and in Which Way Must Competences be Defined?

There is a lively debate among spatial planners and jurists about the question whether and to what extent competences should be defined, or otherwise whether on the contrary they must be assigned case by case by means of consultation.

On the one hand it cannot be denied that the RSV provides a lot of instructions about the distribution of competences between the three levels (Buijs & Gla-

---

[27] Council of State, Apers, n°. 166.439, 9 January 2007, *T.R.O.S.*, 2007, 258-268, with note P.-J. DEFOORT, 'Het subsidiariteitsbeginsel en de taakstellingen uit het RSV als annulatiemiddel voor de Raad van State.'

beke 2007). On the other hand it has to be observed that the distribution of competences is formulated in a non-systematic, incoherent and vague way. Anyway, there seem to be advocates and opponents for clearly defining the competences of the various planning levels. This discussion seems to fit in the permanent area of tension in spatial planning between flexibility and legal certainty.

The outstanding argument *in favour of* establishing and defining competences is the legal certainty or rather the legal uncertainty that would exist if this was not done. The arguments *against* establishing competences are for one thing that a distribution of competences can be difficult to establish in advance and for the other that the distribution of tasks is better sorted out by means of mutual consultation between the levels of government.

The following arguments are in favour of a clear establishment and definition of competences.

- Spatial planning is an instrument to regulate a social struggle for space and is essentially a political event, in which power relations are of vital importance. In this the formal distribution of competences is one of the 'hard' institutional elements that co-determine the content-related negotiation process. In such a context a clear distribution of competences is mainly a protection for the lower authorities against the Flemish Government and/or the Flemish administrative departments, both in view of the (formal) right of initiative and in view of the content-related options of the planning process that have to be made. If the distribution of tasks depends on consultation, the lower authorities are for both points far too much dependent on the higher levels.

  The content of the plans is to a large extent also determined by the supervision of the approval process, as will appear from the case of the provincial RUP for Beaches and Dikes.

- The lack of a clear distribution of competences leads to serious practical problems: the 'plenary meetings' threaten to get bogged down in endless discussions on the distribution of competences. Endless deliberations may reduce decisiveness, can lead to frustration about too slow decision processes and a too unwieldy governmental structures and procedures and may cause conflicts that escalate and have a destructive effect.

- Clearly delimited competences imply identifiable responsibilities, and the lack of these conversely implies a lack of clear responsibilities. If responsibilities are not clearly determined, there is a real danger that all levels of government watch each other, with the result that the stakeholders are left in the cold. This is also illustrated by the provincial RUP for Beaches and Dikes as we will see below.

Apart from these opportunist arguments the principle of legal certainty can also be invoked as an important legal argument to advocate the establishment of competences, and more particularly, the 'material principle of legal certainty'. This is the legal certainty principle as a requirement of a clearly defined legal position.

4.4 Inadequate Formulation of the Distribution of Tasks

It should be noticed that the formulation of the distribution of tasks in the structure plans (and particularly in the RSV) leaves much to be desired, even to the extent that it may threaten the 'formal' legal certainty – the principle of legal certainty as a requirement for accessibility, i.e. distinguishability and clearness of objective law. More particularly there are problems as to legal certainty due to the use of undefined or badly defined terminology, due to a lack of coherence and due to a lack of clear, understandable formulation (*see* Defoort 2005).

5. The Competence to Draw up an RUP for Beaches and Dikes

The issue of competences as well as the distribution of tasks applies just as much to the subject of our case study: an RUP for Beaches and Dikes. In this paragraph we will examine whether the RSV and the Provincial Spatial Structure Plan for West Flanders (PRS W-Vl) assign tasks that provide a starting point for the power to draw up an RUP for Beaches and Dikes. Before doing this, we will first deal with a number of principles necessary for the interpretation of the distribution of tasks.

5.1 General Principles for the Interpretation of the Distribution of Tasks

Inspiration for rules to the interpretation of the distribution of tasks can be found in constitutional law. The distribution of tasks can be interpreted by analogy with the principles that are applied by the Constitutional Court for the interpretation of the rules governing the competences applying to the federal government, the Regions and Communities (Defoort 2007b).

- If a particular issue for which an RUP must be drawn up can fall under several jurisdictions, it should be concretely examined which concept of competence it is most closely related to. The principle of proportionality and effective motivation should justify the final choice.

- The competences should not be implemented or interpreted in a restrictive way. By analogy with jurisdiction of the Constitutional Court it might be decided that the assigned competences should be considered to include the *full* powers to issue regulations that are proper to the competence.

- Since the DRO or the RSV do not contain a provision that is comparable to Article 10 of the Special Act of 8 August 1988 for the Reform of the Institutions ('Bijzondere Wet tot Hervorming van de Instellingen' – BWHI) with regard to the so-called 'implicit competences ', it would probably go too far to also apply this rule governing the competences by analogy to the distribution of competences for drawing up RUPs. According to article 10 BWHI one authority may enter the area of jurisdiction of another authority concerning issues for which the level of government in question is not competent in principle, insofar as those provisions are necessary for the exercise of its own competence.

5.2 The Distribution of Tasks in the RSV Relevant to Beaches and Dikes

The RSV does not contain specific rules about beaches and dikes. At first sight there are mainly two so-called 'substructures' that are important for determining the power to draw up an RUP for Beaches and Dikes: 'tourist-recreational infrastructure' and 'nature'.

5.2.1 Competences Relating to Tourist and Recreational Infrastructure

Commentators rightly observe that there are no clear rules of the game with regard to subsidiarity relating to tourist-recreational infrastructure (David *et al.* 2003). Starting from the text of the RSV, it seems that it is possible to distinguish two 'categories of competences' relating to tourist-recreational infrastructures[28].

- On the one hand the RSV provides for a separate category *"specific tourist-recreational infrastructures that require a decision at Flemish regional level"*[29]. These concern in particular areas for accommodation for outdoor recreation (camping and caravan parks, camping sites and holiday parks), individual weekend cottages, golf links and ULM- and light aircraft airfields. These competences should be considered as exclusive Flemish competences. The RSV explains this 'distribution of tasks' as follows: *"Because of their spatial impact and complexity a number of specific tourist-recreational infrastructures require a decision with regard to their desired spatial development at the level of the Flemish Region"*. Considering the principle of linking between structure plans and implementation plans (*see above*), these should be Regional RUPs or regulations. The Flemish Region has indeed assigned itself a clear task. The topics in the summary do not seem to be directly relevant to the issue of beaches and dikes, however.

- With regard to the competences relating to other tourist-recreational infrastructures the situation is much more complex. This is not least due to the highly inaccurate formulation in the RSV. It is sufficient to observe here

---

[28] RSV, p. 417-423.
[29] Indicative section, p. 421.

that the RSV contains rules for 'highly dynamic' tourist infrastructure (among which disturbing [noisy] forms of sport and recreation) and that with respect to competences it seems to make a distinction between the so-called 'rural areas' and 'urban areas'. For lowly dynamic tourist-recreational infrastructure the RSV does not seem to have established specific rules of the game. This means that for determining competences with regard to structure planning in this respect the subsidiarity principle will prevail and that for the drawing up of RUPs a starting point will have to be found in a structure plan or with a distribution of tasks (Defoort 2004).

So the RSV has already determined a number of rules of the game for tourist-recreational infrastructure, but all the same those rules are highly unclear and incomplete. In practice this lack of clarity seems to lead to a high degree of legal uncertainty. Moreover practice also shows that even for those areas where competences are clearly defined, the rules governing the competences are not always observed (e.g. camping sites, weekend accommodation, moto-cross courses …).

Referring to the issue of beaches and dikes we must consequently first of all ask the question whether 'highly dynamic' tourist-recreational infrastructure is concerned. By 'highly dynamic tourist-recreational infrastructure' the RSV understands *"infrastructure that because of its intrinsic character, causes important changes and dynamics in the functioning of the existing spatial and socio-economic structure of the direct environment and therefore greatly changes the existing spatial use (for example due to a highly concentrated provision of facilities or one large facility in one location, due to the presence of a large group of people in relation to the size of the area, …)"*. 'Lowly dynamic tourist-recreational infrastructure' is according to the RSV *"infrastructure that because of its intrinsic character, causes rather re-stricted changes in the existing spatial and socio-economic structure of the direct envi-ronment and in the existing spatial use"*[30].

The provincial RUP for Beaches and Dikes provides for a number of regula-tions for allocation and layout relating to authorised constructions on beaches and dikes, for example bathing cabins, surf and sailing clubs, points of sale for drinks, authorised constructions on a marked off part of the beach for specific events …. The question is whether that infrastructure should be considered as highly or lowly dynamic. It cannot be denied that the beach as such attracts a lot of people. However it does not seem that the infrastructure mentioned above causes important changes in those dynamics, at least not in the urban-ized coastal towns with a lot of tourist accommodation for single day or longer-stay tourism: the urbanized parts of the coast draw a lot of people any-way, and the presence or absence of bathing cabins, sports clubs, drinks stalls … will fundamentally change very little in those places. From that perspective such infrastructure for those places can be considered to be lowly dynamic. This means that the different levels of planning can regulate it in their respec-

---

[30]   RSV, p. 419.

tive structure plans according to the (extremely vague) subsidiarity principle described above and the (much more concrete) principle of hierarchy.

The West Flanders draft PRS contained a policy framework that aimed at a uniform approach for allowing and prohibiting constructions on the beach. This policy framework was based upon a study (TERRA) that was drawn up on the orders of the Flemish Waterways and Maritime Affairs Administration, Department of Waterways and Coast (now MD&K), in collaboration with the provincial authorities of West Flanders. However, both the provincial authorities and the Department of Waterways and Coast were highly uncertain about the question of which authority was actually competent to issue urban development regulations for beach constructions. That uncertainty finally led to a parliamentary question to the Minister for Spatial Planning asking whether the Province of West Flanders was competent to include a policy framework about beach constructions in its structure plan and more generally which supra-local authority was competent to draw up a regulatory instrument for beach constructions, the province or the Flemish Region (*see next chapter*). In his answer the Minister stated quite cryptically that it was obvious that the province would take the initiative, either in the form of a provincial RUP, or with a provincial urban development regulation, "*since the development of a spatial vision of tourism and recreation is part of the provincial planning tasks*"[31]. As a result of this the above mentioned policy framework was maintained in the definitive PRS W-Vl.

Considering the principle that every level of government is competent to draw up RUPs in implementation of its own structure plan, the drawing up of an RUP for Beaches and Dikes falls under the competence of the provincial authorities of West Flanders, at least insofar as a regulation of lowly dynamic tourist-recreational structures on beaches and dikes is concerned. The latter implies that the competence of the province appears to be restricted to spatially urbanized areas, since it cannot just be supposed that providing the possibility of all kinds of beach constructions in more remote (non-urbanized) locations would not bring about a highly dynamic situation and would not change the spatial utilization. Such places seem to fall rather under the Natural Structure than under the tourist-recreational structure anyway (*see below*).

There might be some doubt about the question whether the allocation of a 'beach for events' – as happened in Zeebrugge (Bruges) and Knokke – should not anyhow be considered as highly dynamic, also in urbanized areas. To answer that question one may appeal to the afore-mentioned interpretation principles on the one hand, determining that the competence for a certain issue should be supposed to include full jurisdiction on that issue, and on the other hand that it should be examined with which jurisdiction a specific issue

---

[31] Request for explanation by VAN NIEUWKERKE, A. d.d. 17 May 2001 to Minister VAN MECHELEN about the drawing up of an urban development regulation with regard to activities on the beach, *Handelingen*, Fl. Parl., 2000-2001, N° 183.

is most closely related, in which the principle of proportionality is determining. Remembering these principles it may be stated that the competence to regulate construction on beaches and dikes includes the competence to lay down rules relating to a beach for events, considering the relatively limited size of such zones (in Zeebrugge restricted to the already existing platform for events and in Knokke restricted to maximum 5000 m²) and the non permanent character of this (only between 15 March and 15 October).

During the public inquiry on the provincial RUPs of the policy framework of the PRS W-Vl there arose a number of questions about subsidiarity. On the one hand some municipalities thought that the urban development regulation for beach and dike constructions was part of the competences of the municipality. Some other municipalities argued on the other hand that the RUPs were too detailed and left no room for a municipal policy. The answer here might be that the policy framework of the PRS and the RUP aim at a uniform approach for the whole coastal area with regard to allowing or prohibiting constructions on the beach. The fact that there is a need for common regulations for a larger area is indeed an argument that may be used to decide that centralisation is appropriate, rather than decentralisation (Defoort 2005).

5.2.2 The Competence to Designate the Natural Structure

It is obvious that certain parts of the coast include important natural values and that the power of drawing up an RUP therefore should also be assessed from the viewpoint of the spatial substructure 'nature'.

From the viewpoint of the distribution of competences, the designation of the *natural structure* is quite clear. The RSV determines that this is done in regional spatial implementation plans. The designation of the natural structure should happen simultaneously with and on an equal basis with the designation of the agricultural structure, at the initiative of the department responsible for spatial planning and in collaboration with the government departments responsible for nature, agriculture and forest as well as in consultation with the provincial and municipal authorities. With regard to the designation it has been statistically determined how many Large Units of Nature ('Grote Eenheden Natuur' – GEN), Large Units of Nature in Development ('Grote Eenheden Natuur in Ontwikkeling' – GENO), agricultural area, forest extension area and Nature Interweaving Areas (IVON) the Flemish Region must designate[32]. Apart from the RSV, the Decree on Nature Conservation[33] also provides for the designation of natural areas, which does not make things simpler. As a matter of fact the RSV applied a different planning horizon (2007 versus 2002) and different terminology ('Natural Structure' versus 'Flemish Ecological Network ('Vlaams Ecologisch Netwerk' – VEN) (Bogaert 2004).

---

[32] Indicative section p. 392; binding section p. 585.
[33] Decree of 21 October 1997 with regard to nature conservation and the natural environment.

But also the provinces have competences relating to nature. The RSV pre-scribes that Nature Corridor Areas are designated in provincial RUPs. Accord-ing to the RSV this should be done subject to the Flemish designation of the natural structure and by means of guidelines drawn up at the level of the Flemish Region. Nature Corridor Areas are only designated insofar as their connecting function cannot be guaranteed by another part of the Natural Structure (usually by Nature Interweaving Areas)[34]. The provincial compe-tences for Nature Corridor Areas has to be seen as a 'limited competing com-petence' (*see above*). On the one hand it is a competing competence because the provinces are competent in parallel to the Flemish Region for (an aspect of) the designation of the Natural Structure. De facto there is a hierarchy, since the provinces are dependent on the Flemish designation. On the other hand the competing competence is 'limited' both temporally and conditionally. The exercise of competence of the province is indeed (temporally) suspended until after the Flemish designation of the Natural Structure and moreover the pro-vincial competence must be exercised on the basis of Flemish guidelines. Strictly speaking this means that the province could not designate Nature Corridor Areas for beaches and dikes before the Flemish Region had finished the designation of the Natural Structure at the coast, or at least had started this designation. It should be noticed that the Flemish Region had not yet started the designation of the Natural Structure at the time when the provincial RUPs were drawn up.

Although the rules for the distribution of competences with regard to nature are quite clear, there are numerous problems from a policy and process point of view. Custers *et al.* (2003) justly observe that the Flemish Region has bur-dened itself with a tremendous responsibility (Custers *et al.* 2003). The Flemish authority was indeed convinced that it would be possible to quickly wrap up the designation process for nature and agriculture, but in practice the proc-esses seem to run much less smoothly than had been hoped. The long-term character of the designation process is problematic for the provinces and mu-nicipalities, because the competence of designation relating to nature and par-ticularly to agriculture implies a considerable restriction of their competence. As long as the Flemish authority has not definitively decided where the natu-ral structures are located, it is for example absolutely uncertain for the prov-inces where they can exercise their powers of designation of Nature Corridor Areas. This is even more the case because the RSV did not make any selection of areas that should be part of the Natural Structure at Flemish level.

This issue is a relevant one for the provincial RUP for Beaches and Dikes. It is obvious that the province cannot designate an area with (important) natural values as an area mainly classified for recreational use. Provincial RUPs have classified certain more isolated areas with natural values as 'recreation-nature conservation transition area', 'nature conservation area with limited ancillary recreational use' or 'nature conservation area with ancillary recreational use'.

---

[34] RSV, p. 392.

Obviously the provincial authorities consider these areas as Nature Corridor Areas, where light recreational ancillary use was deemed to be acceptable. Initially those parts were called 'solitary beach zones', but this was amended on the advice of the Minister for Spatial Planning, who argued that provincial RUPs "*cannot change the actual use and finality of the VEN area (main function being nature conservation and use nature conservation area), (but that) the area specific regulations may include provisions and preconditions for subordinate functions that are compatible with the main function*"[35].

On the occasion of the approval of the provincial RUPs the Minister finally withheld his consent to a number of the afore-mentioned Nature Corridor Areas with ancillary recreational use in a number of RUPs (for example RUP Bruges, RUP Bredene), as will appear further on in the case study. It should be noted here that the exclusion was not made because any competence was infringed but because of the impact on the existing European Special Protection Area or Special Area of Conservation or the lack of an appropriate assessment (Birds or Habitats Directives).

6. Conclusions

In view of the provincial RUP for Beaches and Dikes case study, we can draw the following provisional conclusions on the basis of a legal-technical analysis.

The RUP Establishment Procedure: a Straitjacket with a Low Level of Ambition with Regard to Participation

The formal procedure for the establishment of an RUP sits in a fairly tight straitjacket from its preliminary adoption by the Provincial Council until its publication in the Belgian law gazette. During the phase of preliminary draft and the plenary meetings, it is however possible to deal with the procedure in a very flexible way, since jurisprudence states that possible procedural mistakes in that phase cannot lead to the annulment of the RUP afterwards.

The formal procedure is also fairly strict with regard to participation. It should be noted that participation in the preliminary draft phase is restricted to official and political consultation. The public consultation only comes late in the policy process. Participation of individual citizens only takes place *after* the preliminary adoption of the RUP by the Provincial Council, through the classic instrument of public inquiry. According to jurisprudence, any fundamental change of the plan at a later time should be subject to a new public inquiry. Due to this, the authorities will be rather reluctant to thoroughly change the preliminarily adopted plan.

---

[35] For example Ministerial Decree on the subject of the draft provincial spatial implementation plan "Strand en Dijk Bredene (Beaches and Dikes Bredene" of the Province of West Flanders, d.d. 15 September 2004.

In order to provide for truly full participation of individual citizens and interest groups, they might be involved in the planning process during the preliminary draft phase, for example by means of hearings and with the opportunity to formulate comments in writing afterwards. At the moment this is not the case.

The Question of Competences: a Complicated Tangle

From the analysis above the distribution of competences with regard to spatial planning and the drawing up of RUPs in particular, appears to be a very complicated tangle. This is mainly due to a lack of clear rules governing the competences and the distribution of tasks in the RSV, on the one hand, and inadequate alignment with the Nature Decree on the other hand. The rules governing the competences and the distribution of tasks are not only unclear and often inaccurately formulated, but they are also scattered over the entire RSV. This is for example illustrated by the rules governing the competences for tourist-recreational infrastructure – or rather the lack of (clear) rules in this respect.

The competence for the designation of the Natural Structure is then an illustration of the fact that the Flemish Region has taken over a lot of competences. Due to capacity problems (lack of people and resources) and public support problems (e.g. tensions between issues relating to agriculture and nature) the competences cannot be adequately exercised and within a reasonable period of time. This endangers the exercise of competence by lower authorities according to the principle of hierarchy. The question is whether the Flemish Region is actually able to carry out the various planning processes itself, and whether it would not be more realistic to consign more planning processes to the lower authorities, so that the Flemish Region can mainly focus on safeguarding the main spatial principles of the RSV by means of consultancy as well as administrative supervision. The latter requires of course that this administrative supervision is carried out in a correct way. The case will show that this is not always so.

A different approach to hierarchy and the establishment of clear rules governing the competences can provide a solution to some of the problems discussed in this chapter. Such rules should however not be formulated in too detailed and rigid way and must be applied by means of a number of reasonable interpretation rules.

References

BOGAERT, D. (2004). *Natuurbeleid in Vlaanderen. Natuurontwikkeling en draagvlak als vernieuwingen?* Brussel: Instituut voor Natuurbehoud.
BUIJS, X. & A. GLABEKE (2007). 'Taakstelling in de ruimtelijke plannen: wie is bevoegd voor wat?'. *T.R.O.S.*, 284-291.

CABUS, P. & P. SAEY (2000). 'Subsidiariteit in het nieuwe Vlaamse planningssysteem: plaatsbepaling en eerste evaluatie'. *T.R.O.S.*, (Bijzonder nummer: Subsidiariteit in de ruimtelijke planning), 31-45.

CUSTERS, S., H. LEINFELDER & C. VANDEVOORT (2003). 'Afbakening van natuur en landbouw in Vlaanderen. Een nauwe trechter en een lelijke mozaïek'. In P. Schrijnen (ed.) *De cultuur van het bestuur. Over Nederlandse trechters en Vlaamse mozaïeken.* Delft: Stichting Planologische Diskussiedagen.

DAVID, P., H. LEINFELDER, A. PISMAN & P. TOTTE (2003). 'De kunstige nuance tussen een realistische en een expressionistische mozaïek: subsidiariteit in de praktijk'. P. Schrijnen (ed.) *De cultuur van het bestuur. Over Nederlandse trechters en Vlaamse mozaïeken.* Delft: Stichting Planologische Diskussiedagen.

DEFOORT, P-J (2004). *Bevoegdheidsverdeling in de ruimtelijke planning. Subsidiariteit: feit of fictie?* Scriptie ingediend tot het behalen van de academische graad van gediplomeerde in de aanvullende studies GAS – Ruimtelijke Planning. Gent: Universiteit Gent.

DEFOORT, P.-J. (2005). 'Bevoegdheidsverdeling in de ruimtelijke planning. Subsidiariteit: feit of fictie?'. *T.R.O.S.*, 281-335.

DEFOORT, P.-J. (2007a). 'Geldt het subsidiariteitsbeginsel voor (sectorale) BPA's? Over de verhouding tussen BPA's en structuurplannen'. *T.R.O.S.*, 134-149.

DEFOORT, P.-J. (2007b). Het subsidiariteitsbeginsel en de taakstellingen uit het RSV als annulatiemiddel voor de Raad van State'. noot onder R.v.St. Apers, nr. 166.439, 9 januari 2007, 260-268.

DEFOORT, P.-J. & G. Goedertier (in press). 'Delegatie van beslissingsbevoegdheden inzake ruimtelijke ordening, monumenten en landschappen aan de leden van de Vlaamse Regering'. *T.R.O.S.* (48).

DE WAELE, T. (2007). 'Van ontwerp tot definitief plan: overheid, bezint eer ge begint!'. (noot onder R.v.St., Dethier, nr. 149.576, 28 september 2005). *T.R.O.S.*, 50-53.

VERHOEVEN, D. (2007). 'Bestemmingswijzigingen tijdens de goedkeuringsprocedure van plannen van aanleg: naar meer tegenspraak in openbare onderzoeken ? noot onder R.v.St. Hanotiau, nr. 160.169, 15 juni 2006'. *T.R.O.S.*, 169-173.

CHAPTER 5

The Provincial Spatial Implementation Plan (PRUP) for Beaches and Dikes.
An Analysis of the Decision Making Process

Dirk Bogaert and Dino De Waen

1. Introduction

After the legal-technical analysis of the new instrument of the 'Spatial Imple-mentation Plan' (RUP) in the previous chapter, we will describe in this chapter the results of the analysis of the policy process of the Provincial Spatial Im-plementation Plan (PRUP) for Beaches and Dikes. The description of the analysis results pays attention to the dimensions distinguished in the Policy Arrangement Approach (PAA): discourse, actors, rules of the game and power (see chapter 1). In the analysis we distinguish three periods: what happened before, the informal preliminary consultation and the formal process.

2. What Happened Before

2.1 The Period of Agenda Setting: Lack of Clarity Leads to Appealing Discourses and a Need for New Rules of the Game

The Belgian coast constitutes a specific case as far as spatial planning is con-cerned. As described in the previous chapter, we had to wait until 1962 before the Belgian federal legislator enacted laws and regulations for spatial planning and urban development. It is noticeable that this legislation and also the later 'zoning plans', hardly pay any attention to sea dikes and beaches. The larger part of the Belgian beaches remained 'non-designated', but not the least 'un-used'. Due to problems of scale on the one hand (insufficiently detailed plans) and due to the highly dynamic character of beaches and dunes on the other hand (mobile ecosystems), particular parts of the beaches, and even parts of dikes, are rather haphazardly designated as nature areas.

Especially in the 1990s coastal recreation and tourism were expanding, due to which there was also a growing demand for all kinds of beach constructions (viz. MIRONA 2000). Constructions of a temporary to semi-permanent and even permanent character appeared in an uncoordinated way in all possible locations. This new dynamics exceeded the capacity of the Belgian coast that is only 67 kilometres long, causing increasing problems with regard to various users, to the quality of the public space and to specific natural values. Thus water sports were mainly kept outside of the central areas, using the argument of safety, so that in most cases they were located near to or in nature areas. Due to lack of legal certainty the managers of for example surf clubs were not happily inclined to invest in their infrastructure, which initially lead to not particularly aesthetic constructions. According to various respondents this was only possible because the authorities had been exercising a policy of tolerance for decades at the various levels of government (regional and municipal). In certain cases the constructions were even built with the consent or approval of local authorities, as was the case with 'Surfers Paradise' in Knokke (*see text box*).

'You must know that the Mayor has morally committed himself: 'Do build', he said, 'if you have to wait for every Tom and Dick and Harry.... I will arrange it!' But it did not get arranged ....'

Within the Flemish authorities the current MD&K (Flemish Agency for Maritime and Coastal Services) plays an important role with regard to developments on beaches and dikes. In the past MD&K granted permission to build constructions, but lacked clear rules for that. Still in 1988 MD&K sent a letter to the municipalities containing nine guidelines*"to control bigger and bigger constructions on the beach"* (Letter 28 june 1988). In the interviews users and local government officials however indicated that applications for constructions were usually dealt with individually and on an ad hoc basis without an overall framework. Public servants, local politicians (at municipal and provincial level) as well as market players state that not everything was permitted, though *'nevertheless quite a lot'*. The proliferation of constructions on the Flemish beaches, and by extension also on the sea dikes, could be largely attributed to a lack of clear rules of the game, with regard to precision of prescription as well as to formality and authority.

In 1995 the Flemish Government issued a decision concerning beach concessions, which regulated this whole issue (*see previous chapter*). But this was not enough, as was shown among other things by the fact that in the coming years there were appealing discourses for better regulation of the use of beaches and dikes, from politicians, civil servants as well as nature conservation associations. Thus questions were put to the competent Ministers of the Flemish Government in Parliament. On 4 November 1998 the Flemish Member of Parliament, Andre Van Nieuwkerke, for example asked a question to the then Ministers for Spatial Planning and Environment[1], raising the urbanization of the beach. He defined this urbanization as the *"apparently disorderly proliferation of large shacks"*, which in his view *"are threatening not only the intrinsic natural values of the beaches, but also the scenic appearance of the North Sea beach as the last more or less intact open space along the coast, and a fortiori the attraction for tourists."* As a concrete example of the proliferation of shacks threatening the natural values, reference was made to the surf clubs VVW Heist and 'Surfers Paradise' (*see text box*).

Local politicians too considered the issue of constructions without permits as a priority. During the annual consultation of the mayors of coastal municipalities with the Governor of the Province of West Flanders (Minutes 1999) the mayors presented a list of 90 problematic constructions to the Governor, for which a solution was required before summer (MIRONA 2000). A few days later this request was given further support by a second question in parlia-

---

[1]   Question by Van Nieuwkerke, 4 November 1998 to Minister Stevaert about *North Sea beaches – Urbanization*, Fl. Parl., 1998-1999, N° 69.

THE PROVINCIAL SPATIAL IMPLEMENTATION PLAN (PRUP) FOR BEACHES AND DIKES.

AN ANALYSIS OF THE DECISION MAKING PROCESS

ment by the Flemish Member of Parliament Devolder with regard to beach constructions without permits[2].

The combination of parliamentary questions and the initiative of the mayors of the coastal municipalities finally put the issue of beach constructions on the Flemish political agenda. During the in-depth interviews the respondents confirmed that the problem of proliferation of beach constructions was not only signalled by politicians, but just as much by the administrative agencies (MD&K, AROHM) *and* by a nature conservation organisation ('Natuurpunt'). In an internal note in preparation for discussions between various ministerial offices (internal note) we see that among other things the parliamentary questions have urged the competent Ministers to commission MD&K to develop a policy framework.

2.2 Knowledge Building as an Important Resource: the TERRA Report

To develop a policy framework you need knowledge. In order to add to that knowledge MD&K requested a study from the department 'Milieu Ruimtelijke Ordening en Natuur' (Environment, Spatial Planning and Nature – MIRONA) of the Province of West Flanders. The concrete task was to draw up a *"planning and legal framework for the use of the seawall and in particular of the beaches and dikes"* (MIRONA 2000). The study fitted into a European project of which MD&K was the leader, the so-called TERRA project that was part of the demonstration programme for Integrated Coastal Zone Management of the European Commission of the European Union.

Thanks to this study an inventory was made up for the first time of existing beach and dike constructions along the Belgian coast and of the then prevailing legislation and regulations. The report points out the following problem areas: the aesthetic quality of the constructions, the visual nuisance, the problem of detached and disused constructions.

> *"Particularly with regard to surf clubs it is observed that often containers are used in which the surfing material is stored and, in some cases, these are even used as a bar. In most cases the containers are corroded or have been covered with graffiti."* (MIRONA 2000: 18)

Subsequently a policy vision was developed with a view to drawing up assessment criteria making a distinction between new and existing, temporary and permanent constructions, with and without permits. The vision developed took into account environmental aspects, tourist economic aspects as well as aesthetic aspects. The authors of the TERRA report proposed among other

---

2   Topical Question of Devolder, 27 January 1999 to Minister Stevaert about the development of urban development regulations with regard to activities on the beach, *Handelingen (Record of Debates)*, Fl. Parl., 1998-1999, N° 30.

things to provide for a zoning of the Belgian coast with the corresponding detailed regulations. The following zones and regulations were anticipated:

- Zone A: Beach – dike – continuous building. Temporary and permanent constructions possible.
- Zone B: Beach – dike – scattered building. Temporary and permanent constructions possible.
- Zone C: Beach – only scattered building. If next to A: idem zone B. If next to B: idem zone D.
- Zone D: Beach – (possibly dike or road) – dunes/parks/woods. No permanent constructions possible. Few temporary constructions possible.

The TERRA report also contains a description of specific problematic issues per municipality after implementation of the proposed criteria and zoning. In total this led to 72 problem areas, which were unevenly spread among the coastal municipalities. Of this, the authors of the TERRA report say:

"Finally we observe that there are no considerable differences between the various municipalities as to the way in which they deal with constructions. But some municipalities are conspicuous in a negative way." (MIRONA 2000: 48)

	Badly zoned and without permit	Properly zoned and without permit	Unaesthetic sights	Number of problem areas
De Panne		2	3	5
Koksijde	1	3		4
Nieuwpoort		4	3	7
Middelkerke	1	2	1	4
Oostende		3	2	5
Bredene	3			3
De Haan	7		2	9
Blankenberge	3	1	1	5
Zeebrugge	1	2		3
Knokke	2	19	6	27
TOTAL	18	36	18	72

Table 2: overview of problem areas with constructions on beaches and dikes in the year 2000 (authors' own table, source data MIRONA 2000)

The drafting of the TERRA report did not only produce a considerable increase in information with regard to constructions on beaches and dikes, but also provided important experiences in the process of consultation with internal and external steering committees, coastal municipalities and sectors. According to various respondents, the experience acquired by public servants in provincial authorities was later used of in the drafting of the final PRUP for Beaches and Dikes. It provided the civil servants who were involved with the necessary legitimacy and the required authority. Building up knowledge by means of the TERRA report can be considered as an important resource for the Province of West Flanders.

THE PROVINCIAL SPATIAL IMPLEMENTATION PLAN (PRUP) FOR BEACHES AND DIKES.

AN ANALYSIS OF THE DECISION MAKING PROCESS

2.3 Parallel Processes and New Rules of the Game

Of course spatial planning of beaches and dikes does not take place in a vacuum. During the period under consideration there were important innovations with regard to Flemish legislation and regulations (*see previous chapter*). Perhaps the most important new rule of the game in spatial planning was the concept of structure planning, via which it was possible to respond to the reality of a dynamic society – in contrast to the earlier rather static land use plans. The Planning Decree[3], and the following Decree on Spatial Planning[4] (DRO) provided not only a legal basis for this concept, but also fully involved lower levels of government (municipalities and province) in the development of plans. For the Province of West Flanders this implies that for the first time it could draw up a Provincial Spatial Structure Plan West Flanders (PPD 2002), which finally was approved by the competent Minister on 6 March 2002. It is remarkable that the policy framework that was elaborated by TERRA was included in the indicative and directive sections of PRS-WV as *"specific policy framework with regard to tourism and recreation"* (PPD 2002: 259 ff), and not in the binding section. This only meant a partial formalization of the policy framework, but at that moment it had not yet gained authority. Still, the binding section of the PRS-WV held out the prospect of drawing up a PRUP or regulation for the desired spatial structure for tourism and recreation.

> *"Draw up a provincial spatial implementation plan (or regulation) for beach constructions"* (PPD 2002: 305).

This binding clause is seen as the formal reason for drawing up the PRUP for Beaches and Dikes (Claessens 2004; PPD 2005).

We observe important developments in adjacent policy areas that were partly at the basis of the (necessary) search for solutions to the issue of constructions on beaches and sea dikes. Thus for example, the so-called 'Duinendecreet' (Dunes Decree)[5] was approved in 1993 in order to protect the remaining dunes, and in 1997 there followed the 'Natuurdecreet' (Nature Decree)[6] for the conservation, restoration and development of natural values in Flanders.

In the 1990s parallel processes and new rules of the game could be observed in Spatial Planning and Nature policy, and this would inevitably lead to a policy with regard to constructions on beaches and dikes.

---

[3]   Decree of 24 July 1996 with regard to Spatial Planning.
[4]   Decree of 18 May 1999 with regard to the Organisation of Spatial Planning (and later amendments).
[5]   Decree of 14 July 1993 with regard to the Protection of the Coastal Dunes.
[6]   Decree of 21 October 1997 with regard to Nature Conservation and the Natural Environment.

2.4 The Initiator and the (Re)positioning of Actors

From what precedes it is clear that the Province of West Flanders was not only a 'new' player in the area of Spatial Planning, but also seemed to be willing to seize the opportunity with both hands. In a short period of time the province invested in people and means for drawing up a study assignment (MIRONA 2000) *and* the PRS-WV, and moreover it also held out the prospect of drawing up a PRUP or a regulation. Shortly after the approval of the PRS-WV the Province of West Flanders started to develop the PRUP. It is remarkable that once again the choice was made to have the provincial department for spatial planning to develop this PRUP on its own instead of outsourcing it to firms specialised in making studies. A first preliminary draft PRUP was already discussed in the autumn of 2002. The partial approval followed three years later on 19 September 2005 (*see below*).

The new legislation (Planning Decree, DRO, RSV...) led to (re)positioning of actors, amongst other things due to the principles of subsidiarity and hierarchy (*see previous chapter*). Nearly all respondents indicate during the interviews that 'the province' is seen as initiator in drawing up the PRUP, whether encouraged or not by the higher government level (Flanders). Most respondents state that the PRUP is a continuation of the TERRA report, some even make no distinction between these. To a number of respondents it is clear that this also automatically implied implementation of the PRS-WV. The PRUP would provide for a legally binding sequel supplement.

> *'When we were dealing with the initial plans and asked ourselves whether we had to draw up a regulation or a PRUP, we discussed this with AROHM, which also had a lot of experience with the permits in Flanders, together with MD&K and AMINAL. They also sat around the table.'*
>
> *'It may also have been the province that due to subsidiarity became responsible for tourism and recreation.'*

One respondent thinks that the fact that the province played the role of the driving force in this can partly be explained by the fact that the Flemish authorities did not want to take a stand on this dossier. Beaches and dikes were no priority for this level of government – except for protection of the coast – although the RSV does describe the coast as *"structure determining"* at Flemish level (see among others AROHM 1998: 333,353 and 584). On the other hand the Flemish Government had asked the provincial authorities by means of a circular letter[7] to formulate a vision of the tourist recreational infrastructure. The observation that many problem areas with regard to tourism and recreation are systematically passed on from the Flemish Region to the province promoted a *"strong tourist profile for the provinces"* and can also partly explain the initiative to look for solutions for beach constructions (Claessens 2004: 57).

---

[7] Circular letter RO/96/06 with regard to the substantive distribution of tasks for the provincial spatial structure plan.

THE PROVINCIAL SPATIAL IMPLEMENTATION PLAN (PRUP) FOR BEACHES AND DIKES.

AN ANALYSIS OF THE DECISION MAKING PROCESS

The mayors of coastal municipalities who were interviewed emphasize the role of the municipalities in obliging the province to take action.

'We got it started. That is what the coastal mayors had asked for under the previous government.'

At the same time they emphasize that the principle of subsidiarity also raised the question whether the provincial level was more appropriate than the municipal level for the drawing up of an RUP anyway. Other respondents argue that the province is indeed more appropriate by referring to the importance of an approach across municipal boundaries and the increased opportunities for integrated management of coastal areas.

'(...) the province had taken the initiative because it wanted to contribute to the integrated management of coastal areas.'

The search for solutions for constructions on beaches and dikes caused a repositioning of actors. The province presented itself as initiator and driving force, partly on the authority of the Flemish authorities (MD&K) and partly at the request of some municipal authorities that wanted solutions for some unsolved problematic issues.

2.5 Definition of the Objectives. The Need for a Framework and Legal Certainty

In the finally approved PRUP for Beaches and Dikes the authors formulated the following objective "to organise the tourist recreational activities within the area of the plan, particularly with regard to all constructions, both of temporary and permanent character and the associated activities." (PPD 2005: 5 and 23). Taking into account the purpose of defence from the sea, as well as the economic and the environmental functions of beaches and dikes the authors thought it necessary to aim at a "careful use of space" (ibidem: 23). Rather than creating new things the aim was a qualitative upgrade of existing sites.

At governmental level however there was a second important objective. The drawing up of a PRUP for Beaches and Dikes meant indeed the implementation of a provision of the previously approved PRS-WV. The authors explain their preference for an RUP over a regulation, because of the nature of the issue that required a decision on designation of use and because of the need for a public inquiry. Both elements are not involved in case of a regulation (ibidem: 4).

Although the respondents formulated quite heterogeneous answers when they were asked to give the objectives of the PRUP for Beaches and Dikes, we think that we can distinguish two lines: the creation of a comprehensive policy framework for beaches and dikes along the whole of the Belgian coast and the creation of legal certainty. The need for a comprehensive policy framework was mentioned by respondents from state (politicians and civil servants), civil society and market. Some talked about the *'creation of a framework'* or even of *'creating order on the beach'*. With regard to the latter they referred among other things to conflicts among users or between tourist recreational activities and natural values. A beach life guard put it as follows:

> *'The problem was proliferation; clubs were established on the beaches in a permanent way without permit and nature conservationists got angry about it and to some extent they were right.'*

The problem of 'proliferation' was seen along the whole of the Belgian coast and was dealt with in a different way by every coastal municipality, for lack of a comprehensive framework.

> *'I think that all local councils had problems with bathing cabins, playgrounds, ...'*
> *'After all it was also out of concern for tourism, we promoted the massive use of the coast, and the local councils do that too. We observed that there was an unrestrained use of the beaches and that every municipality had another vision.'*

These differences in local policies and the growing number of conflicts created the need in particular among authorities that granted permits such as MD&K, for an obligatory framework of evaluation.

> *'We had to grant permits and needed guidelines. (...) Moreover a balance was needed between nature and recreation.'*

A second element the respondents perceived as an objective of the PRUP is that it had to meet the need for legal certainty. It is striking that this need for legal certainty is also mentioned by respondents from state (politicians and civil servants), civil society as well as market, although they all emphasized different things. The permit granting authorities mainly talked about legal certainty in the sense of clarity with regard to the complex legal situation relating to beaches and dikes, such as, for example, the existence of non-designated areas. A representative of the water sports associations and of a surf club mainly talked about legal certainty in the sense of a clear policy with regard to permits and possibilities of regularisation.

> *'Give us a permit. Now we must do everything illegally with a wink.'*
> *'I was also glad about it, for it was indeed time to have regulations on the beach.'*

People from the nature conservation sector not only pointed at the possibility of regularisation so as to create legal certainty, but also at other (sub)objectives:

> *'There was a twilight zone, it was not properly described.'*
> *'To stop and if possible reverse the proliferation of shacks by letting undesired constructions disappear or by having them removed.'*

THE PROVINCIAL SPATIAL IMPLEMENTATION PLAN (PRUP) FOR BEACHES AND DIKES.

AN ANALYSIS OF THE DECISION MAKING PROCESS

To sum up it may be said that according to the respondents the definition of the objectives was mainly concerned with the lack of clear rules of the game, and contained elements that were related to problems with regard to formality, authority as well as precision of prescription.

3. The Informal Preliminary Consultation

3.1 Content-related and Instrumental Arguments for Informal Rules of the Game

In the preceding chapter (the legal technical analysis) we indicated that the formal procedure for the development of an RUP is in a rather tight straitjacket and is not very ambitious with respect to participation. In the preliminary draft stage participation is restricted by decree to official and political consultation. Public consultation is only later in the policy process.

The planning process for the PRUP for Beaches and Dikes is an exception to that. The authors of the PRUP chose to 'reinforce' the procedure provided by decree with informal rules of the game by adding a phase of informal preliminary consultation. In November 2002 a consultation took place on the basis of a first proposal of a preliminary draft involving the 10 local councils as well as the user groups involved (hotel and catering industry, bathing cabin proprietors, sports clubs, beach life guards, nature conservation associations and fishermen). This was done through a combination of information meetings, bilateral consultation, open days where civil servants provided information to individual citizens and finally a hearing. In this phased consultation the choice was made to work per region (west coast, central coast, east coast and Knokke) and to consult the sectors separately during a first phase. Between the first proposal of a preliminary draft and the second proposal, feedback was given to the Flemish agencies (AROHM, MD&K and ANB) and an opinion was also asked of 'Westtoer', the West Flemish provincial organisation for tourism and recreation. The second proposal was then informally presented for advice to the 10 local councils and the Flemish and provincial agencies involved in June 2003. On the basis of this whole process a preliminary draft was drawn up and this constitutes the first formal step in the procedure that is provided by decree (PPD 2005).

One might ask why the province attached such great importance to participation through informal preliminary consultation. An important explanation seems to lie in content-related and instrumental arguments. With regard to content it had been learnt from the development of the TERRA report that knowledge building is an important resource that generates power. The TERRA report was also drawn up in consultation with, and with the input of various stakeholders. One of the authors of the PRUP writes in this connection: *"The most important objective was on the one hand to inform, but on the other hand to include from the first stage elements that had been overlooked or underesti-*

mated" (Claessens 2004: 58). At the same time it was understood that the issue of constructions on beaches and dikes is a very complex question, involving an amalgam of often conflicting interests. From an instrumental point of view the provision of informal preliminary consultation can be seen as a means of defusing potential sources of conflict or in other words of creating support for the process ahead. A civil servant who was involved in the process put it as follows:

> *'They chose this approach, because they hoped to solve all problems before the legal procedure, or if this was not possible to know at least which problems there were, hoping they would find enough arguments to be able to refute them.'*

Also the stakeholders interviewed consider the instrumental perspective to be an important explanation. It is remarkable that various respondents in this context refer to experiences concerning the designation of Marine Protected Areas, in which policy was initially developed without any form of consultation (*see chapter 3*). Referring to this, a representative of a water sports association said:

> *'They had understood that it is no longer possible to do something in a corner.'*

A representative of the nature conservation sector agrees, but at the same time points to possible disadvantages of so much preliminary consultation:

> *'Consultation disarmed. There was a certain reassurance. But the disadvantage is that you actually already make concessions to most of them. There is no protest then, but part of your initial plans cannot be achieved any more.'*

Another explanation why the province attached so much importance to participation is probably to be found in the fact that this was the first PRUP that was drawn up in Flanders. The province could present itself as a 'new' player at policy level, both vis-à-vis higher and lower levels of government. The latter certainly should be interpreted in the context of subsidiarity and hierarchy, given that not everybody was convinced that the province was the most appropriate level of government for the development of policy with regard to beaches and dikes (*see before*).

> *'We still had to prove ourselves. There were no PRUPs yet. At the time of the RSV an RUP had been drawn up at Flemish level with regard to camp sites and this was then converted into a PRUP, but that was all. It was also an ideal topic to develop further at a supra-local level and it was perfect for cutting an image as a province.'*

In the interviews local politicians pointed out that they observed a (re)positioning. Two mayors of coastal municipalities talk in this respect of a shift in the province's approach from a rather patronizing (*'paternalistic'*) authority to a supportive authority:

THE PROVINCIAL SPATIAL IMPLEMENTATION PLAN (PRUP) FOR BEACHES AND DIKES.

AN ANALYSIS OF THE DECISION MAKING PROCESS

'I have been mayor for some time now, but never before have I seen such an intensive enquiry.'

'That the province has taken a different approach and is now confirmed in that. When I became mayor the province was a wicked stepmother. The lady everybody was afraid of. Now we already call the province to ask questions.'

3.2. Present and Absent Actors

The authors of the PRUP aimed at a maximum involvement of actors in the informal preliminary consultation:

'We have involved everybody that we could involve, and indeed they all came and we also consulted with the administration.'

Still the participation at this informal preliminary consultation was characterized by who was present and who was absent. The most prominent parties that were present seem to be the local councils and some, particularly commercial user groups. Nature conservation associations, the association of self-employed entrepreneurs (UNIZO) and the beach fishermen seem to be the most important absentees (*see internal reports*). The conspicuous absence of nature conservation associations and UNIZO at this stage of the process can probably be explained in part by the fact that both organisations were assigned a role in the procedure provided by decree through the PROCORO (*see below*), so that they focused their attention on the formal procedure. Moreover respondents see various other explanations for the relative absence of nature conservation associations. People interviewed state for example mistakenly that nature conservation associations were not invited, whereas other respondents explain their absence by the fact that these associations are not *'real users'*:

'NGOs? No. They are not real users.'

The nature conservation movement itself also explains its relative absence from the informal preliminary consultation by the low expectations of nature conservationists at the beginning of this process.

'Maybe it was despondency. We already knew that those PRUPs were a losing game! Now we know that it is possible to have an impact.'

On the other hand the scope of the dossier and its very technical nature are considered to partly explain the low level of enthusiasm of nature conservation associations.

'No, it was also a technical dossier and it dealt with current issues, it was not about possible damage to what was new.'

There are differing opinions as to the question whether the 'ordinary citizen' should have been involved, although the problem of the very technical nature of the dossier and a lack of involvement can be given as counter-arguments.

'They could have approached it in a broader way, the non-organised part of population was not included. The group was very one-sided, they all had their own interests, but ordinary people have a broader view. But that is very difficult to organise.'

Finally it should be noted that the provincial administrative departments (the authors) in this stage of official consultation mainly focused on lower level authorities. The preliminary consultation for example provided a role for the provincial organisation 'Westtoer' but not for 'Toerisme Vlaanderen' (the Flemish Region Tourist Office). Vis-à-vis the Flemish agencies, and in particular the competent Agency of Nature and Forests (ANB), a civil servant stated that there was

'...rather the attitude of 'we will keep them informed'.'

This was explained by saying that a more active involvement of this specialised agency at this stage would have complicated the process too much. Among many users of the coast the agency concerned had indeed a rather negative, severe image on the basis of its action in former dossiers.

The presence and absence of actors was obviously determined by strategic considerations on both sides – participants and the authors.

3.3 Different Perceptions of Power and Influence

From the enquiry it appears that various respondents appreciated the way of working with the informal preliminary consultation. People from local authorities (civil servants and politicians) even indicated that this informal preliminary consultation was maybe even more important than the later consultation in the formal PRUP procedure. Through this informal consultation municipalities could refer to current or planned projects. Moreover they could provide arguments for maintaining existing constructions before decisions were taken.

'For the municipalities those moments of consultation were very important! In that way it was possible to complete projects that were running or that were about to start.'
'We had a number of bathing cabins here and it was not desirable to reduce that number. So in this respect that consultation was important to indicate the needs of the municipalities.'

Various respondents from state (politicians and civil servants), civil society and market think that local councils and commercial users had some consider-

THE PROVINCIAL SPATIAL IMPLEMENTATION PLAN (PRUP) FOR BEACHES AND DIKES.

AN ANALYSIS OF THE DECISION MAKING PROCESS

able power and influence at this stage, in contrast to the 'absent' nature conservation associations.

> 'They (the nature conservation associations, editor's note) stand up for the public interest. They have attributed much less importance to the decision-making process than commercial users and local councils.'

The nature sector (civil servants and civil society) signals that precisely from a perspective of power and influence there are a number of drawbacks to investing in informal consultation at such an early stage in the policy process.

> 'The study phase went by in an objective and correct way (TERRA, editor's note). But then there was so much consultation of mainly local councils that the participation and the influence of those councils became too large. This resulted in the continuation of the existing use of the space and in some cases even an increased use of the available space.'

The perception of power and influence is not shared by all respondents and seems to be largely based upon their private expectations on the one hand and the experiences they had on the other. Thus a bathing cabin proprietor says that there was *'little consideration for'* what was discussed, whereas the mayor of the neighbouring seaside resort says: *'and the bathing cabin proprietors have also had the opportunity to speak their minds. Their concerns were even taken into consideration.'*

From the assessment of the informal preliminary consultation it also appears that the sharing of information in two directions is important. Overall people thought that a lot of information was provided by the authors of the PRUP and that they also had the opportunity to provide information to the authors. This did not only concern factual information on constructions, but also feedback on the intended policy. According to the authors of the PRUP in certain cases this finally also led to adjustments:

> 'I also remember the first meetings where my department had compiled a list of everything it wanted to settle. Of course they were not thanked for that by the mayors. We actually went too far. We wanted to sort everything out and in this we went too far. Which was not so bad actually. Because afterwards we came back after consultation to where we are now and everybody is satisfied with that. If we had not started so ambitiously, it might have been different.'

3.4 Discourses. Between Opportunity and Threat

Thus far (*paragraph 2*) we have explained that although everybody wanted a policy framework and more legal certainty, not everybody had the same motives. Not all actors had the same relationship to the process that had been started. During the in-depth interviews we tried to find out to what degree the respondents experienced the PRUP as an opportunity or as a threat.

The authors of the PRUP and the politician responsible for it, clearly saw it as an opportunity. The drafting of a PRUP was pioneering work and allowed the mainly young public servants and the province to make a name for themselves in terms of administration. At the same time it put things in perspective to meet with 'all' actors from the coastal region for the first time.

Nevertheless not all actors considered the PRUP as an opportunity. Although local councils had asked for 'clarity' themselves, various mayors, aldermen and local officials say that the PRUP was initially also perceived as a threat to their own autonomy. A local public servant for example explains that in the beginning he experienced the PRUP as:

'Just another thing coming from above ...'

It was also feared that this new instrument would make everything more complicated.

'Then we were afraid that instead of simplifying things it would make them more difficult'.

Among the 'users' there is an important distinction between the nature conservation associations and the commercial users. The commercial users saw the PRUP as an opportunity to regularise existing constructions, but still they feared that they might not succeed and that certain constructions would have to disappear.

'I remember I was invited together with everybody who was involved in the beach in one way or another. Initially I was glad that we were involved, because this is not always the case. During that meeting they also told us that they intended to map and to regularise everything, well not word for word.(...). So I was happy about that as it was a sign of recognition. I had been there for 15 years and I had a permit from the local council to run a surf club there.'

The nature conservation associations at first saw it as an opportunity to get the multitude of constructions at the coast sorted out. However, this took on the nature of a threat as soon as the first plans were drawn. Whereas many commercial users hoped to get regularisation, this regularisation actually constituted the major fear of nature conservation associations. For them regularisation meant in certain cases a continuation of spatial disorder at the expense of open space and natural values.

3.5 Provisional Outcome. Content and Process

The elaborate informal preliminary consultation produced important insights with regard to content and process. In *'Some Conclusions by the Author'* one of the authors of the PRUP formulates findings that are connected with both aspects (Claessens 2004). On the basis of those conclusions and from the re-

THE PROVINCIAL SPATIAL IMPLEMENTATION PLAN (PRUP) FOR BEACHES AND DIKES.

AN ANALYSIS OF THE DECISION MAKING PROCESS

ports of the various initiatives during the preliminary consultation, we can conclude that during the preliminary consultation two clearly distinct tensions became clear: one tension of tourism and recreation versus nature *and* a tension of global approach (interests) versus an individual approach (interests). The first has mainly to do with content and the second with the management of the process, but both cannot be completely separated from each other.

The municipal councils involved are mainly interested in tourist recreational aspects and to a (far) lesser degree in natural values, which are considered to be 'makeable' things because of their dynamic character. Apparently these latter interests were nearly exclusively defended during the preliminary consultation by the competent Flemish agency for nature (ANB), which according to the author *"predominantly adopted a very rigid attitude and was only prepared to make minor concessions to the tourist and recreational needs"* (Claessens 2004: 59).

A remarkable phenomenon at this phase was the very neutral attitude of the competent Flemish agency for the coast (MD&K) which initially commissioned the TERRA project, with which the whole process was started. A representative of the agency explains this as follows:

> *'Our objective was that the process would be successful. But we did not have demands ourselves. For us any outcome was fine, as long as a consensus was found.'*

Still the author of the PRUP observes that MD&K adopted *"a rather suspicious attitude vis-à-vis spatial planning and also vis-à-vis provincial authorities with autonomous jurisdiction and powers."* (Claessens 2004: 59)

As far as the process is concerned, it became clear during the informal preliminary consultation that the vast majority of actors involved advocated that individual, private dossiers should be dealt with and not a comprehensive approach. This is of course not completely surprising for users who participate out of self-interest, and often commercial interest. But it is remarkable that those users are often supported in this by their local authorities, who are not successful in advocating a more global vision and/or approach either. It is slightly surprising that the same phenomenon is observed among the majority of provincial politicians (members of the Provincial Council), who just as much look at supra-local plans from a very local perspective. Claessens (2004) thinks that the main explanation for this lies in the 'double mandates', since some members of the Provincial Council also carry out a mandate at local level. Other respondents refer to the importance of lobbying as another possible explanation, in which users argue their dossier with friendly politicians.

4. The Formal Process

4.1 ICZM and Shifts in Discourse

Under the definition of the objectives (*see paragraph 2*) we described that two important objectives could be distinguished for drawing up the PRUP: creation of legal certainty on the one hand and creation of a comprehensive policy framework for beaches and dikes along the whole Belgian coast on the other hand. Although it was not described in this way, the need for a comprehensive policy framework can be considered as a need for integrated coastal zone management (ICZM). The Flemish authority (AROHM 1998), followed in this by the provincial authority (PPD 2002) and spatial planners, wanted an integrated approach for the whole Belgian coast, across the boundaries of 10 coastal municipalities and across the various sector boundaries (housing, recreation and tourism, nature ...).

Initially this also resulted in the idea of developing one comprehensive plan, one PRUP for the Belgian coast. In the end we can see that already during the informal preliminary consultation the idea of one PRUP was abandoned and that the choice was made of drawing up 10 sub-PRUPs. From the survey of respondents we think that we can distinguish two possible explanations for this shift in discourse: a strategic and a content-related explanation. Representatives from state (politicians and civil servants), civil society as well as market refer to strategic arguments. A politician responsible says the following:

> 'So in the beginning we wanted to put the whole coast in a PRUP. But pretty soon this appeared not to be possible. Then we opted to make one RUP per municipality. Because, if people would want to go to the Council of State ('Raad van State' – RvS), then only one has to be amended and not all of them. For, if a change has to be introduced in Knokke, the other municipalities do not have to be involved and do not have to organise a public inquiry either.'

The division into 10 sub-plans provided the strategic advantage that if there were problems, the formal procedure did not have to be gone through again for the whole coast but only for those sub-plans with which there were problems. After all it was feared that the whole process would get stuck or would have to be repeated on the basis of a number of contentious dossiers. It is noteworthy that respondents in this context nearly exclusively referred to one coastal municipality (Knokke).

With regard to content it was argued that in this way it was more possible to reflect the individual characters of the 10 different coastal municipalities, although the same principles were applied to the various municipalities.

> 'The approach was fine too. They first dealt with the coast as a whole to determine principles, which they then applied to the individual municipalities.'

THE PROVINCIAL SPATIAL IMPLEMENTATION PLAN (PRUP) FOR BEACHES AND DIKES.

AN ANALYSIS OF THE DECISION MAKING PROCESS

Not everybody subscribed to this analysis. Representatives from the PRO-CORO and the nature conservation movement deplored these 'salami tactics', although they also admit that it was perhaps the only practicable solution. The division was at the expense of the initial objective of spatial coherence and is explained by the fact that – in spite of subsidiarity – the municipalities in this way wanted to safeguard their autonomy to a maximum extent. A case in point is that none of the local councils interviewed indicates that this division was at the expense of quality.

A second important shift in discourse that took place was the introduction of so-called blank areas. Whereas the initial intention was to use a cross-sectoral approach, we observe that during the process it was decided to keep nature out of the process to a considerable extent. In practice this meant that the PRUP became a basically tourist recreational PRUP, in which no or hardly any decisions were made about areas of natural interest (except for the so-called solitary beach zones). In other words, the Belgian coastline was not completely designated from De Panne to Knokke, but now showed a number of blank areas. One of the authors says about this:

'Now we have a tourist PRUP that pays attention to nature.'

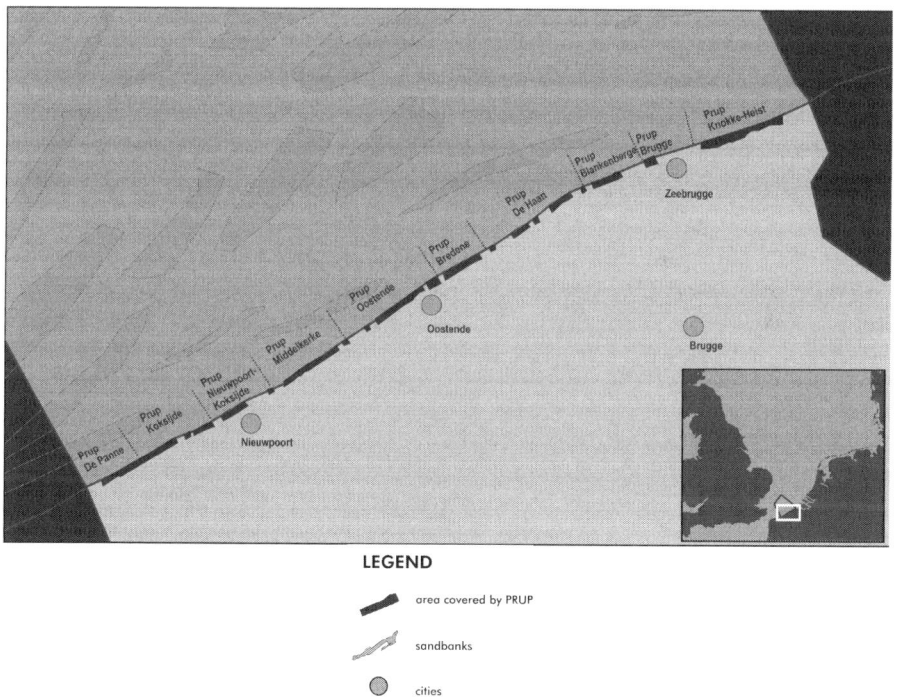

LEGEND

area covered by PRUP

sandbanks

cities

Figure 5: Belgian coastline with blank areas

155

It is difficult to find out precisely where, when and by whom it was decided to keep the natural areas out of the process. Both from the analysis of the documentation and from the interviews, this appears to be mainly a consequence of official consultation. From both, it also appears that content-related as well as strategic arguments were used and that the assessment of arguments was often sensitive. The latter is among other things illustrated by the fact that the following passage was deleted from the draft minutes of a consultation meeting with the Flemish agencies and 'Westtoer': *"The provincial planning department proposes that the parts of the beaches that will be included in the VEN (Flemish Ecological Network) will not be part of the PRUP, but to leave the layout to the Flemish Community."* (Minutes 2003a). In the definitive minutes it says: *"The proposed preliminary draft does not pronounce upon the 'green areas' (white in the plan). These overlap partly with the designation of the VEN (1st phase) and fall under the jurisdiction of the Flemish Region."* (Minutes 2003b). The subsidiarity principle is mentioned as the major argument for working with blank areas, considering 'nature' to be within the competence of the Flemish authorities. This is confirmed during the discussion by among others the civil servants of the Flemish agency for nature (ANB). In that sense it is striking that the PRUP does provide *"recreation-nature transition zones"* and particularly *"solitary beach zones"* that get the main function 'nature' with ancillary recreational use (PPD 2005: 25). The latter are designated in places where there is concentration of buildings or areas with accommodation provision behind the line of dunes, due to which a local pathway was created through the dunes to the beach. One of the authors of the PRUP says with regard to this:

> *'But we were stuck with those solitary beach zones in Flemish water. Actually we never thought that those would remain in the plan after approval.'*

The use of blank areas led to questions during this stage too, mainly from 'Westtoer', which still advocated one plan for the whole beach. 'Westtoer' also uses both content-related and strategic arguments for this. With regard to content 'Westtoer' thinks that one plan covering the whole area would create clarity for local authorities. Strategically speaking 'Westtoer' fears not being involved if the Flemish authorities designate the blank areas, so that tourist recreational access cannot be guaranteed.

The authors of the plan (the province) had strategic considerations as well. By leaving the nature zones out of the PRUP they largely got round the difficult discussion between tourism and recreation on the one hand and the nature sector on the other, thus hoping that the process would advance more rapidly and more efficiently. As far as the competent Flemish nature agency is concerned, it remembered the experience of the informal preliminary consultation, in which regularisation seemed to prevail over the development of a comprehensive spatial framework, mainly advocated by local authorities.

THE PROVINCIAL SPATIAL IMPLEMENTATION PLAN (PRUP) FOR BEACHES AND DIKES.

AN ANALYSIS OF THE DECISION MAKING PROCESS

'But on the other hand we somewhat feared that the influence of the local level would erode the urban development regulations of the green areas that had to be designated in such a way that it would not make any sense.'

An important argument for ANB was also that at the same moment the designation of the natural structure had been put on the rails in Flanders, by which the blank areas could get filled in. However, this designation was seriously delayed because of tensions with regard to the agricultural structure, so that the planning process of the Flemish authorities did not mesh any longer with that of the PRUP.

It should be noted that the discussions about drawing up one PRUP or 10 sub-PRUPs and providing for blank areas or not were largely carried out under the heading of subsidiarity. In principle it should always be checked which level of government is most appropriate to develop a policy, but the PRUP process showed that apart from legal considerations there are also pragmatic and in particular strategic considerations that play a role in this respect. For the choice between one PRUP or 10 sub-PRUPs this concerned mainly the relationship between the local authorities and the province, in the case of the blank areas this had to do with the relationship between the province and the Flemish authorities.

4.2 The Formal Procedure and the Impact of the Informal Rules of the Game

The formal procedure of an PRUP prescribes that the preliminary draft PRUP should be the object of political and official consultation through one or more plenary meetings (*see previous chapter*). Given the fact that during the preparatory study stage the option was taken to develop one PRUP per coastal municipality, it was also decided to organise 10 plenary meetings in November 2003. These plenary meetings were extremely poorly attended, and even some Flemish agencies were systematically absent ('Toerisme Vlaanderen', 'De Lijn' (Flemish Public Transport Company), ANB) or only participated in a limited number of cases ('Agentschap Ruimtelijke Ordening en Onroerend Erfgoed Vlaanderen' – Flemish Agency for Spatial Planning and Heritage Properties). This can be partly explained by the fact that it was possible to formulate written opinions. On the other hand so much had been invested in the informal preliminary consultations that various respondents considered the plenary meetings rather as obligatory, as the authors initially had intended.

'Because we intended to organise the informal procedure in such a way that the official procedure could be considered as a formality.'

One of the consequences was that respondents minimised the impact of those meetings, as a chairman of a Municipal Advisory Council for Spatial Planning (GECORO) indicated:

> *'Well yes, we had all those plenary meetings and so on, but the decisions have been taken beforehand, you see.'*

Other respondents also referred to the relationship between the informal and the formal procedure. Nearly all respondents point out in this respect that the informal procedure had a larger impact on the entire process. A mayor of a coastal municipality put it as follows:

> *'The formal side was also fed by the informal. If you say to a member of the Provincial Executive: you are making life impossible for our bathing cabin proprietors, this actually has an impact. He will then see what he can do informally.'*

From this quotation it appears that when some respondents are talking about the informal procedure, they do not only refer to the informal preliminary consultation but also to informal contacts and lobbying. This concerned contacts with the civil servants responsible but also with friendly politicians or politicians who were involved in the matter. In the course of the process most actors had gained more confidence in the civil servants of the province, whereas in the beginning they were afraid that there would be interference from above (the province). Representatives from state (politicians and civil servants), civil society and market describe the provincial civil servants as competent, interested and enthusiastic. Three characteristics from which they seem to draw their authority. The solid official preparation and supervision of the process may also explain why hardly anybody refers to the role of the PROCORO, a public consultation body that nevertheless played an official role by providing advice and later by dealing with the objections (*see below*).

The formal procedure also resulted in a shift in the actors. Thus we see that 'Toerisme Vlaanderen', an agency of the Flemish Community, and the Flemish Agency for Spatial Planning and Heritage Properties (Agentschap Ruimtelijke Ordening en Onroerend Erfgoed Vlaanderen) played a role in the policy process by means of consultancy or through the plenary meetings. Thanks to the participation of the Flemish Agency for Spatial Planning and Heritage Properties the nature sector was no longer standing alone in defence of collective interests such as nature and landscape. Thanks to 'Toerisme Vlaanderen' a second government partner intervened to defend the tourist recreational interests. It is remarkable that 'Toerisme Vlaanderen' emphasized different things in defending those interests than the West Flemish provincial enterprise for tourism and recreation 'Westtoer'. In the thorny dossier of 'Surfers Paradise' (*see text box*) for example, 'Toerisme Vlaanderen' pointed out that it did not dispose of an urban development permit and that the infrastructure was rather inaccessible, so that it was proposed that another location should be sought (Advice Toerisme Vlaanderen 2003). With regard to the same dossier 'Westtoer' defended the regularisation of 'Surfers Paradise' during the informal preliminary consultation.

THE PROVINCIAL SPATIAL IMPLEMENTATION PLAN (PRUP) FOR BEACHES AND DIKES.

AN ANALYSIS OF THE DECISION MAKING PROCESS

On the basis of the plenary meetings and the opinions provided the draft plans were partly amended and subsequently provisionally adopted by the Provincial Council (24 July 2004). These draft plans were the subject of the public inquiry that took place from 19 July 2004 to 16 September 2004.

4.3 Public Inquiry

4.3.1 All Actors in the Game?

A next step in the formal procedure of drawing up the PRUP is the organisation of a 60 days public inquiry, during which in principle all actors (also individual citizens) can lodge an objection. In the previous chapter we explained that, in accordance with the procedure provided by decree, the public inquiry is essential to the bringing about of modifications. Various respondents question the importance of the public inquiry, among other things because of the lack of interest among ordinary people. A local civil servant, who was involved in the organisation of the public inquiry, says the following on the subject:

'There were not many people present. No, and if they were there, it was mainly the organised elements of the population. You do not reach ordinary people by saying: here it is. Still it brought up important issues, for example for the hotel and catering sector.'

A colleague from another seaside resort adds:

'...people only react when they see a plan, and even then it is always about NIMBY (Not in my backyard). If it gets too abstract then there is no reaction.'

According to well-informed experts it is very difficult to reach the individual citizen by means of a public inquiry because of a lack of involvement due to, among other things, the level of abstraction, as well as the often over-technical and over-complex nature of the subject. Moreover, the multitude of procedures and public inquiries result in the fact that people can no longer see the wood for the trees. Also the moment of the public inquiry may be decisive in determining if individual citizens will attend or not, although this is put in perspective by a local civil servant:

'It has already happened that we have held a public inquiry in summer, and then they cannot attend because they are working. But there's always something the matter, in winter they are closed and in summer they are working.'

An objection to the public inquiry as an instrument for participation in PRUP procedures also seems to be the moment at which it enters the policy process. A representative of the PROCORO, competent for examining the objections, put it as follows:

'It comes too late in the process. Juul is right and Bertha is right, but we will not start everything over again now. So Juul and Bertha are not right ...'

For the public inquiry procedure relating to the PRUP for Beaches and Dikes 207 objections were eventually lodged. As indicated above, the public inquiry did not lead to 'massive' involvement of individual citizens. In all they account for somewhat more than half of the objections, a major part of which dealt with the disappearance of private bathing cabins. Moreover there is a remarkably unequal distribution between the coastal municipalities. Once again Knokke appeared to be the seaside resort with the highest number of objections (more than half of the total number!).

It is also striking that civil society played a relatively modest role during the public inquiry. Only 'Natuurpunt' (10), UNIZO (3), the surf clubs (2), a yachting federation (1), an association of bathing cabin proprietors (1) and traders associations (2) lodged objections. It is remarkable that mainly 'Natuurpunt' showed itself actively during the public inquiry. It is the only association that lodged objections to the 10 draft PRUPs. This is particularly conspicuous because the association had taken a rather low profile during the preliminary process. With regard to discourse this meant that nature interests were no longer only defended by the Flemish agencies alone (ANB, followed by M&L), but also by civil society.

'Yes, that was AMINAL (i.e. ANB) that during the public inquiry got the support of 'Natuurpunt'. That was striking, because before they did not say anything. They were present, but less visible.'

During the PRUP process few respondents referred to the existence of supporting or challenging coalitions. Most respondents do consider the local authorities as those who support and defend the interests of the users. In Koksijde this resulted among other things in an identical objection by the local council and by the GECORO. Also the bathing cabin proprietors, who usually acted in an uncoordinated way, used standard objections in *one* municipality (Knokke). During the public inquiry there was also – to a certain degree – a discourse coalition between the Flemish agency for nature (ANB) and the nature conservation associations.

Only the problem dossiers seem to have led to mobilisation. Thus a petition with 30,000 signatures was handed in during the public inquiry to support 'Surfers Paradise' (*see text box*). This dossier resulted in this period also in political tug-of-war between the various levels of government (municipality, province and Flemish Region).

' 'Surfers Paradise' will be best remembered. There was even a lot of discussion about it at a high political level. (...) There were even demonstrations in the Provincial Council. It really became a symbolic dossier.'

THE PROVINCIAL SPATIAL IMPLEMENTATION PLAN (PRUP) FOR BEACHES AND DIKES.

AN ANALYSIS OF THE DECISION MAKING PROCESS

4.3.2 Europe and the Appropriate Assessments

The content of the objections can be divided into general objections and PRUP specific objections. The objections from local councils, users and individual citizens fall nearly completely under the second category, and usually only concern matters of self-interest. Local authorities restricted themselves virtually exclusively to the area of their municipality and moreover asked for attention to constitutional principles like legal certainty. Appealing to the subsidiarity principle, they tried to strengthen the specific local situation (Minutes 2002).

The general objections were related to a considerable extent to the rapport with nature in general and overlaps with protection of areas in particular. This concerned areas that the Flemish authorities had already designated as areas with main function 'nature' in the framework of the Flemish Ecological Network (VEN), or areas that were designated as Special Protection Areas (SPA) (*see chapter 2*). With regard to these SPAs, ANB noticed during the public inquiry that, in accordance with the European regulations, appropriate assessments had to be developed and presented for advice. ANB was followed in this by the regional agency for spatial planning and by 'Natuurpunt' (composite objections). According to a respondent from ANB the province had been too casual about this and considered it as a *'simple formality'*. Since this only became clear during the public inquiry and hence after the provisional adoption of the provincial RUP, the province had a problem. A number of zones (*transition zones, solitary beach zones* and even a part of the central zone) could no longer be justified (see objections).

It should be noted that the argument of appropriate assessment, or at least the seriousness of it, appears only so late in the process.

> *'Suddenly, during the public inquiry this appeared to be a fundamental problem. It appeared from this that we could not justify a number of things. But at that moment it was of course too late to have a one year study carried out. (...) It was also the first time that we had done this and we did not know very well what to do. In the end the Minister told us, after the PRUP had already been discussed in the Provincial Council and after AMINAL (ANB) had given its opinion, that we should check that appropriate assessment with AMINAL (ANB). So then we could not start over again and then he judged whether our appropriate assessment was correct or not.'*

The authors of the PRUP explain the lack of appropriate assessments on the one hand by the lack of experience, but on the other hand also by the lack of concrete guidelines for drawing these up.

> *'It was also AMINAL (ANB) that asked for that, but when we then asked what they wanted, they didn't know either. Therefore we never took it seriously.'*

In any case it is clear that the lack of or the inadequacy of the appropriate assessments led to tensions during the public inquiry between the province on the one hand and the competent Flemish agency on the other. Still, everything seems to indicate that out of pragmatic considerations (given the well-advanced stage of the procedure) they certainly wanted the PRUP process to continue and did not want to burden it with additional studies or surveys for making more detailed appropriate assessments (*see below*).

After examination by the PROCORO an opinion was submitted to the Provincial Executive of the Province of West Flanders, after which the PRUP for Beaches and Dikes was definitively adopted by the Provincial Council of West Flanders on 12 May 2005. Finally the definitively adopted PRUP was submitted for approval to the Flemish Government, together with the decision of the Provincial Council and the opinion of the PROCORO.

4.4 Definitive Approval and Shifting Balances of Power

As described in the previous chapter the Flemish Government is competent in the supervision of the approval process for the provincial spatial implementation plans. Although the Flemish Government has a broad scope of discretion, it can in principle not make amendments to the decision that is submitted for approval. If the lower authority (the province) is not prepared to make amendments, the Flemish authority can partially approve the plan and for example delete certain passages. The latter is only possible if this neither affects the coherence of the plan, nor the content that is required by decree. On 19 September 2005 the PRUP for Beaches and Dikes was definitively adopted by the Flemish Minister who was competent for spatial planning. However, six PRUPs were only partially approved: Middelkerke, Ostend, Bredene, Blankenberge, Bruges and Knokke-Heist.

The underlying arguments the Minister referred to were the problems of compatibility with other planning initiatives (Ostend), problems with regard to legal certainty (Blankenberge) and problems of compatibility with legislation concerning nature conservation (Bredene, Bruges and Knokke-Heist). The Minister stated for example that it had not been sufficiently proven that in the case of the surf club 'Surf City', which is situated in a vulnerable area, there would not be any significant harmful effects to the nearby SPA. On the basis of those considerations the zone concerned was deleted from the plan, but the Minister suggested that the province could make a new appropriate assessment (*see text box*). In a reaction the province indicated:

> *"The Provincial Executive does not see how the province, without new legal or factual elements, could make a different 'appropriate assessment'."* (Communiqué 2005)

THE PROVINCIAL SPATIAL IMPLEMENTATION PLAN (PRUP) FOR BEACHES AND DIKES.

AN ANALYSIS OF THE DECISION MAKING PROCESS

The definitive approval strongly disturbed the balance of power between province and Flemish authorities. A press release of the Provincial Executive of the Province of West Flanders speaks volumes:

> *"For a number of those decisions (deletions, editor's note) the Provincial Executive can have an understanding, but for a number of other decisions the Provincial Executive has objections of a legal nature. More in particular the Provincial Executive thinks that the boundaries of administrative supervision have been exceeded."* (Communiqué 2005)

This press release also mentions *"transgression of jurisdiction"* and *"important legal uncertainty"*. The fact that the Provincial Executive distributed such a press release and sent a letter to the competent Minister, illustrates how sensitive the ministerial decision was. According to the Province of West Flanders the approval supervision was interpreted too broadly and was even exceeded. An illustration is the example of the municipality of Middelkerke where the competent Minister introduced the following amendments (deletions): "A ~~limited~~ *extension of the body of the dike in the immediate proximity of the casino, on the seaward side, is admissible".* The 'explanation/vision' contains the following deletions: "By '~~limited~~ *extension is e.g. meant a '~~balcony~~-construction' that increases contact between dike and sea. It can* ~~not at all~~ *be the intention to build a 'pier' in the sea perpendicular to the casino".* It is clear that by deleting the words 'not at all' the supervisory authority interprets the supervision of the approval process in a broad way, particularly after the long procedure of informal and formal (preliminary) consultation. Various respondents from state (civil servants as well as politicians), civil society and market say that in spite of all the consultation, there are apparently other 'forces' at play in the phase of the definitive approval. Concretely allusions are made here to the existence of political party networks.

> *'The province approves the PRUP and then Van Mechelen (the Minister, editor's note) rejects it. Mere politics.'*
> *'Yes, I know what it is, it is plain politics. We have to be honest about the [political] colour of the mayor ... The Minister was (mis)led and he also said that he probably had let himself be misled.'*
> *'The Minister is not very favourably disposed towards the province. I suppose there will have been informal contacts between some local councils (Koksijde, Blankenberge) and the office of the Minister.'*

When they are asked to give an explanation, some respondents point at the double mandate of a local politician (alderman, member of the Provincial Council *and* ministerial staff member) as a factor of power. The person referred to was at the time of the PRUP process not only alderman of a coastal municipality, but also member of the Provincial Council *and* staff member at the office of the Minister of Spatial Planning. One of the authors indicates that the person concerned played a double role, since his support was also indispensable for the success of the process:

'If he did not approve of it, he might very well have thrown a spanner in the works.'

This quotation clearly shows that the balance of power was not only shifting between the various levels of authority (province versus Flemish Region) but also in the relationship between civil servants and politicians. Whereas provincial civil servants according to many respondents were strongly influencing the decision making process due to their expertise and commitment (*see above*), we see that at the end of the process political decisions are taken. When the competent Minister was questioned about this shortly after the adoption in the parliamentary Commission for Spatial Planning, he answered as follows: *"I actually do not intend to become notary of spatial planning in Flanders. Either I am Minister of Spatial Planning and I can direct or I am a notary. But in that case the Director-General can sign the plans tomorrow and I am no longer interested."*[8]. From this answer it appeared that the problems of subsidiarity and hierarchy, either manifestly or not, prevailed during the whole PRUP procedure. Whereas in the beginning of the process there was mainly discussion between the province and the municipalities, with the municipal autonomy at stake, we see that at the end of the process there is mainly discussion between the province and the Flemish Region, with the municipalities as an argument. The explanation the Minister provided in the Commission on the occasion of the PRUP Middelkerke (*see above*) exemplifies this: *"The problem arising in this context amounts to the way in which we must apply the subsidiarity principle. The question arises whether it is up to the Provincial Executive or to me as Minister to decide whether the extension of a limited walking pier as desired by the local authority on that location is spatially acceptable or not. If you ask me, the answer to both questions is no."* Thus the Minister indicated that he wanted to give more autonomy to the local authorities.

At the end of the process the issue of subsidiarity and the shifting balance of power between the province and the Flemish Region resulted in a public conflict. A reminder of the Province of West Flanders and the commotion in the press had caused resentment with the competent Minister who pressed for consultation. A politician who was in a position of responsibility says about this:

'... first it was suddenly revealed in the press and then the Minister was angry because the man in the street could read it. Then we were sent for and we told each other how the matter stood (...). We had a discussion in private and then we said that no legal measures were necessary. (...) At the moment (2007) it is quiet.'

It is remarkable that this political deliberation came so late in the process and only after a conflict had occurred. Both the provincial politicians and the com-

---

8   Request for explanation by mister Carl Decaluwé, 13 October 2005 to minister Dirk Van Mechelen about the Provincial Spatial Implementation Plans for Beach and Dike Constructions., Fl. Parl., 2005-2006, C029-LEE05.

THE PROVINCIAL SPATIAL IMPLEMENTATION PLAN (PRUP) FOR BEACHES AND DIKES.

AN ANALYSIS OF THE DECISION MAKING PROCESS

petent Minister acknowledge that there has been little political consultation between the two levels of government. Both declare after the event that they experience this as a problem. After this political crisis there was no further political consultation regarding this dossier.

5. Conclusions

What Happened Before. Subsidiarity and the Province as a 'New' Player

The expansion of recreation and tourism on the Belgian coast in the 1990s caused further growth of temporary and permanent constructions on beaches and dikes. The lack of clear rules of the game and the policy of tolerance of the various authorities with regard to spatial planning resulted in a 'proliferation', which made it essential to adopt a clear policy framework. By means of the so-called TERRA report there was knowledge building (among other things inventory of problem areas) and moreover the initial impetus was given to providing assessment criteria and to linking zoning with regulations. By means of an interactive approach, paying a lot of attention to consultation and participation mainly of local authorities, provincial civil servants acquired legitimacy and authority. The knowledge building through the TERRA report can be considered as an important resource for the province.

Moreover the Province of West Flanders was also legitimised as a 'new' player in the area of spatial planning due to new Flemish rules such as the Planning Decree and the Decree on Spatial Planning. Those new rules led to a repositioning of actors, among other things as a consequence of the principles of subsidiarity and hierarchy. In this way there was a new instrument of structure planning, through which lower levels of government could also get fully involved in the development of plans. By means of the development of a Provincial Spatial Structure Plan the Province of West Flanders formalised the policy framework of the TERRA report. The binding section provided for the drawing up of a PRUP, and thus in the light of subsidiarity the province put itself clearly on the map as initiator and driving force. This happened partly by order of the Flemish authorities and partly at the request of some local councils, who wanted solutions to unsolved problem areas. Beaches and dikes were not a priority for the Flemish Government – except for coastal protection. Of course the situation was different in the coastal municipalities, so that the issue of subsidiarity was more difficult there. The fear for losing administrative autonomy was outweighed as an argument by the possibility of achieving a more integrated approach beyond the boundaries of the coastal municipalities. According to the respondents the creation of a comprehensive policy framework and the creation of legal certainty constituted the double objective of the PRUP. The definition of the objectives concerned a lack of clear rules of the game, with regard to formality, authority as well as precision of prescription.

The Informal Preliminary Consultation. Participation, but then Mainly Intended for Local Actors?

The province decided to extend the formal procedure for drawing up an RUP with an informal phase of preliminary consultation mainly with local councils and users. One might wonder why the province attached so much importance to participation in the form of an informal preliminary consultation. An important explanation seems to lie in content-related and instrumental arguments. By means of consultation it was not only the intention to achieve knowledge building, but also to defuse potential sources of conflict and create support for the subsequent process. It is remarkable that the province mainly addressed itself to lower levels of government, rather than to the supervisory authority of the Flemish Region. This is explained by referring to negative experiences in the past, when policy processes got stuck after protest from local authorities and users because of a lack of participation (*see among other things chapter 3*). An additional explanation probably lies in the fact that, in this way, the Province wanted to safeguard its own autonomy vis-à-vis Flanders as far as possible.

A number of actors such as associations of trades people, nature conservation associations and individual citizens were almost absent during the phase of the informal preliminary consultation. The very technical nature, the lack of involvement (interest) and the perspective of the formal procedure were given as explanations for this absence. Later it appeared that waiting for the formal procedure had not been the best strategic choice, since the results of the informal preliminary consultation influenced the PRUP that was eventually approved. But the participants greatly appreciated the provision of consultation at such an early stage of the policy process, mainly because of the experience that in this way it was possible to influence the process itself and the (provisional) policy results. The perception of influence and power seems to be largely determined by the private expectations and experiences of the various actors. Thus respondents from the nature sector stated that the initial objectives of the PRUP were put under pressure by the extensive informal preliminary consultation. The influence of local officials and users resulted in a continuation (regularisation) and in some case even a reinforcement of use of space. The latter provides an illustration of the fact that, although everybody wanted a policy framework and more legal certainty, not everybody had the same motivation.

The extensive informal preliminary consultation finally resulted in important understandings concerning content and process. With regard to content the tension became clear between tourism and recreation on the one hand and nature on the other, in which the tourist recreational discourses were mainly argued by local councils and users, and the nature discourse was virtually exclusively argued by the competent Flemish agency ANB. With regard to the process it became clear that the vast majority of the actors involved advocated

THE PROVINCIAL SPATIAL IMPLEMENTATION PLAN (PRUP) FOR BEACHES AND DIKES.

AN ANALYSIS OF THE DECISION MAKING PROCESS

an individual treatment of dossiers and not a global approach, although this was one of the objectives of the PRUP.

The Formal Process. Shifting Discourses and Balances of Ppower?

Before the formal process got started the provincial authority decided not to aim any longer at one comprehensive plan for the whole of the Belgian coast, but rather at 10 sub-plans. This decision was both inspired by strategic and content-related arguments. As far as content was concerned it was hoped that in this way it would be possible to take into account the specific character of the municipalities. Strategically speaking there was the advantage that in case of any problems it would not be necessary to repeat the whole procedure, but only that relating to the sub-plan in which there were problems. Both arguments can be considered as an illustration of the way in which the province hoped to deal with the subsidiarity principle. On the one hand the province wanted to show sufficient respect for the autonomy of the municipalities, but on the other hand the province also wanted to build in sufficient certainty to safeguard its own autonomy.

The subsidiarity principle and the lack of clarity in this regard also played an important role in a second shift in discourse that took place. Initially it was the intention to use a cross-sectoral approach, but it could be observed that during the process it was decided to largely keep nature outside of the process. For this too, strategic and content-related arguments prevailed. Strategically speaking the authors could get round the often difficult discussion between tourism and recreation on the one hand and nature on the other hand by leaving out nature, so that the process would progress more quickly. With regard to content, nature basically falls under the jurisdiction of the Flemish Government. But due to the delay in designation of the natural structure by the Flemish authorities, large stretches of beach are still undesignated today. This illustrated that subsidiarity can be an obstacle to an integrated approach if planning processes are badly harmonized at various government levels. Moreover the PRUP process exemplified that the subsidiarity issue was playing a role until the end. In the choice between one PRUP or 10 sub-PRUPs what was mainly at stake was the relationship between the local authority and the province. In case of the introduction of the blank areas (leave out nature) it was about the relationship between the province and the Flemish Region.

The tension between the province and the Flemish authority became heated on the occasion of the definitive approval of the PRUP for Beaches and Dikes, when six of the 10 PRUPs were only partially approved. As underlying argumentation the competent Minister referred to problems of compatibility with other planning initiatives, with legislation on nature conservation and to problems concerning legal certainty. In practice this meant that no solution was provided for a number of tricky dossiers like the surf clubs, which were partially behind the search for a comprehensive policy framework (*see text box*).

The definitive approval disturbed the balance of power between the province and the Flemish authorities. According to the province the Flemish authority exceeded its supervisory jurisdiction by deleting words in some sub-PRUPs. According to the same Flemish authority the province did not meet the European requirements by attaching too little importance to appropriate assessments. Whereas at the beginning of the process there was mainly discussion on subsidiarity and hierarchy between the province and the municipalities, with the autonomy of the municipalities at stake we see that at the end of the process there is mainly discussion between the province and the Flemish Region, with the autonomy of the municipalities as an argument.

The result was that the PRUP did not realise the comprehensive approach that was hoped for.

What was the Role of Participation in the Whole Process?

For this last paragraph we go back to the central question of our survey: *'How did the policy process work out and what was the role of participation?'*. During the interviews the respondents were asked to describe the management style used by the province. The respondents could refer to more than one category of answers.

Management style 'The province …	Politicians N=4	Civil servants N=8	Civil Society N=5	Market N=1
Mainly facilitated other actors			●	
Searched for active forms of collaboration	● ●	● ●	●	
Delegated to other actors		●	●	
Allowed actors to participate in policy	● ●	● ● ●		
Consulted with the actors	● ●	● ● ● ● ●	● ● ●	
Informed the actors		● ● ●	● ●	●
Used a rather closed authoritarian style	●			●

Table 3: management style used according to respondents

In the answers of the respondents it is conspicuous that the majority does not only describe the management style as informative, but also as consultative and even collaborative (*table 3*). A minority describes the management style used as a rather closed authoritarian style. This concretely concerns one mayor of a coastal municipality and the manager of a surf club that was not regularised through the PRUP. Personal experiences and the impact of the PRUP on the individual's situation seem to be conclusive in the assessment of the management style, certainly in this ex-post evaluation. Also the predominantly positive assessment of the management style used can be explained from that perspective. The majority of respondents from state, civil society and market

THE PROVINCIAL SPATIAL IMPLEMENTATION PLAN (PRUP) FOR BEACHES AND DIKES.

AN ANALYSIS OF THE DECISION MAKING PROCESS

state that they are satisfied with the process, because the objections and expectations raised were taken into account. But representatives from the nature sector (authority and civil society) stated that they thought that due to the type of participation that was practised, the process evolved too far away from the initial objective towards the regularisation of private dossiers.

The type of participation that was practised also resulted in a shift of positions of actors. Two mayors of coastal municipalities talk about a shift of the province from a rather patronizing (*'paternalistic*) authority to a more supportive authority. Looking back at the participation in the context of the PRUP process it is clear that the institutionalised participation through the GECOROs and PROCORO only played a marginal role. Only two GECOROs (out of 10) submitted opinions/objections. The PROCORO did not manifest itself as an advisory council in which there was in-depth public consultation, but limited itself to the role prescribed by decree. To explain this, reference is made to the solid preparation and the extensive knowledge of dossiers of provincial civil servants, who took on all the work. The (relative) power of provincial civil servants can hardly be overestimated in this dossier. Neither can the impact of the informal preliminary consultation. Through this consultation it was possible to substantially anticipate the public inquiry that was provided for by decree. Various respondents did not see this public inquiry as an appropriate instrument for consultation, because of the moment at which it is officially required (too late), the subject of the public inquiry (too complex) and the difficulty of reaching the public to be consulted (antiquated communication and methods of making public announcements).

It should be noted that most respondents only know about the PRUP procedure until the moment of the public inquiry. They do not know about the adoption by the Provincial Council and the definitive ratification by the Minister. Respondents point out that they have never been informed about the eventual outcome of the process. The official procedure indeed does not provide for personal feedback to people who have lodged a complaint. Many respondents – including the authors – find it difficult to answer the question whether the objective has been achieved. Still the division into 10 sub-PRUPs and especially the use of blank areas is seen as a necessary evil, to allow the process to move forward. In addition, the fact that after the intensive PRUP procedure not all parts of the Belgian beaches are yet designated and that for some problematic dossiers no solution has been achieved, is thought to be problematic, mainly because of the continuing lack of legal certainty.

As a side effect reference is sometimes made to the pacifying effect of the PRUP process for local authorities and the majority of the (commercial) users. Thus the PRUP for Beaches and Dikes played an important role, after a number of earlier rather tumultuous dossiers relating to the Belgian coast (*see among others chapter 3*).

Surfing between Subsidiarity and Hierarchy

In the ex-post evaluation of the PRUP process we avoided going too deeply into concrete dossiers. This was not an easy exercise since the PRUP procedure was to a considerable extent dominated by concrete and usually private dossiers, in which individual interests often prevailed over collective interests (*see text*). By way of illustration this text box gives a brief description of two problematic dossiers that were of importance during the entire process, the surf clubs 'Surfers Paradise' (Knokke) and 'Surf City' (Zeebrugge). Both dossiers were subject to changing rules of the game, discourses, coalitions and balances of power.

Surf City

Surfers Paradise

THE PROVINCIAL SPATIAL IMPLEMENTATION PLAN (PRUP) FOR BEACHES AND DIKES.

AN ANALYSIS OF THE DECISION MAKING PROCESS

Some objective facts

The table below compares the situation of the surf clubs at the moment of the preparatory phase.

'Surf City'	'Surfers Paradise'
Fixed construction on the beach of Zeebrugge	Fixed construction on the beach of Knokke
Indicated in BPA 'Strandwijk' (MB 10/01/2000)	No BPA applicable
Nature area according to the Regional plan	No use indicated in the Regional plan
Located in a Special Protection Area of the Birds Directive (Poldercomplex)	Not located in a Special Protection Area
Not located in, but adjacent to a Special Area of Conservation of the Habitats Directive (Dune zones including IJzer estuary and Zwin BE2500001)	Not located in, nor adjacent to a Special Area of Conservation (Dune zones including IJzer estuary and Zwin BE2500001)
TERRA report: wrongly zoned (zone D, nature area) and not licensed	TERRA report: correctly zoned (zone B, transitional zone), but not licensed
Summons, ('Proces Verbaal' - PV) drawn up 3 May 2000	Summons (PV) drawn up 4 March 1998
Summons dismissed by the office of the Public Prosecutor on 23 November 2001	Demolition order 19 May 1998 introduced by the Public Prosecutor Demolition order on 11 January 2000 confirmed by the Public Prosecutor No writ of summons by the office of the Public Prosecutor

Table 4: comparison of the situation of 'Surf City' and 'Surfers Paradise' during the preparatory phase of the PRUP

The constructions of the surf clubs exemplify the policy of tolerance that various levels of government (local councils, MD&K, …) have practised for years on the Belgian coast, resulting in the 'proliferation' described above. Both clubs were established illegally. In both cases it concerned fixed constructions without a permit. Moreover 'Surf City' was located in an area that was protected in various ways – for the sake of nature conservation. Therefore the TERRA report considered the surf clubs as problematic constructions (TERRA, 2000), and they were verbalized (*see table 4*).

The Informal Procedure. Changing Rules of the Game and Changing Coalitions?

The preliminary draft that was used in the informal preliminary consultation took up the zoning as provided for in TERRA. 'Surf City' could 'at most be consolidated'. For 'Surfers Paradise' there was the proposal of a cluster of permanent constructions for (water) sports clubs. For 'Surf City' a question mark was put on the accompanying map. 'Surfers Paradise' was located in a so-called transition area between recreation and nature.

Two important changes took place between the first draft versions and the draft version that was used in the formal procedure. The transitional zone 'Zeebrugge westzijde' (Zeebrugge west side) was extended, so that 'Surf City' now was part of it. The initially proposed transition zone in Knokke was reduced, with the consequence that 'Surfers Paradise' would henceforth fall just outside the draft PRUP – and therefore in principle also outside the further procedure. The explanations for this are not unequivocal. But according to various respondents it seems that local political support has played a role in both dossiers.

The city of Bruges showed itself during the whole PRUP process to be an advocate of the interests of the only local surf club of the city (Zeebrugge is part of Bruges) 'Surf City'. Thus the city of Bruges tried to recognize the surf club in terms of planning by including 'Surf City' when drawing up the specific sub-municipal zoning plan 'BPA Strandwijk'. In consultation with and with the consent of MD&K, there were also investments made in infrastructure by a new layout of the sea dike, with special parking facilities near the surf club. Because according to the regional plan the club was located in a nature area the province initially opted not to include 'Surf City' in the PRUP process in order to leave decisions about the surf club to the Flemish authority – in conformity with the subsidiarity and hierarchy of the plans. After pressure from local politicians – including a member of the Provincial Executive – the city of Bruges and the surf club itself, it was decided to include 'Surf City' anyway.

During the whole procedure Knokke appeared to be a more volatile stakeholder. Initially the local council tolerated the construction of the surf club 'Surfers Paradise', and the mayor even expressed his support on the occasion of the opening of the club. Yet the development of a specific sub-municipal zoning plan 'BPA Finis Terrae' (MB 20.09.2002) also had consequences for 'Surfers Paradise'. With this BPA the municipality wanted to clean up a dilapidated swimming pool complex, on the edge of the Special Area of Conservation 'het Zwin'. The real estate company 'Compagnie Le Zoute S.A.', of which the mayor was at that time managing director, developed plans for building exclusive luxury apartments on a part of the former site. The build-

THE PROVINCIAL SPATIAL IMPLEMENTATION PLAN (PRUP) FOR BEACHES AND DIKES.

AN ANALYSIS OF THE DECISION MAKING PROCESS

ing permit for those plans was granted after a provision had been made for the extension of the nature conservation area 'het Zwin' in compensation. The extension of the nature conservation area implied that 'Surfers Paradise' would henceforth border on the northern part of the nature conservation area that also was designated as Special Area of Conservation under the Habitats Directive. According to the policy framework this implied that 'Surfers Paradise' was now both badly zoned and had no permit. A representative of 'Surfers Paradise' spoke in this respect of a political decision, considering the double role of the mayor, who was not averse to self-interest:

'In consultation with ANB the mayor had extended the line so that 'Surfers Paradise' was now at the wrong side of the line, a mere political decision'.

The arrival of luxury apartments did not only mean a restricted accessibility (reduction of parking space) of 'Surfers Paradise', but according to the manager it also created a new problem. For 'Surfers Paradise' caused visual nuisance for the new owners of the luxury apartments. The former coalition between 'Surfers Paradise' and the local authority was restricted here by a strategic coalition between ANB and the municipality of Knokke, in the person of the mayor. With regard to jurisdiction this implied that no longer the province but the Flemish authority (with advice of ANB) had to give a ruling on this tricky dossier.

The Formal Procedure. 'Surfers Paradise' as a Symbolic Dossier

Also during the formal procedure we see that both dossiers appear regularly. From the analysis of the policy process (documentation, interviews …) it appears that, although 'Surf City' was more badly zoned on the basis of objective data *(see table 4)* there was more resistance to 'Surfers Paradise'. Representatives of the nature sector (civil servants and civil society) explain this partly by the fact that 'Surfers Paradise' had become a symbolic dossier because of the attention of the media. The surf club became a symbol of the spatial mismanagement on the coast which the PRUP wanted to put a check on. Provincial politicians and civil servants believe that this even led to a different approach from the Flemish authorities that were giving advice. In the opinion on the PRUP for Beaches and Dikes Knokke-Heist, the Flemish agency for spatial planning states that 'Surfers Paradise' cannot be accepted. In the opinion for the PRUP for Beaches and Dikes Bruges, the same agency takes a less resolute position with regard to 'Surf-City': *"On the basis of the very limited data provided it is for the time being not possible to take a positive position with regard to 'Surf-City'"*.

The legal uncertainty and legal inequality were also important key elements in the discourse that 'Surfers Paradise' used for its defence and that clearly had a mobilising effect among individual sympathizers and some local politicians. The mobilising capacity was illustrated during the public inquiry, with 49 objections and a petition with 30,000 signatures as the high point. The manager of 'Surfers Paradise' also lobbied among national politicians from various political parties, however without the desired result: 'Surfers Paradise' remained outside the draft PRUP. During a session of the Provincial Council, before adoption of the PRUP, the dossier finally led to a demonstration *and* heated discussions, but once again without any success for the surf club. One of the authors of the PRUP confirmed that this dossier caused the most commotion.

> *'Surfers Paradise will be remembered best. There was even a lot of discussion about it at a high political level. It did not start like that, but that is how it ended. There were even demonstrations in the Provincial Council. It really became a symbolic dossier, if it had not been this before.'*

The PRUP that was eventually adopted by the Provincial Council included 'Surf City' with the proposal *"The construction is restricted to the current surface and the necessary measures should be taken to safeguard the dune zone that lies behind it"* (PRUP, 2005). 'Surfers Paradise' was not included in the PRUP and was located in a blank zone, about which the Flemish authority had to give a further ruling.

The Adoption of the PRUP. Surfing Between Subsidiarity and Hierarchy

The dossier of the surf clubs and that of 'Surfers Paradise' in particular, constitutes a painful illustration of the way in which subsidiarity and hierarchy in difficult dossiers can result in passing on powers and responsibilities from one level of government to another. Until the moment of ministerial ratification the surf clubs were a point of contention between the competent Minister and the provincial authorities. 'Surf City' was one of the cancellations carried out by the supervising authority (*see above*), because according to the Minister *"it was not possible to sufficiently prove that the vulnerable nature area in which it is located would not be significantly affected."* (Press release 2005). According to the Minister the appropriate assessment by the province in implementation of the Habitats Directive and the Nature Decree was not sufficient. However, the Minister held out the prospect of an approval if a more appropriate assessment were obtained. In concrete this implied that the province had to repeat this exercise, but it refused to do so with the explanation: *"The Provincial Executive does not see how the province, without cognisance of new legal or factual elements, would be able to make a different 'appropriate assessment'."*

For 'Surfers Paradise' the competent Minister asked the province for a solution. In its answer the province referred to the fact that it *"had initially planned to include Surfers Paradise in the provincial RUP, but on the basis of unanimous*

THE PROVINCIAL SPATIAL IMPLEMENTATION PLAN (PRUP) FOR BEACHES AND DIKES.

AN ANALYSIS OF THE DECISION MAKING PROCESS

opinions of all Flemish agencies it appeared that the province was exceeding its competences, because the surf club was located in European protected areas and (probably) in a nature conservation area." (Press release 2005). The consequence was that according to the province it had no jurisdiction over 'Surfers Paradise' and that this problem also ended up in the laps of the Minister and the Flemish authority.

After a procedure of more than four years both surf clubs were back in the same uncertainty with which the PRUP story began. In January 2008 the designation of the natural structure by the Flemish authority, under which the empty zones would be allotted a use, had not yet become a fact. The litigation over 'Surfers Paradise' had not yet been settled.

References

ADVICE TOERISME VLAANDEREN (2003). *Advies Toerisme Vlaanderen RUP's 'Strand en Dijk': Knokke-Heist.* Advies gegeven op 26 november 2003. Brussel: Toerisme Vlaanderen.

AROHM (1998). *Ruimtelijk Structuurplan Vlaanderen 1997, integrale versie.* Brussel: Administratie Ruimtelijke Ordening, Huisvesting en Monumenten en Landschappen.

CLAESSENS, S. (2004). *Het provinciaal ruimtelijk uitvoeringsplan als nieuw planningsinstrument: evaluatie case PRUP voor strand en dijk in West-Vlaanderen.* Antwerpen: Thesis Universiteit Antwerpen.

COMMUNIQUÉ (2005). *Bestendige deputatie reageert op beslissingen i.v.m. Ruimtelijke Uitvoeringsplannen strand en dijk.* Persbericht van 6 oktober 2005, 2005/DPC/PB/304. Brugge: persbericht van de Dienst Communicatie van de Provincie West-Vlaanderen.

MINUTES (1999). *Beknopt verslag van de vergadering van de kustburgemeesters.* Verslag van het overleg op 18 januari 1999. Brugge: interne nota van het kabinet van de gouverneur van West-Vlaanderen.

MINUTES (2002). *Overlegronde in het kader van de opmaak van het Provinciaal Ruimtelijk Uitvoeringsplan (RUP) Strand- en dijkconstructies, verslagen gemeentebesturen en gebruikers van De Panne, Koksijde en Nieuwpoort Middelkerke, Oostende, Bredene, De Haan, Blankenberge, Brugge en Knokke-Heist.* Brugge: interne nota van de Provinciale Planologische Dienst West-Vlaanderen.

MINUTES (2003a). *Overlegronde in het kader van de opmaak van het Provinciaal Ruimtelijk Uitvoeringsplan (RUP) Strand- en dijkconstructies, verslag overleg Vlaamse administraties en Westtoer.* Verslag van het overleg op 10 februari 2003. Brugge: interne nota van de Provinciale Planologische Dienst West-Vlaanderen.

MINUTES (2003b). *Overlegronde in het kader van de opmaak van het Provinciaal Ruimtelijk Uitvoeringsplan (RUP) Strand- en dijkconstructies, aangepast verslag overleg (1) Vlaamse administraties en Westtoer.* Verslag van het overleg op 10 februari 2003. Brugge: interne nota van de Provinciale Planologische Dienst West-Vlaanderen.

MIRONA (2000). *Planologische en juridisch kader voor het gebruik van de zeewering en in het bijzonder strand en dijk.* Brugge: Provincie West-Vlaanderen dienst Milieu, Ruimtelijke Ordening en Natuur.

PPD (2002). *Provinciaal Ruimtelijk Structuurplan West-Vlaanderen: Ruimte voor verscheidenheid.* Brugge: Provinciale Planologische Dienst West-Vlaanderen.

PPD (2005). *Provinciale ruimtelijke uitvoeringsplannen (RUP) STRAND EN DIJK.* Brugge: interne nota van de Provinciale Planologische Dienst West-Vlaanderen.

LETTER (1988). *Keten op het strand.* Brief van 28 juni 1988 aan het college van Burgemeester en schepenen van De Panne, Koksijde Nieuwpoort, Middelkerke, Oostende De Haan, Blankenberge, Knokke/Heist, Brugge en Bredene. Oostende: Brief van het Ministerie van openbare werken.

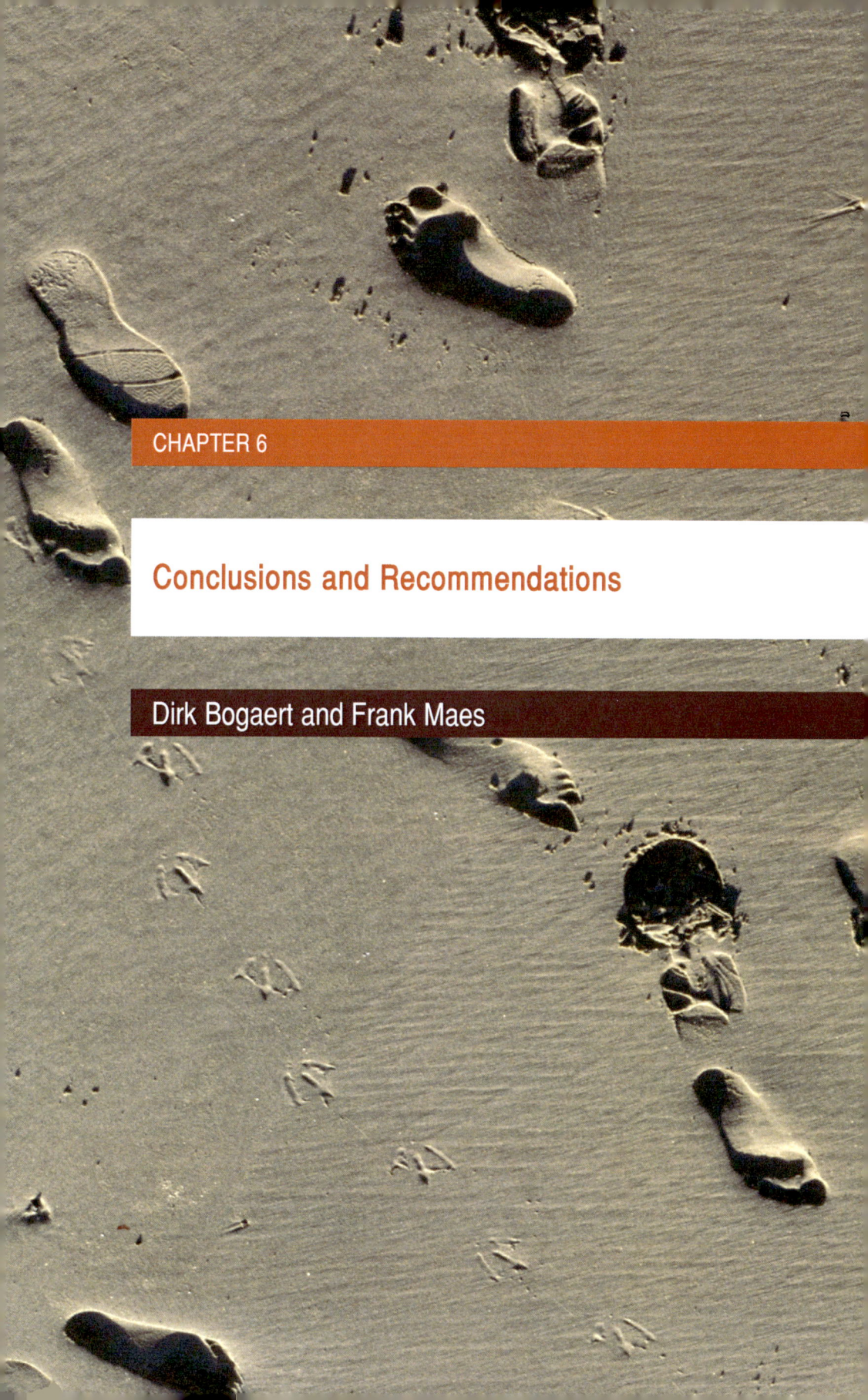

CHAPTER 6

Conclusions and Recommendations

Dirk Bogaert and Frank Maes

Who rules the coast? This book has tried to answer this multi-faceted question on the basis of two recent dossiers on the Belgian coast: the designation of the Marine Protected Areas (MPAs) and beach spatial planning by means of an Provincial Spatial Implementation Plan (PRUP). In both cases we have analysed the legal framework as well as the way in which policy processes worked out in practice, paying special attention to the role of participation. From the analyses it appears that the answer to the question *'Who rules the coast?'* can neither be reduced to one actor nor to one level of government. In both dossiers an amalgam of actor from state, civil society and market, whether or not in complex informal and/or formal relationships determines the outcome of policy processes with regard to the coast.

In both dossiers the policy makers or bodies responsible aimed at participation, albeit from completely different starting positions and with varying levels of ambition. But we can observe an important difference here. Whereas the designation of the MPAs was initially set up according to a classic top-down approach, the process of the PRUP for Beaches and Dikes decisively opted for various forms of participation from the very start of the policy process.

Based upon the observation of similarities and differences between both policy processes a number of lessons can be drawn with regard to participation:
- A classic top-down approach leads to policy processes getting bogged down;
- Bilateral consultation can depolarize policy processes, but is at the expense of transparency in those processes;
- Participation requires clarity in matters of competences;
- The paradox of extensive participation and collective interest;
- The need for a 'middle-ground' approach;
- The need for policy *after* participation.

A Classic Top-down Approach Leads to Policy Processes Getting Bogged Down

The initial MPA designation process in Belgium in 1999 is a classic example of a top-down approach. A central authority imposed policy decisions on local authorities and stakeholders without any form of consultation. It should not be surprising that this policy process got bogged down. Local authorities and stakeholders felt ignored and had the impression that their autonomy was compromised. The central authority was confronted with questions of legitimacy and a problem of lack of trust, which finally led to the policy process becoming deadlocked.

As an explanation for the inadequate attention to participation we have referred to capacity problems in the form of a lack of adequate means and experienced people within the federal authorities of that time. Moreover we also have considered strategic and content-related arguments. Strategically speaking it was the intention to complete the policy process quickly before the government's term of office was over. With regard to content the initial policy was almost exclusively based upon scientific knowledge and the federal authorities hardly based itself upon so-called layman's knowledge, or did not do so at all. On the basis of the ex-post evaluation we can draw conclusions about both arguments.

- Putting less effort into participation does not necessarily lead to saving time. The initial non-provision of information, let alone participation appeared not to result in saving time. The strategic argument 'time' could not be maintained since the opposition to the policy carried out resulted in delaying and finally discontinuing the process. The first Marine Protected Areas were established only six years after the Marine Environment Act (1999).
- Usually it is better not to pursue policy only based on scientific knowledge (*see below*). As a consequence of the nearly exclusive attention to scientific knowledge, local stakeholders (state, market and civil society) did not identify with the intended policy. The almost completely scientific discourse of the federal authorities did not correspond to the layman's knowledge of hands-on experts of the coastal region and considerably contributed to the protest against the intended policy. It is advisable to better align the policy discourse to that of the stakeholders.

In the PRUP dossier we see that the authority responsible rather chose a bottom-up approach and on top of the formal rules provided additional rules of the game with regard to participation. In contrast with the MPAs dossier it provided forms of participation with local authorities and users at an early stage (before the formal procedure). This investment seemed to pay off since it was possible to wind up the formal procedure within the planned timeframe. Still we should ask ourselves whether this process did not focus too much on the 'bottom' and too little on the 'top'. The authority responsible (the province) mainly concentrated on consultation with, and participation of local authorities and users and much less on the higher levels of government.

- In policy processes the 'bottom' is as important as the 'top'. Ignoring higher policy levels can have a negative influence on policy processes and the desired outcome, particularly if there are uncertainties about the distribution of competences and issues of subsidiarity. It is advisable to maintain optimal involvement of various levels of government in all phases of the policy process.

Bilateral Consultation Can Depolarize Policy Processes, but is at the Expense of the Transparency of those Processes

In the analysis of the MPA designation process we have described a shift towards more interactive forms of governance. The scientific literature refers to content-related, democratic and instrumental arguments for more interactive forms of governance. In the dossiers studied instrumental arguments seem to have prevailed. The major leitmotif seemed to be reducing the power to obstruct, restoring confidence and creating support.

Bilateral consultation appeared to play a crucial role in depolarizing the MPA designation process. In a first attempt at designation the policy was prepared top-down and subsequently this was (at best) communicated to the parties involved. On the occasion of a new designation initiative six years later the parties involved were contacted with a question for information, instead of with an announcement. The choice of bilateral consultation seems to have one important advantage, in particular in case of polarized dossiers. Through bilateral consultation actors more easily give up their often rigid positions and role patterns, which are inspired by all kinds of group dynamic processes. This is essential for restoring confidence and gathering information. From our ex-post evaluation it appears that the most important disadvantage seems to be the risk of loss of transparency in policy processes both with regard to the choice of participating actor as well as to content.

- Criteria are needed for the selection of actors. What matters in bilateral consultation is not only 'how' this participation is achieved, but in particular also 'who' is involved or – even more important – 'who' is 'not'. In the cases we have examined the selection criteria seem to be described in no more detail than 'people involved with the coast' from state, market and civil society. It is for example remarkable that for the MPA designation process in Belgium there was preliminary bilateral consultation with 'heavy economic' sectors (sand and gravel and wind turbines) about zoning and concessions for their economic activities. Once there was clarity on this issue the MPAs dossier was taken up again. The economic criteria played an important role, perhaps too important, in the selection of actors without their being made more explicit. Therefore, it is advisable to make the criteria used more explicit.
- Sometimes the dividing line between bilateral consultation and 'backroom politics' disappears. Bilateral consultation implies that the process is not transparent for people who are not involved. The dividing line between this kind of consultation and backroom politics without democratic control on the course of the process and the outcome of the process is often vague. It is advisable to communicate more openly with everyone whether involved or not.

Participation Requires Clarity on Competences

Both process evaluations have confronted us with a question that is important with regard to participation: *'who organises participation and about what?'*. A common characteristic of both dossiers is the multi-level dimension. A multitude of government levels from local through provincial, regional, federal, European to international seem to play a role in the dossiers under examination. Lack of clarity with regard to subsidiarity and hierarchy lead in both dossiers to jurisdictional issues (regional-federal, provincial-regional...), delay and in case of the PRUP to postponement of policy implementation.

The cases examined in this book show that issues of subsidiarity and hierarchy in sensitive dossiers can lead to the passing on of competences from one level of government to another, and from that perspective constitute an alibi for not carrying out policy.

- Participation requires clarity on competences before, during *and* after the policy process. The fact that decisions are not taken in sensitive dossiers does not only foster legal uncertainty for (some) participants, but also undermines their confidence in interactive forms of governance in particular and the functioning of 'authorities' in general. Participation requires clarity on competences before, during *and* after the policy process and this not only from the perspective of the participant but also from the perspective of the civil servants and politicians involved.

The Paradox of Collective Interest and Extensive Participation

Seas and landscapes are traditionally public goods that belong to everyone. In the evaluation of the policy processes we have observed that participants from civil society and market in both processes emphasize their individual interest. Only representatives of nature conservation associations and some authorities invoke 'the collective interest' as an argument in the participation procedures. However, among public authorities this strongly depends on the level of government. Comparatively local authorities seem to pay more attention to individual interests (of the municipality, of private persons ...) than higher level authorities. The PRUP dossier showed among other things that politicians who have double mandates (holding office at one or more levels: local, provincial and/or regional) can also result in individual interests prevailing over collective interests at higher levels of government. Both in the MPAs dossier and in the PRUP dossier, participation resulted in the adjusting of initial objectives and certain stakeholders talked about *'the erosion of the plan objectives'* at the expense of the collective interest. In the case of the PRUP this resulted in the introduction of 'blank (undesignated) areas', and in this way virtually no pronouncement was made on natural values (public goods). In case of the MPAs it resulted in the designation of 'paper reserves' in which hardly or no adequate management measures and effective protection are provided.

- Both dossiers confront us with a paradox of extensive and collective interest and also with questions such as '*who* can participate *in what* and in *which phases* of the policy process?'. Just as it is better not to make and carry out policy on the basis of scientific knowledge alone, neither should it be done exclusively on the basis of (a mixture of) economic, social and political interests. In other words there is a need for a kind of *'middle-ground' approach* (*see also* Jones 2002).

Need for a 'Middle-ground' Approach

A 'middle ground' approach combines top-down and bottom-up approaches in the management of a process. From the ex-post evaluations described in this book it appears that this requires a middle ground position with regard to 'knowledge' as well as to the rules of the game used. Policy should neither be based upon scientific knowledge alone, nor exclusively on formal legislation and regulations. In both cases, there is a need for a kind of 'middle-ground' approach, both with regard to discourse as well as to rules of the game.

- A 'middle-ground' approach concerning 'knowledge' does not presuppose a middle ground position between scientific opinion and so-called layman's know-how, but it does presuppose that scientific opinion will be supplemented by, or checked against layman's know-how. In this way actors are involved in the policy process at an early stage and there is more chance of successfully developing a shared discourse.

- Attention is needed to 'authority', 'formality' *and* 'precision of the prescription' in the rules of the game that are used. Starting up policy processes without clarity about possible consequences, results in (legal) uncertainty among actors, eroding confidence and trust and issues of legitimacy, which eventually bring policy processes to a standstill. Rather than exclusively aiming at formal legislation and regulations based upon strict prohibitions, the aim should also be to achieve informal rules and elements such as voluntariness, co-responsibility and confidence. Nevertheless, it is crucial for the success of policy processes that it is clear from the outset what the possible consequences of the intended policy will be for all stakeholders. Clarity about possible consequences is also a condition for follow-up, evaluation and feedback. Although the user agreements, as applied with regard to MPAs in Belgium, may be useful for making various stakeholders more responsible, they provide no guarantee for efficient and effective management of the MPAs due to, among other things, a lack of follow-up and feedback. In other words there is also need for policy *after* participation.

Need for Policy after Participation

In our conclusions and recommendations we finally want to point out the importance of follow-up or the importance of policy *after* participation. In both dossiers we observe that once the policy decisions have been taken (MPAs designated, PRUP approved) the follow-up leaves much to be desired. By follow-up care we mean not only the importance of follow-up, supervision and enforcement, but also 'aftercare' for actors who participated in the policy process.

- Follow-up, supervision and enforcement require more attention. Follow-up, supervision and enforcement constitute a difficulty, among other things because various actors know very little about the policy decisions, the multitude and complexity of legislation and regulations, but also because of the rather low priority given to this by the responsible authorities.

Moreover supervision at sea (in this case for the MPAs) requires other resources than supervision on land.

- Attention is needed to the dissemination of information *after* policy decisions have been taken. From our study it appears, however, that there is a particular need for follow-up care (policy) *after* the end of the participation process and the decision-making. Information on the policy outcomes does not reach the individual participant, or at least not sufficiently so. By paying more attention to information on policy decisions *and* the underlying arguments there is more chance of creating a feeling of involvement and shared responsibility.

Who Rules the Coast?

As we have indicated above there is no unequivocal answer to the question *'Who rules the coast?'*. What is unequivocal is that we are confronted with shifting relationships and power positions between state, market and civil society on the one hand and between various levels of government on the other. It remains to be seen to what extent the resulting new (in)formal relationships and power balances will adequately ensure the sustainable use of public goods such as marine ecosystems and open space.

Post Scriptum

Coastal zone policy is a dynamic process, as was shown in the two cases described in this book. New developments occurred after finalising this book. In february 2008 the Belgian Council os State annulled the designation of the SAC Vlakte van de Raan, following the complaint by the energy firm Electrabel *(see chapter 5.8)*. The main argument by the Council of State is the insufficient motivation for the designation. It is yet unclear if the government will start a new procedure for the designation of the area as an SAC.

LIST OF ABBREVIATIONS

AHTEG	Ad Hoc Technical Expert Group
AMINAL	Administratie Milieu-, Natuur-, Land- en Waterbeheer afdeling Natuur (Flemish Nature Conservation Administration)
ANB	Agentschap voor Natuur en Bos (Flemish Nature Conservation Administration, used to be AMINAL)
APA	Algemeen Plan van Aanleg (General Municipal Zoning Plan)
AROHM	Administratie Ruimtelijke Ordening, Huisvesting en Monumenten en Landschappen (Flemish Spatial Planning Administration)
BBL	Bond Beter Leefmilieu (federation of the Flemish environmental movement)
BNVR	Belgische Natuur en Vogel Reservaten (Belgian Nature and Ornithological Reserves, nature association)
BPA	Bijzonder Plan van Aanleg (Specific Sub-municipal Zoning Plan)
BPNS	Belgian Part of the North Sea
BS	Belgisch Staatsblad (Belgian Law Gazette)
BWHI	Bijzondere Wet tot Hervorming van de Instellingen (Special Act for the Reform of the Institutions)
CBD	Convention on Biological Diversity
CFP	Common Fisheries Policy
COP	Conference of Parties (COP) of United Nations Conventions
DRO	Decreet houdende de Organisatie van de Ruimtelijke ordening (Decree of 18 May 1999 With Regard to the Organisation of Spatial Planning)
EC	European Community
EEZ	Exclusive Economic Zone
EU	European Union
GECORO	Gemeentelijke Commissie Ruimtelijke Ordening (Municipal Advisory Commission for Spatial Planning)
GEN	Grote Eenheden Natuur (Large Units of Nature)
GENO	Grote Eenheden Natuur in Ontwikkeling (Large Units of Nature in Development)
GRUP	Gewestelijk Ruimtelijk Uitvoeringsplan (Regional Spatial Implementation Plan)
ICZM	Integrated Coastal Zone Management
ILVO	Instituut voor Landbouw- en Visserijonderzoek (Institute for Agricultural and Fisheries Research)
INBO	Instituut voor Natuur- en Bosonderzoek (Research Institute for Nature and Forest, used to be IN: Institute for Nature Conservation)

IUCN	International Union for the Conservation of Nature
IVON	Integraal Verwevings- en Ondersteunend Netwerk (Nature Interweaving Areas)
KB	Koninklijk Besluit (Royal Decree)
MB	Ministrieel Besluit (Ministrial Order)
M&L	Dienst Monumenten en landschappen
MD&K	Vlaams Agentschap voor Maritieme Dienstverlening en Kust (Flemish Agency for Maritime and Coastal Services)
MER	Milieueffectrapportage (Environmental Impact Assesment)
MIRONA	Provincie West-Vlaanderen dienst Milieu, Ruimtelijke Ordening en Natuur (Provincial Spatial Planning Administration)
MPA	Marine Protected Area
MUMM	Management Unit of the North Sea Mathematical Models and the Scheldt Estuary (a department of the Royal Belgian Institute of Natural Sciences)
NIMBY	Not In My Back Yard
N.V.	Naamloze Vennootschap (Public Limited Company)
OJL	Official Journal Legislation
OSPAR Convention	Convention for the Protection of the Marine Environment of the North-East Atlantic
PAA	Policy Arrangement Approach
PROCORO	Provinciale Commissie Ruimtelijke Ordening (Provincial Advisory Commission for Spatial Planning)
PRS-WV	Provinciaal Ruimtelijk Structuurplan West-Vlaanderen (Provincial Spatial Structure Plan West Flanders)
PRUP	Provinciaal Ruimtelijk Uitvoeringsplan (Provincial Spatial Implementation Plan)
RSV	Ruimtelijk Structuurplan Vlaanderen (Flemish Spatial Structure Plan)
RUP	Ruimtelijk Uitvoeringsplan (Spatial Implementation Plan)
SAC	Special Area of Conservation
SBSTTA	Subsidiary Body on Scientific, Technical and Technological Advice
SBZ	Speciale Beschermingszone (Special Protection Areas)
SCI	Site of Community Importance
sp.a	Socialistische Partij Anders (Flemish Socialist Political Party)
SPA	Special Protection Area
UNCED	United Nations Conference on Environment and Development
UNIZO	Unie van Zelfstandige Ondernemers (Union of Tradespeople)

V.V.H.V.	Vlaamse Vereniging Hengelsport Verbonden
	(Flemish Association for Angling Unions)
V.Y.F.	Vlaamse Yachting Federatie
	(Flemish Yachting Federation)
VEN	Vlaams Ecologisch Netwerk
	(Flemish Ecological Network)
VVW	Vlaamse Vereniging voor Watersport
	(Union of Flemish Watersports Associations)
vzw	Vereniging Zonder Winstoogmerk
	(non-profit organization)
WWF	World Wide Fund for Nature

A PARTIAL EDITION
OF *LES FAIS DES ROMMAINS*,
WITH A STUDY OF ITS STYLE AND SYNTAX

A Medieval Roman History